Organic
Places to Stay
in the UK 2nd edition

Organic
Places to Stay

in the UK ^{2nd} edition

Linda Moss

green books

This edition first published in the UK in 2008
by Green Books Ltd
Foxhole, Dartington, Totnes, Devon TQ9 6EB

Maps: ©MAPS IN MINUTES™ / Collins Bartholomew (2007)

Photo credits

Page 1: Garden Rooms, Kingsbridge, Devon
Page 10: Leckmelm, Ullapool, Ross-shire
Page 29: Buttervilla, Looe, Cornwall

Front cover
Top row: all photos from The Austwick Traddock, Settle, Yorkshire
Main picture: Pen-Y-Dyffryn Country Hotel, Oswestry, Shropshire

Back cover
Mushrooms: Botelet, Liskeard, Cornwall
Apples: Lantallack Farm, Saltash, Cornwall
Eggs: Aspen House, Hoarwithy, Herefordshire
Cauliflower and redcurrants: The Rumblie, Laggan, Inverness-shire

ISBN 978 1 900322 19 5

Text printed on Revive 75% recycled paper
by Latimer Trend, Plympton, Devon, UK

CONTENTS

FOREWORD
by Patrick Holden

Food pilgrimage is my idea of 21st-century travel. You set off on a journey – perhaps the underlying motive is 'inner' travel – but your aim is to enter into the spirit of the places you visit.

You can do this through the impressions of the landscapes, the geography, the geology, the rock, the soil and the architecture, and of course the people. But the ultimate and most intimate contact you can have with the place of your destination is to taste its food.

By tasting the food of the place you visit you are entering into an enduring relationship, which will make a permanent impression through your senses. I can think of no better way of achieving this than through visiting farms and guest houses which offer organic food. That way, you also make contact with the local inhabitants, thus adding a social and cultural element to your pilgrimage.

Just browsing through the pages of this book evokes in me a sense of longing to visit many of the listings, not least because I have met some of those who run them or have already visited, and can testify to the beauty of their homes and surroundings as well as the quality of their produce.

Making good use of this book will help those who run these places to build relocalised and self-sufficient food systems for the future.

Patrick Holden CBE
Director
Soil Association

HOW TO USE THIS BOOK

There are four categories of accommodation in this book. The first lines of the entries are colour-coded for ease of recognition. Green denotes places that cater for guests, which have been divided into 'B&B' and 'Hotel'. Brown denotes places that are self-catering, which have been divided into 'S-C' and 'Camping'. The colours are also used on the maps to identify the type of accommodation.

39	LOOE *(B&B)*	BUTTERVILLA
224	KINGTON *(Hotel)*	PENRHOS MANOR HOUSE
341	HOWDEN *(S-C)*	THE STRAW BALE CABIN
407	ULLAPOOL *(Camping)*	LECKMELM FARM

Please note that the maps do not pinpoint the exact location of a particular place to stay. For directions, contact the accommodation owner.

There are a number of organic certification bodies in the UK. Where a place to stay is on a certified organic farm, or has a different organic certification (for example has its own organic restaurant or organic kitchen garden, or provides an organic breakfast), the name of the certifying body appears to the right of the photo.

A number of the organic farms in this book are members of the World Wide Opportunities on Organic Farms (WWOOF) network. The aims of WWOOF are:

• to enable people to learn first-hand about organic growing techniques
• to enable town-dwellers to experience living and helping on a farm
• to help farmers make organic production a viable alternative, and
• to improve communications within the organic movement.

You can find out more at www.wwoof.org.uk.

The term 'CL' after the name of a caravan site means Certified Location. These are privately owned sites, which only allow five units on at any one time.

My advice to anyone with any particular dietary and other requirements is to ask the owners when you first contact them regarding availability, as they will all try to be as flexible as possible in order to make their guests feel very welcome.

This second edition of *Organic Places to Stay in the UK* includes the following symbols:

 Accommodation which accepts children. Please note that some places displaying this symbol will only accept children under the age of one, others will only accept children over a certain age, and most people have opted not to display the child symbol if they only accept children over twelve.

 Accommodation which accepts dogs. Bear in mind that there will be exceptions regarding the number of dogs, the size and behaviour of the dog etc, and most farmers will not accept dogs in the lambing season.

 Accommodation within one mile of a train station. If this is a main line station, you will be able to complete your journey by taxi or bus.

 Accommodation within one mile of a bus stop. Please bear in mind that a number of accommodations are very rural and buses only run infrequently.

Some of the hosts will pick you up from the train station or bus stop if you arrange this beforehand – ask when you book – and if you are arriving after dark, and walking the last part of your journey, don't forget your torch!

We will be grateful for any feedback on the places where you stay, and there is a form on page 304 for this purpose.

MAPS

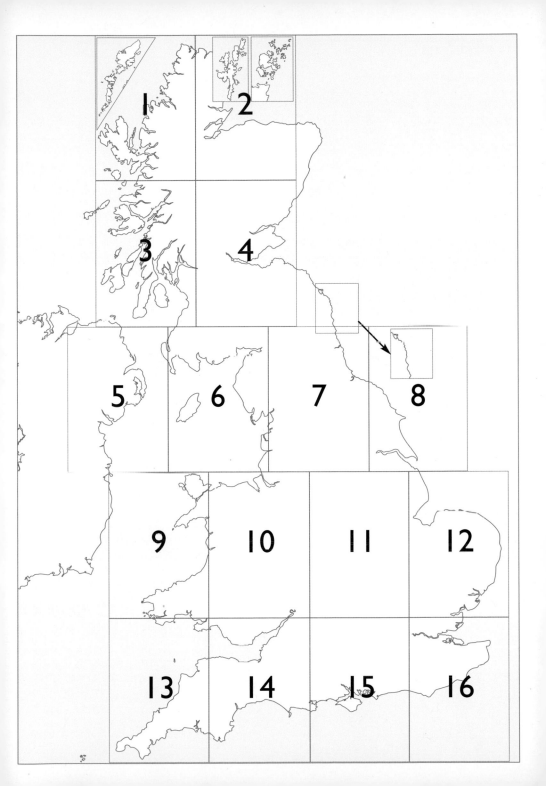

MAP I

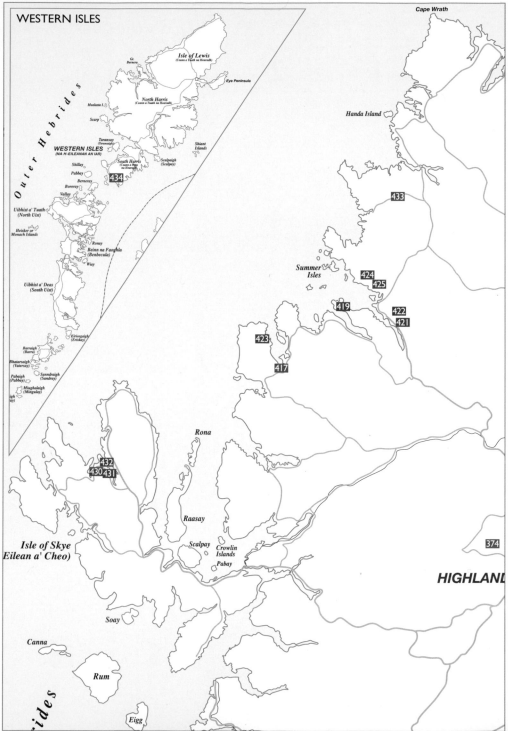

WESTERN ISLES

Outer Hebrides

Gt. Bernera
Isle of Lewis
(Ceann a Tuath na Hearadh)
Eye Peninsula

Mealista I.
North Harris
(Ceann a Tuath na Hearadh)
Scarp
Taransay
(Tarasaigh)
WESTERN ISLES
(NA H-EILEANAN AN IAR)
Shiant Islands
Shilley
South Harris
(Ceann a Deas na Hearadh)
Scalpaigh
(Scalpay)
Pabbay
Berneray
Boreray
434
Vallay
Uibhist a' Tuath
(North Uist)
Heisker or
Monach Islands
Ronay
Beinn na Faoghla
(Benbecula)
Wiay
Uibhist a' Deas
(South Uist)
Eiriosgaigh
(Eriskay)
Barraigh
(Barra)
Bhatarsaigh
(Vatersay)
Sandraigh
(Sandray)
Pabaigh
(Pabbay)
igh
ay)
Miughalaigh
(Mingulay)

Cape Wrath

Handa Island

433

Summer Isles
424
425
419
422
421
423
417

Rona

432
430 431

Raasay

Isle of Skye
Eilean a' Cheo)

Scalpay
Crowlin Islands
Pabay

374

HIGHLAND

Soay

Canna

Rum

rides

Eigg

MAP 2

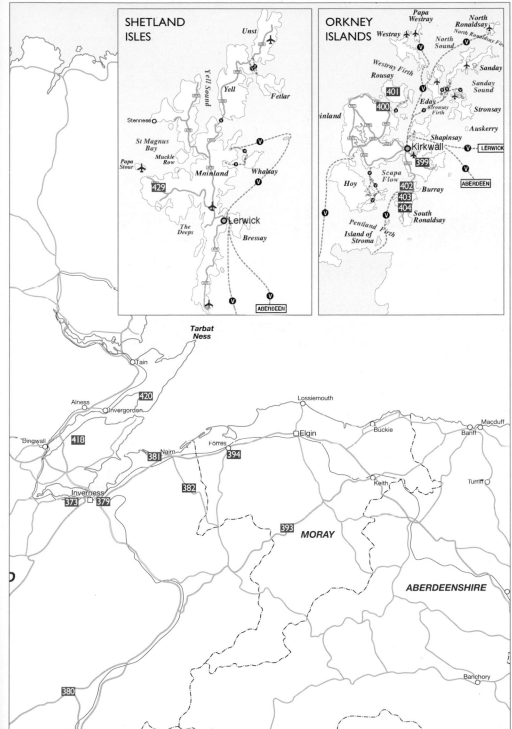

SHETLAND ISLES

Unst
Yell Sound
Yell
Fetlar
Stenness
St Magnus Bay
Muckle Row
Papa Stour
Mainland
Whalsay
429
The Deeps
Bressay
Lerwick
ABERDEEN

ORKNEY ISLANDS

Papa Westray
North Ronaldsay
North Ronaldsay Firth
Westray
North Sound
Westray Firth
Rousay
Sanday
401
400
Sanday Sound
Mainland
Eday
Stronsay
Stronsay Firth
Kirkwall
399
Shapinsay
LERWICK
Auskerry
Hoy
Scapa Flow
402
403
404
Burray
South Ronaldsay
ABERDEEN
Pentland Firth
Island of Stroma

Tarbat Ness
Tain
Alness
420
Invergordon
Lossiemouth
Dingwall
418
Elgin
Buckie
Banff
Macduff
Nairn
381
Forres
394
Keith
Turriff
Inverness
373   379
382
393   MORAY
ABERDEENSHIRE
380
Banchory

MAP 3

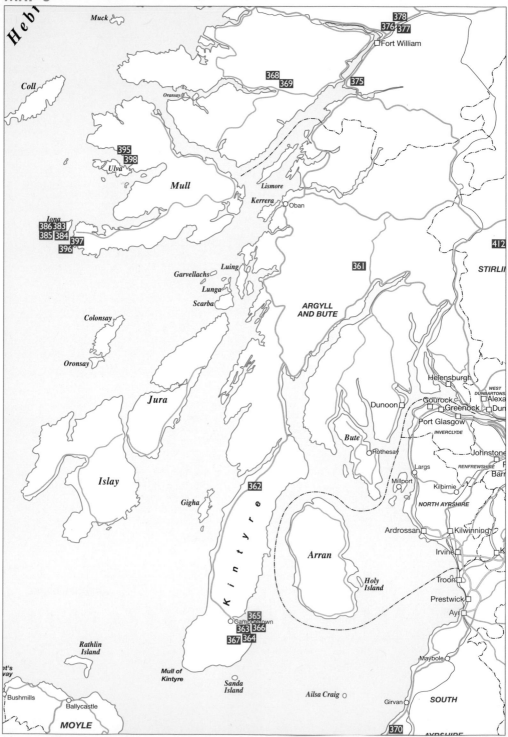

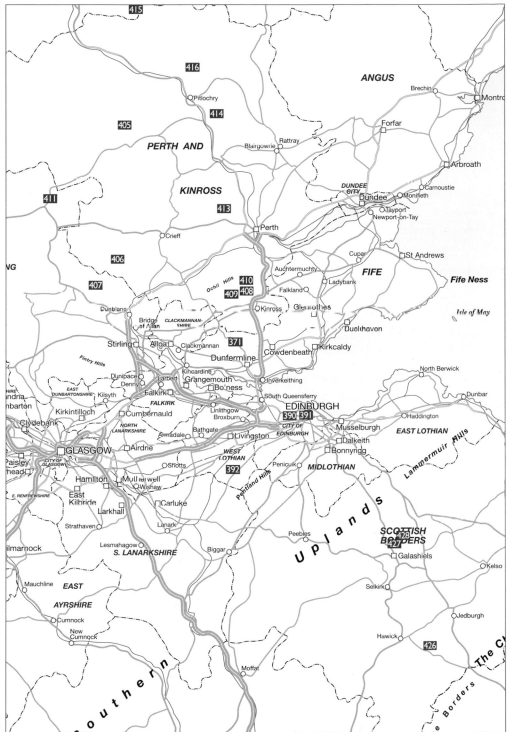

MAP 4

ANGUS

Brechin

Montro

415

416

Pitlochry

Forfar

414

405

Blairgowrie Rattray

Arbroath

PERTH AND

Carnoustie

DUNDEE
CITY

Dundee Monifieth

KINROSS

Tayport

413

Newport-on-Tay

Perth

411

Cupar

St Andrews

Crieff

FIFE

Fife Ness

406

Auchtermuchty

407

Ochil Hills 410 408

Ladybank

Falkland

409

Isle of May

Dunblane

Kinross Glenrothes

Bridge
of Allan

CLACKMANNAN-
SHIRE

Duelthavon

Stirling Alloa Clackmannan

371

Fintry Hills

Dunfermline Cowdenbeath Kirkcaldy

EAST
DUNBARTONSHIRE

Dunipace

Kincardine

North Berwick

Denny

Larbert

Grangemouth

HIRE

Falkirk Bo'ness

Inverkeithing

Dunbar

ndria
nbarton

Kilsyth

FALKIRK

South Queensferry

Kirkintilloch

Cumbernauld

Linlithgow

EDINBURGH

Haddington

Clydebank

NORTH
LANARKSHIRE

Broxburn

390 391

Musselburgh

EAST LOTHIAN

Paisley
head

GLASGOW

Airdrie

Armadale Bathgate Livingston

CITY OF
EDINBURGH

Dalkeith

Lammermuir Hills

CITY OF
GLASGOW

WEST
LOTHIAN

Bonnyrigg

E. RENFREWSHIRE

Shotts

392

Penicuik

MIDLOTHIAN

ilmarnock

Hamilton

Motherwell

Pentland Hills

Wishaw

East
Kilbride

Carluke

Larkhall

U p l a n d s

Strathaven

Lanark

SCOTTISH
BORDERS

Peebles

428

Lesmahagow

Biggar

427

S. LANARKSHIRE

Galashiels

Kelso

Mauchline

EAST

Selkirk

AYRSHIRE

Cumnock

Jedburgh

New
Cumnock

Hawick

426

Moffat

The Ch

S o u t h e r n

e Borders

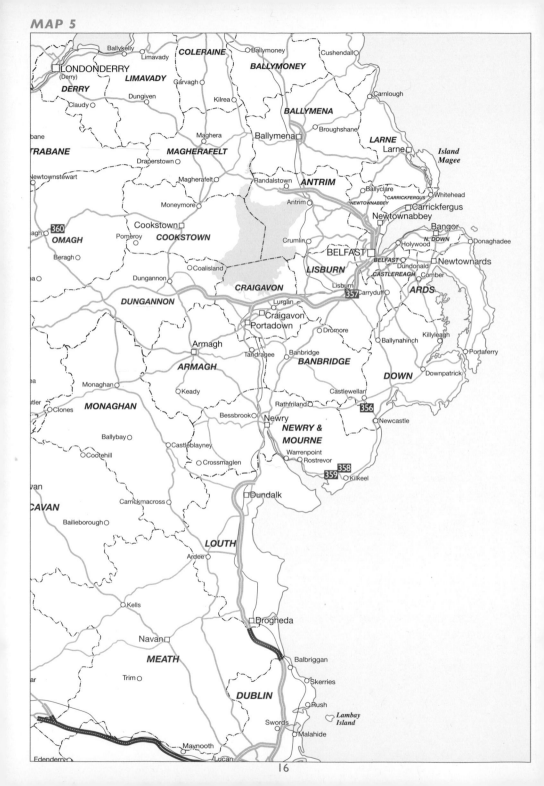

MAP 5

MAP 6

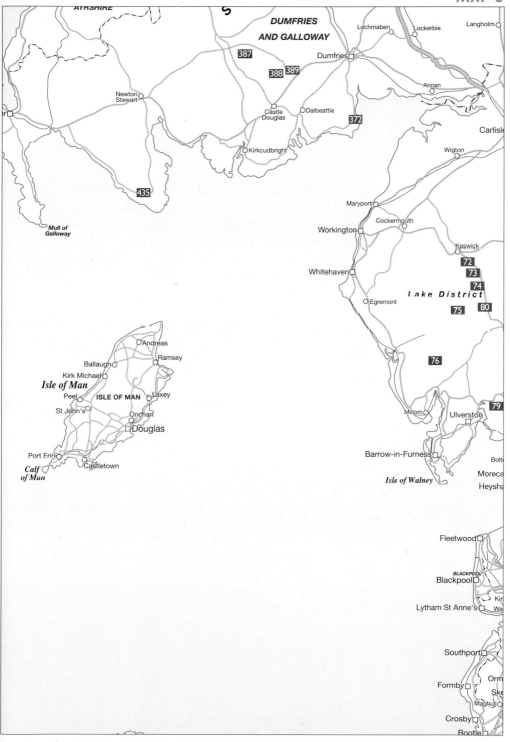

AYRSHIRE

DUMFRIES
AND GALLOWAY

Lochmaben
Lockerbie
Langholm

387

Dumfries

388 389

Annan

Newton
Stewart

Castle
Douglas
Dalbeattie

372

Carlisle

Kirkcudbright

Wigton

435

Maryport

Cockermouth

Mull of
Galloway

Workington

Keswick

72
73

Whitehaven

74

Lake District

75   80

Egremont

76

Andreas

Ballaugh
Ramsey

Kirk Michael

Isle of Man

Peel
Laxey

ISLE OF MAN

St John's
Onchan

Millom
Ulverston

79

Douglas

Port Erin

Barrow-in-Furness

Bolt

Calf
of Man
Castletown

Isle of Walney

Morec

Heysha

Fleetwood

BLACKPOOL
Blackpool

Kir

Lytham St Anne's
Wa

Southport

Orm

Formby

Ske

Maghull

Crosby

Bootle

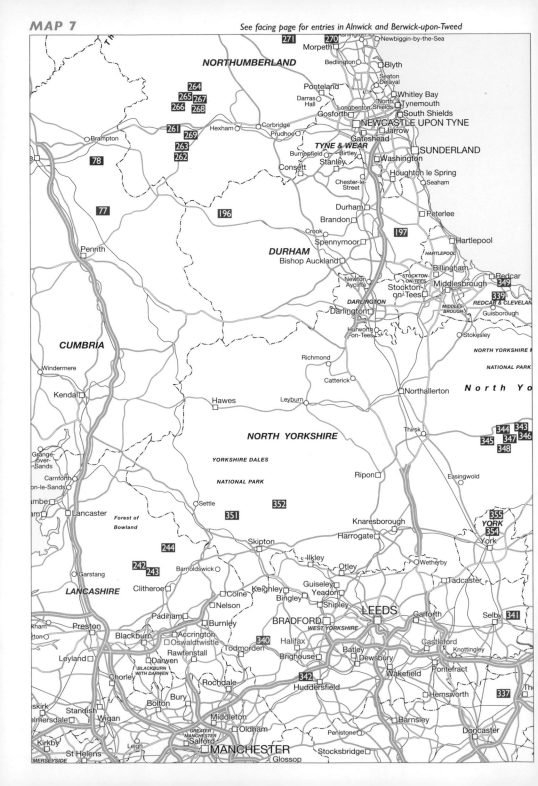

MAP 8

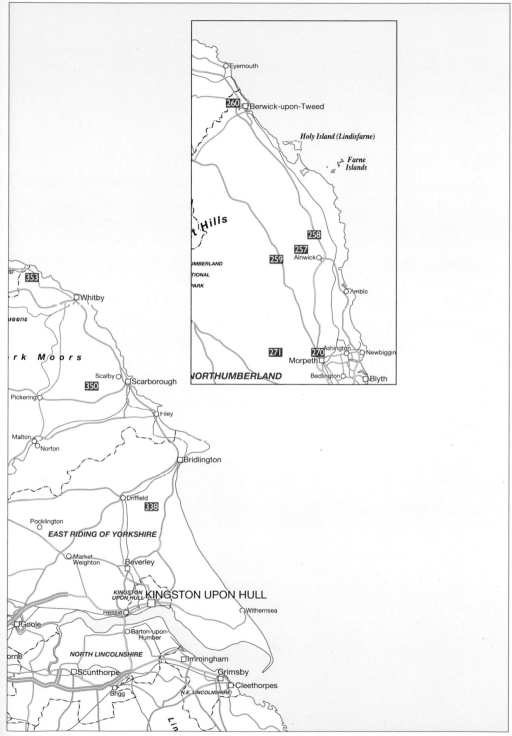

Eyemouth

260 Berwick-upon-Tweed

Holy Island (Lindisfarne)

Farne Islands

t Hills

UMBERLAND

TIONAL

PARK

258

257

259 Alnwick

Amble

271 270 Ashington Newbiggin

Morpeth

NORTHUMBERLAND Bedlington Blyth

353

Whitby

reene

r k Moors

Scalby Scarborough

350

Pickering

Filey

Malton

Norton

Bridlington

Driffield

338

Pocklington

EAST RIDING OF YORKSHIRE

Market Weighton Beverley

KINGSTON UPON HULL KINGSTON UPON HULL

Hessle Withernsea

Goole

Barton-upon-Humber

NORTH LINCOLNSHIRE

orne Immingham

Scunthorpe Grimsby

Cleethorpes

Brigg *N.E. LINCOLNSHIRE*

Lin

MAP 9

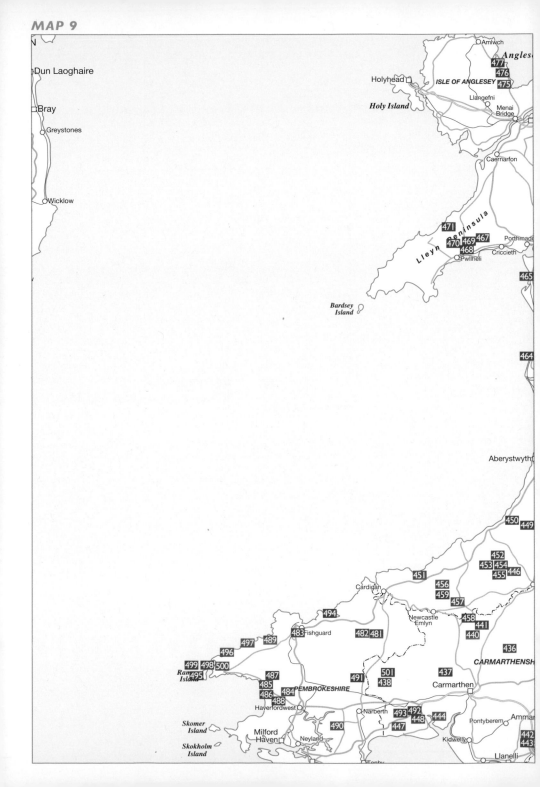

MAP 10

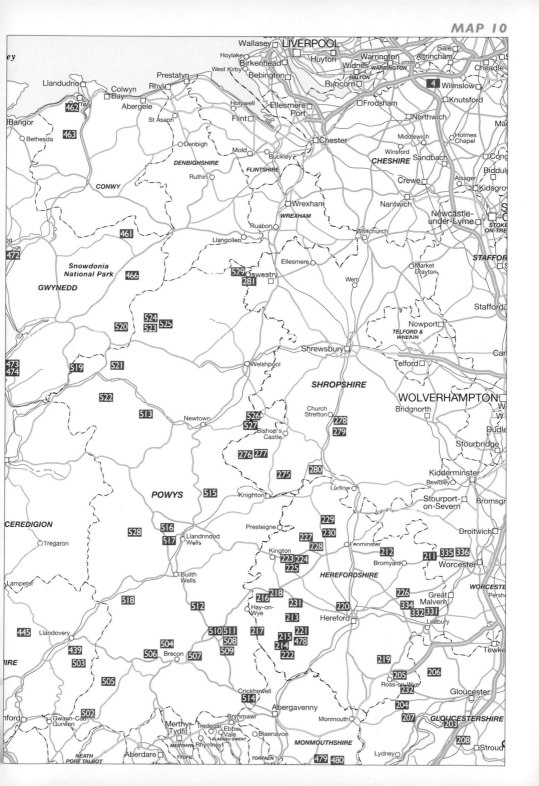

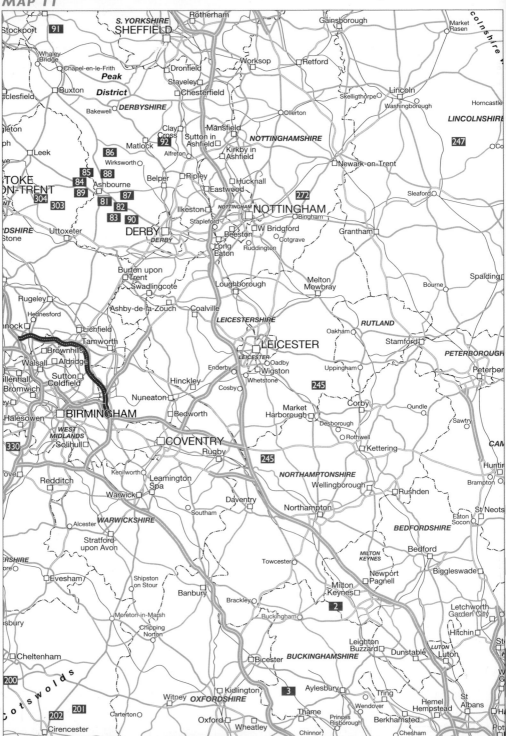

MAP 11

MAP 12

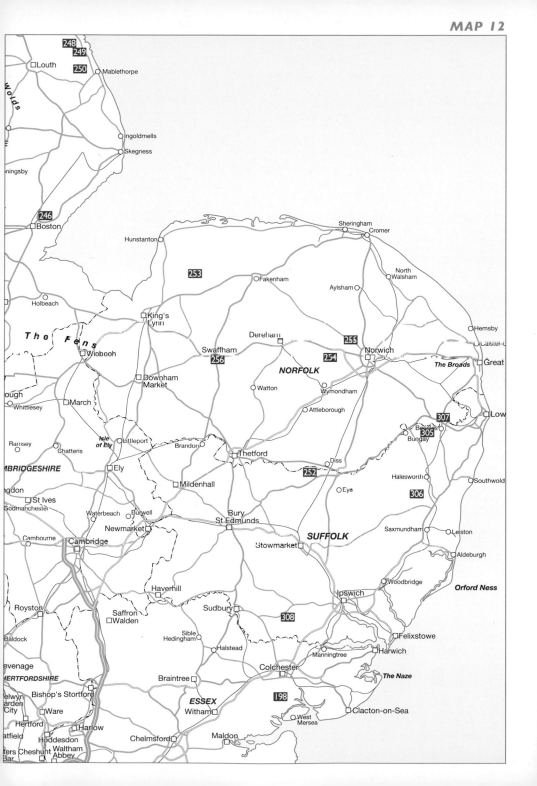

248
249
250

Louth
Mablethorpe

...wolds

Ingoldmells

Skegness

...ningsby

246

Boston

Hunstanton

Sheringham
Cromer

253

Fakenham

North
Walsham

Aylsham

Hemsby

Holbeach

Caister-o...

The Fens

King's
Lynn

Dereham

255

Norwich

The Broads

Great

Wisbech

Swaffham

256

254

NORFOLK

Downham
Market

Watton

Wymondham

307

Low...

...ough

Whittlesey

March

Attleborough

305

Be...s

Bungay

Ramsey

Chatteris

Isle
of Ely

Littleport

Brandon

Thetford

Diss

252

Halesworth

Southwold

...MBRIDGESHIRE

Ely

Mildenhall

Eye

306

...gdon

St Ives

Waterbeach

Burwell

Bury
St Edmunds

Saxmundham

Leiston

Godmanchester

Newmarket

SUFFOLK

Cambourne

Cambridge

Stowmarket

Aldeburgh

Woodbridge

Orford Ness

Haverhill

Ipswich

Royston

Saffron
Walden

Sudbury

308

Felixstowe

Baldock

Sible
Hedingham

Halstead

Manningtree

Harwich

...evenage

Colchester

The Naze

...HERTFORDSHIRE

Braintree

ESSEX

198

...elwyn
...arden
City

Bishop's Stortford

Witham

West
Mersea

Clacton-on-Sea

Ware

Hertford

Harlow

Chelmsford

Maldon

...atfield

Hoddesdon

...ers Cheshunt

Waltham
Abbey

...Bar

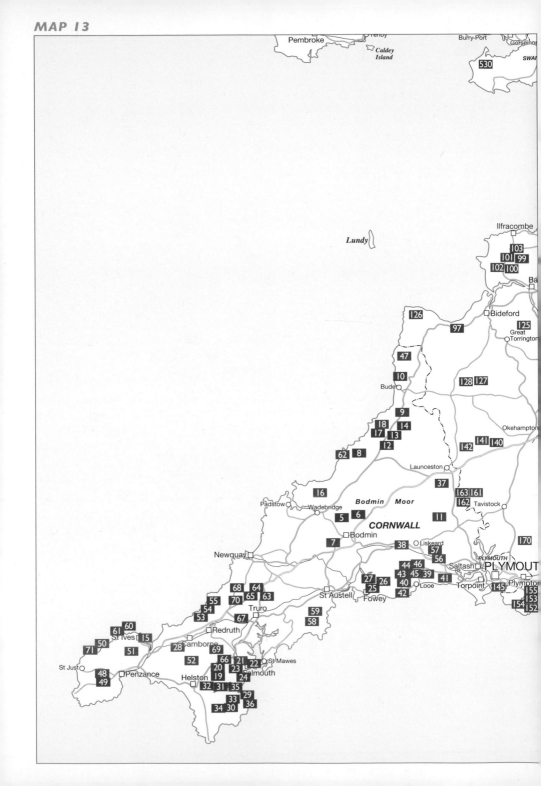

MAP 14

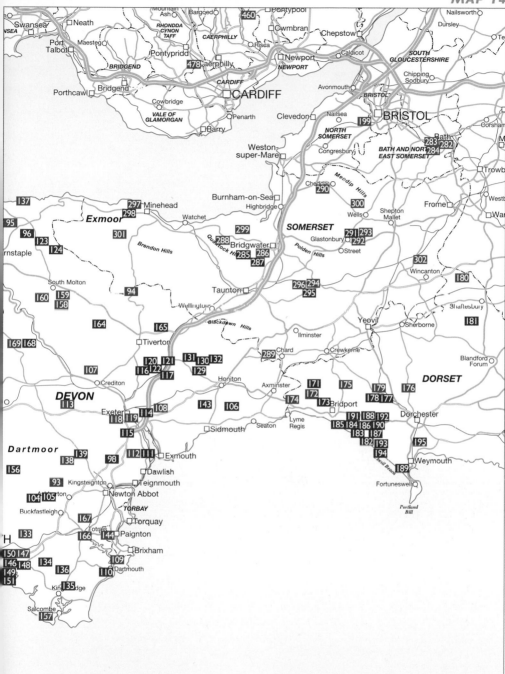

MAP 15

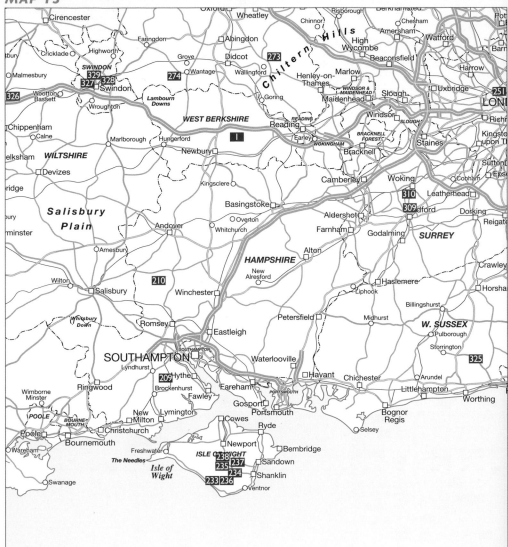

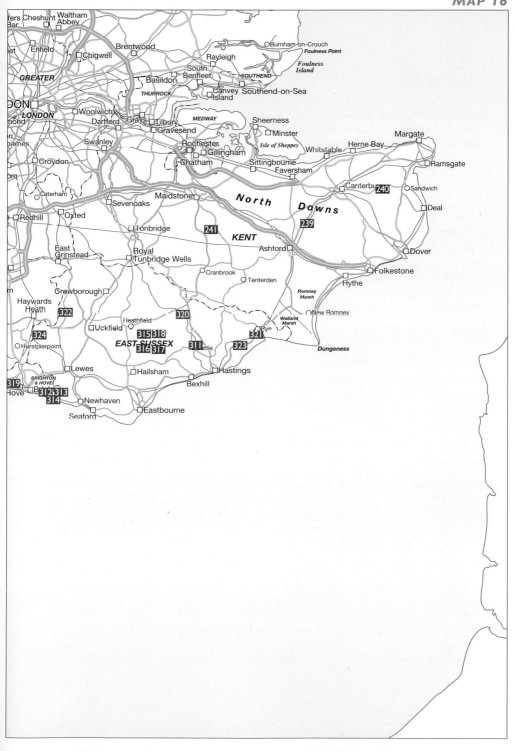

MAP 16

"To take the organic approach to life is to take responsibility for our impact on this planet. When it comes to food, organic production means sustainability and a huge reduction in our carbon footprint, both through eco-friendly farming and the implicit focus on local seasonal shopping. Once awareness is raised, it is wonderful to discover just how many dedicated producers are out there. I know from my own experience that it is surprisingly easy to buy all the fresh produce we need within a ten mile radius – direct from the producers."

– Rob Elliott, Author of The Food Maze

"When I decided to farm organically in the 80s I spent several weeks travelling around the UK gleaning as much information from the old school practitioners as possible. I encountered such generous and open hospitality that I never needed a hotel eatery. Many organic farmers are on a mission to make the world a better place and want to share both the fruits of their efforts and their philosophy with anyone who will listen. They tend to be more interested in food, more interested in the aesthetic and more interested in people, and as a result make good, if idiosyncratic, hosts."

– Guy Watson, Organic Farmer and Founder of Riverford Organic Vegetables

"As an organic farmer and self-catering provider in Northern Ireland, this publication is a must for promoting what we have to offer, and also to make the discerning traveller aware of the standards of excellence and luxury available from the variety of organic places to stay in the UK today."

– Margaret O'Hare, Director, Lurganconary Organic Farms

"Deciding what we eat is one of our biggest influences on sustainable development. Increasingly people want to be sure that the money they spend on holiday is going to improve the area they are visiting. This book tells them how."

– Hugh Raven, Director, Soil Association Scotland

"Many farmers are being encouraged to diversify and in Wales over 160 organic farmers are engaged in various tourism activities. With an annual expenditure by tourists in Welsh rural areas of £1 billion, this business is becoming increasingly important to those organic producers who provide accommodation or have on-farm retail outlets."

– Carolyn Wacher, Consumer and Events Co-ordinator, Organic Centre Wales

HUNGERFORD *(B&B)*

WILTON HOUSE I

33 High Street
Hungerford RG17 0NF
Tel: 01488 684228

Town House Bed and Breakfast
Double, from £70 pn

80% organic (local farm and home-grown)

Wilton House offers the very highest standard of accommodation and comfort in an historic, classic English town house with a documented history that predates 1470. An early 18th-century façade conceals its medieval origins. Described by Pevsner as 'the most ambitious house in Hungerford'. The two guest rooms and dining room are in the elegant 18th-century part of the house, which has wood panelling, open fireplaces and many other period features. The delicious wholesome English breakfast is made with local farm and home-grown organic produce. It's four minutes walk from Hungerford railway station. The River Kennet and the Kennet and Avon Canal both run through the historic market town.

welfares@hotmail.com   www.wiltonhouse-hungerford.co.uk

BEACHAMPTON *(B&B)*

FULLERS FARM HOUSE 2

Manor Farm
Beachampton MK19 6DT
Tel: 01908 562412

Bed and Breakfast
Double, £60 pn

Breakfast includes our own home-grown organic produce

Organic Farmers & Growers

Manor Farm is the last remaining working farm in the village of Beachampton. Our charming period farmhouse is situated on the edge of the picturesque village. We offer very comfortable and stylish bed and breakfast accommodation in the old dairy, giving you independence from the main house. Breakfast is served in the farmhouse in the elegant and cosy breakfast room, where we provide guests with our home-grown and home cured bacon, homemade sausage from our old native breed pigs, along with locally produced preserves. Enjoy the peace and beauty of the unspoilt countryside around us or explore the historic towns of Stony Stratford and Buckingham, both only five minutes drive away.

info@fullersatmanorfarm.co.uk   www.fullersatmanorfarm.co.uk

WORMINGHALL *(B&B)*

LOWERBROOK FARM B&B   3

Ickford Road
Worminghall HP18 9LA
Tel: 01844 339641

Bed and Breakfast, double £80 pn, single £65
Dinner 3 course £30, Supper £15

Honest food using produce in season, home-grown, local and organic whenever possible

500 year old farmhouse set in lovely well kept grounds on a 15-acre farm in the village of Worminghall, five miles from Thame and ten from Oxford on the Bucks / Oxon border. We have one large oak beamed guest suite (sitting / breakfast room, ensuite bathroom) with its own private entrance off an outside patio area, excellent for breakfast when the sun shines. We serve quality food made with the freshest of ingredients using produce in season, home-grown, local and organic whenever possible. Meals are available by prior arrangement. Mary has been a chef for fifteen years; her background is in New Zealand cuisine. Her cookery is essentially based on good food cooked well, partly invented or inspired.

james_cox@talktalk.net   www.lowerbrookfarm.typepad.com

ASHLEY *(B&B)*

SUGAR BROOK FARM   4

Mobberley Road
Ashley WA14 3QB
Tel: 0161 928 0879

Farmhouse Bed and Breakfast
Double, £50 pn

100% organic breakfast on request

Soil Association

Sugar Brook Farm is a working organic farm set within the picturesque location of the Cheshire countryside. We breed sheep and grow cereal crops. Environmental issues are given highest priority, and the farm has recently joined the Countryside Stewardship Scheme to encourage wildlife further. If time allows, you can explore the farm's nature walks and discover its hidden gems – a Grade A site of biological interest at Arden Wood, a Grade B site at Erlam's Pasture in the old tile yard, the brook by the Birkin, and Sugar Brook itself. The proximity of Manchester airport (five minutes away) and Tatton Park does not encroach upon the peaceful setting; rather they add to the convenience of its location.

mail@sugarbrookfarm.co.uk www.sugarbrookfarm.co.uk

BODMIN *(Camping)*

Greyhayes
St Breward PL30 4LP
Tel: 01208 850670

Yurts: sleep 2-6, £295-£475 per week
Short Breaks (available out of season)

Organic sausages, beefburgers, minced beef, bacon, eggs usually available

One 16ft and one 20ft yurt on a 40-acre organic smallholding on the edge of Bodmin moor. The yurts, professionally built on the farm from locally coppiced wood, stand on wooden decks, each with a woodburning stove to one side (wood supplied), and carpets and rugs on the floor. They are totally secluded in two separate fields surrounded by gnarly oaks, granite stones, moorland and pasture. The coast is twelve miles away, the cycle path along the River Camel is less than two miles away, and the moor is underfoot. Depending on the time of year fresh organic produce from the farm or local producers is available (sausages, burgers, minced beef, bacon, eggs), as is locally produced charcoal.

info@yurtworks.co.uk www.yurtworks.co.uk/holidays/index.htm

BODMIN *(Camping)*

Blisland
Bodmin PL30 4LH
Tel: 01208 850491

Yurts: sleep 2-6, £190-£320 per week;
VW camper van hire, £70-£100 per day

Organic meat available on farm

Soil Association

Working organic sheep farm (200 acres) situated high on Bodmin Moor between the villages of Blisland and St Breward. The small campsite (open May-Sep £3-£5 pppn) is intended to have a low impact on the surroundings. The four yurts are well spaced in their own field on the campsite, with stunning views across the moors. Organic meat available on farm. Our local village shop will provide all your daily needs. As well as running a flock of 300 ewes and a herd of 20 cows the farm is rich in archaeological remains and wildlife. A demonstration farm for the SA and West Country Rivers Trust, the farm walk takes in diverse wildlife habitats, 1500m of beautiful river bank, and a Bronze Age hut settlement.

thefarm@bodminmoor.co.uk www.southpenquite.co.uk

BODMIN *(B&B)*

STEPHEN GELLY FARM 7

Lanivet
Bodmin PL30 5AX
Tel: 01208 831213

Bed and Breakfast
From £20 pppn

Nearly everything in the wholefood breakfast is home-grown or homemade

Soil Association

We offer one double ensuite and one family room in our comfortable Victorian farmhouse. Your wholefood breakfast of cereals, milk, eggs, yogurt, fruit, bread, butter, jams, honey, etc is served in the south-facing conservatory. Stephen Gelly Farm is a pleasant rural retreat, situated in a quiet lane south of Bodmin. It's a 120-acre traditional grassland farm with small fields and wildlife friendly hedgerows. We organically farm a herd of Devon suckler cows, a small flock of sheep, free-range chickens and laying hens. Our home produced organic meats are sold directly from our farm. We have a large kitchen garden and keep a house cow, geese, bees and horses. Water comes from a spring on the farm.

stephengelly.farm@btinternet.com   www.stephengellyfarm.co.uk

BOSCASTLE *(S-C)*

OSTLERS 8

Helsett Farm
Lesnewth PL35 0HP
Tel: 01840 261207

Converted Barn: sleeps 4-10
Contact for prices

Organic dairy produce, organic beef and pork

Soil Association

Ostlers is a converted barn which sleeps up to ten people, tastefully furnished in a farmhouse style. Helsett Farm is a 265-acre organic dairy farm, which is home to a pedigree herd of a hundred Ayrshire cows and their calves. The organic milk from the cows is processed in the on-farm factory to produce a variety of organic dairy products – milk, ice cream, yogurt, smoothies, mascarpone, clotted cream, soured cream and frozen yogurts. Organic beef and pork are also available. With stunning views across the farm, visitors are welcome to roam through the fields and woods, watch the cows being milked, feed the young stock, and generally enjoy living on this working organic farm in North Cornwall.

helsettayrshires@aol.com   www.helsettfarm.com

BUDE *(B&B)*

Poundstock
Bude EX23 0DP
Tel: 01288 361297

Bed and Breakfast, £55-£70 pppn
Bed, Breakfast, Dinner, £80-£95 pppn

All food at breakfast and in the restaurant is 100% certified organic

Soil Association

An elegant restored Victorian house from which Gill and Neil Faiers run the UK's first certified 'Bed and Organic Breakfast'. The main house has fabulous views towards the sea, and offers two spacious ensuite double bedrooms, both with roll top baths and separate showers. The adjoining coach house comprises two newly created luxury suites, each with a bedroom, bathroom and private sitting room. We offer a three course dinner on most evenings in our totally organic restaurant, where we serve seasonal home-grown organic food. The emphasis is on freshly picked, carefully prepared, simple and delicious dishes. All the fresh ingredients we use are grown in our own organic gardens and greenhouse.

info@bangorsorganic.co.uk www.bangorsorganic.co.uk

BUDE *(S-C)*

BEACHMODERN NO. 28   10

Downs View Road
Bude EX23 8RG
Tel: 01288 275006

Self-Catering: £1,300-£5,000 per week
Optional private chef

Organic welcome pack, organic meals available, organic dining locally

Beachmodern No. 28 is one of the most luxurious, stylish and contemporary self-catering destinations in Cornwall, and can provide a private chef serving organic modern cuisine using fresh local and organic ingredients sourced from the best Cornish suppliers. We supply an organic welcome pack. No. 28 is perfectly located 400m from Crooklets Beach and overlooking Bude's links golf course on the stunning North Cornwall coast. When the tide is high and the surf is big you can hear the roar of the waves breaking from every room in the house. Large living rooms, open fires, high ceilings, eight bedrooms, three bathrooms (sleeps up to twenty). Two gardens and a barbecue area outside.

stay@beachmodern.com www.beachmodern.com

CALLINGTON (B&B)

BROWDA FARM 11

Linkinhorne
Callington PL17 7NB
Tel: 01579 362235

Farmhouse Bed and Breakfast
£35-£45 pppn

Traditional farmhouse breakfast made with organic and / or local ingredients

Soil Association

A large comfortable 17th-century Grade II listed Cornish farmhouse set within the beautiful unspoilt Lynher Valley, with spectacular views to Bodmin Moor. We offer a traditional farmhouse breakfast made with organic and / or local ingredients wherever possible. The house is the heart of a 250-acre organic farm specialising in the production of quality meat from a pedigree herd of South Devon cattle and a flock of Lleyn sheep. The farm is environmentally rich and varied, supporting an abundance of wildlife within a variety of habitats. These include 40 acres of woodland, one mile of river frontage and a couple of lakes, which our guests may explore and enjoy along with the remains of an Iron age hill fort.

www.thespringerspaniel.org.uk/bedandbreakfast.htm

CAMELFORD (S-C)

NUTMEG COTTAGE 12

Old Newham Farm
Otterham PL32 9SR
Tel: 01840 230470

Cottage: sleeps 4
£275-£595 pw

Local shop (less than 2 miles) sells fresh and local produce

Soil Association

Nutmeg Cottage is one of three old stone and slate cottages formed around the centre of a 30-acre organic beef and sheep farm dating back to medieval times. The cottages have been restored and converted with great care taken to retain as much character as possible. Deep in the country yet only a few miles from North Cornwall's most spectacular unspoiled coastal scenery. The land is grazed in the traditional manner by cattle and sheep, and the owners also keep horses and other smaller livestock. There's plenty of room to get away from it all here, and to find the real peace of Cornwall's unspoiled countryside. The cottage has two bedrooms (a double and a twin), an open log fire, and Wi-Fi internet.

orghol@old-newham.co.uk www.old-newham.co.uk/Nutmegs.htm

CAMELFORD *(S-C)*

SKYBER COTTAGE 13

Old Newham Farm
Otterham PL32 9SR
Tel: 01840 230470

Cottage: sleeps 2
£200-£320 pw

Local shop (less than 2 miles) sells fresh and local produce

Soil Association

One of three cottages formed from the old stone and slate buildings around the centre of a 30-acre organic beef and sheep farm. Dating back to medieval times, the farm is found at the end of a quiet country lane. Deep in the country with no passing traffic, yet only a few miles from the West Country's most spectacular unspoiled coastal scenery. The land is grazed in the traditional manner by cattle and sheep, and the owners also keep horses and other smaller livestock. The cottages have been restored and converted, with great care being taken to retain as much character as possible. There's plenty of room to get away from it all here, and to find the real peace of North Cornwall's unspoiled countryside.

cottages@old-newham.co.uk www.old-newham.co.uk/Skyber.htm

CAMELFORD *(S-C)*

THE STABLES 14

Old Newham Farm
Otterham PL32 9SR
Tel: 01840 230470

Cottage: sleeps 4
£275-£595 pw

Local shop (less than 2 miles) sells fresh and local produce

Soil Association

One of three old stone and slate cottages formed around the centre of a 30-acre organic beef and sheep farm dating back to medieval times. The Stables has two bedrooms, a double four-poster bed with ensuite bathroom and a twin with shower room. Wi-Fi internet. The cottages have been restored and converted with great care taken to retain as much character as possible. Deep in the country, yet only a few miles from North Cornwall's most spectacular unspoiled coastal scenery. The land is grazed in the traditional manner by cattle and sheep, and the owners also keep horses and other smaller livestock. There's plenty of room to get away from it all and find the real peace of the unspoiled countryside.

orghols@old-newham.co.uk www.old-newham.co.uk/TheStables.htm

CARBIS BAY *(B&B)*

COAST   15

St Ives Road
Carbis Bay TR26 2RT
Tel: 01736 795918

Bed and Vegetarian Breakfast, £26-£34 pppn
Vegetarian Restaurant

Local and organic products whenever
possible (50%-70% organic)

Coast Bed and Breakfast is a stylish and contemporary B&B with a restaurant and a gallery. All rooms are ensuite, and most have sea views. Coast has residents' parking, a residents' lounge, decking and a garden outside. In the unique location of Carbis Bay the accommodation is within walking distance to the ancient market town of St Ives. Carbis Bay beach is ten minutes walk away. Breakfast is provided by the Bean Inn vegetarian restaurant, where a range of vegetarian and vegan breakfast options are offered. The emphasis on food at the Bean Inn is on taste, health and value. All food is freshly prepared on the premises, using local and organic products whenever possible (between 50% and 70% organic).

info@coastcornwall.co.uk   www.coastcornwall.co.uk

CHAPEL AMBLE *(B&B)*

DAVID'S HOUSE   16

Chapel Amble
Wadebridge PL27 6EU
Tel: 01208 814514

Bed and Breakfast £35-£45 pppn

100% organic breakfast, locally sourced or
homemade

Chemical-free, organic bed and breakfast. A spacious guest house with warm, friendly hospitality situated close to the dramatic north coast of Cornwall. The stunning beaches of Daymer Bay and Polzeath are both within five minutes drive. We provide delicious organic breakfasts. All the food served is locally produced and organic. Special diets can be catered for. All bedding, furniture and cleaning products are organic / environmentally friendly. Drinking and bathing water is filtered. Chapel Amble is in a conservation area, and is surrounded by National Trust land and organic farmland. Explore the quaint fishing villages of Port Isaac and Port Quin, and the bustling market town of Wadebridge.

info@davidshouse.co.uk   www.davidshouse.co.uk

CRACKINGTON HAVEN *(S-C)*

WOODA FARM COTTAGE 17

Wooda Farm
Crackington Haven EX23 0LF
Tel: 01840 230129 / 230140

Cottage: sleeps 4, £285-£595 pw
Short Breaks, from £150

Organic lamb, eggs, home-grown apples and
vegetables in season, home baking

Soil Association

Spectacular walks, stunning surf and total seclusion on this 20-acre organic farm. Explore our pastures bordered by Cornish banks and hedgerows. Discover our old orchard, bluebell woods, wildflower meadows and stream. Walk the two miles to the magnificent beach at Crackington Haven. Simple and comfortable accommodation in Wooda Farm Cottage, a self-contained annexe of the 16th-century farmhouse. Organic lamb and eggs produced on the farm, seasonal fruit and vegetables, and organic home-baking to order. Organic dairy products (milk, ice cream, etc) are available from a nearby farm. Natural spring water comes from a well. A beautiful art studio is also available with the cottage.

max@woodafarm.co.uk www.woodafarm.co.uk/cottage.html

CRACKINGTON HAVEN *(B&B)*

WOODA FARMHOUSE 18

Wooda Farm
Crackington Haven EX23 0LF
Tel: 01840 230140 / 230129

Stay and Work at Wooda, £145 pp 2 nights
all inc; from £350 pppw all inc (see website
for details)

Organic lamb, eggs, vegetables, fruit from farm

Soil Association

Find comfort, space and freedom in an inspirational setting. Wooda is a working organic farm set in a secluded south-facing valley two miles from the sea. A place for creative people to come and work away from their usual routine. The 16th-century farmhouse is available to those who are also using our award-winning barn space or stunning stable studio for creative work, retreats, celebrations. Groups of up to 12 are then invited to join us as house guests with all their meals included. We naturally turn to our own organic produce first, and you're guaranteed some exciting cooking. Our setting provides the focus, our delicious organic food is the fuel. Bring your creative ideas to Wooda and let them take flight.

max@woodafarm.co.uk www.woodafarm.co.uk

FALMOUTH *(S-C)*

BENS 19

Goongillings Farm
Constantine TR11 5RP
Tel: 01326 340630

Converted Barn: sleeps 4
Contact for prices

Good local shops in the village (ten minutes walk)

Soil Association

Large barn conversion on a beautiful creekside farm on the famous Helford River. The farm covers 150 acres of land, of which 25 acres are made up of attractive woodland. We produce traditionally reared suckled beef calves. We are part of the Countryside Stewardship Scheme, which promotes environmentally friendly farming and encourages wildlife habitat conservation. Numerous species can be found in the fields and woods, including badgers, foxes, buzzards and waterfowl. To preserve them from development the cottages and farm are covenanted to the National Trust. The quay at the end of Goongillings Farm provides a lovely spot for swimming, watersports and boating when the tide is in.

enquiries@goongillings.co.uk www.goongillings.co.uk/bens.htm

FALMOUTH *(S-C)*

GYPSY CARAVAN 20

Goongillings Farm
Constantine TR11 5RP
Tel: 01326 340630

Gypsy Caravan: sleeps 2+1
£30 pn (min 3 nights), £150-£200 pw

Good local shops in the village (ten minutes walk)

Soil Association

Restored gypsy caravan on a beautiful creekside farm on the famous Helford River. The farm covers 150 acres of land, of which 25 acres are made up of attractive woodland. We produce traditionally reared suckled beef calves. We are part of the Countryside Stewardship Scheme, which promotes environmentally friendly farming and encourages wildlife habitat conservation. Numerous species can be found in the fields and woods, including badgers, foxes, buzzards and waterfowl. To preserve them from development the cottages and farm are covenanted to the National Trust. The quay at the end of Goongillings Farm provides a lovely spot for swimming, watersports and boating when the tide is in.

enquiries@goongillings.co.uk www.goongillings.co.uk/gypsy.htm

FALMOUTH *(Hotel)*

HAWTHORNE DENE HOTEL 21

12 Pennance Road
Falmouth TR11 4EA
Tel: 01326 311427

Small Edwardian Hotel, £40-£60 pppn
Dinner (table d'hôte and à la carte)

The finest locally produced meat, fish and
vegetables (around 55%-85% organic)

Family-owned and run, the Hawthorne Dene is a small Edwardian hotel of character and distinction. Steeped in tradition, the hotel has fine rooms furnished to a very high standard. Most have fantastic sea views overlooking Falmouth's magnificent bay and a panorama that stretches from the Roseland to the Lizard. We are committed to green tourism and sustainable practices. We serve only the finest locally sourced produce, organic or free-range where possible. All our food is prepared fresh here on the premises by our award-winning kitchen team. Special diets catered for. We are members of the Soil Association and the CoaST Project, and involved with Organic South West and Recycle Cornwall.

enquiries@hawthornedenehotel.co.uk www.hawthornedenehotel.com

FALMOUTH *(S-C)*

BARN AT GOONGILLINGS 22

Goongillings Farm
Constantine TR11 5RP
Tel: 01326 340630

Converted Barn: sleeps 6-8
Contact for prices

Good local shops in the village (ten minutes walk)

Soil Association

Spacious barn conversion on a beautiful creekside farm on the famous Helford River. The farm covers 150 acres of land, of which 25 acres are made up of attractive woodland. We produce traditionally reared suckled beef calves. We are part of the Countryside Stewardship Scheme, which promotes environmentally friendly farming and encourages wildlife habitat conservation. Numerous species can be found in the fields and woods, including badgers, foxes, buzzards and waterfowl. To preserve them from development the cottages and farm are covenanted to the National Trust. The quay at the end of Goongillings Farm provides a lovely spot for swimming, watersports and boating when the tide is in.

enquiries@goongillings.co.uk www.goongillings.co.uk/barn.htm

FALMOUTH *(S-C)*

FARM AT GOONGILLINGS 23

Goongillings Farm
Constantine TR11 5RP
Tel: 01326 340630

House: sleeps 8
Contact for prices

Good local shops in the village (ten minutes walk)

Soil Association

19th-century farmhouse on a beautiful creekside farm on the famous Helford River. The farm covers 150 acres of land, of which 25 acres are made up of attractive woodland. We produce traditionally reared suckled beef calves. We are part of the Countryside Stewardship Scheme, which promotes environmentally friendly farming and encourages wildlife habitat conservation. Numerous species can be found in the fields and woods, including badgers, foxes, buzzards and waterfowl. To preserve them from development the cottages and farm are covenanted to the National Trust. The quay at the end of Goongillings Farm provides a lovely spot for swimming, watersports and boating when the tide is in.

enquiries@goongillings.co.uk www.goongillings.co.uk/farmhouse.htm

FALMOUTH *(S-C)*

THE FLOWER HOUSE 24

Goongillings Farm
Constantine TR11 5RP
Tel: 01326 340630

Cottage: sleeps 2-4
Contact for prices

Good local shops in the village (ten minutes walk)

Soil Association

Pretty stone cottage on a beautiful creekside farm on the famous Helford River. The farm covers 150 acres of land, of which 25 acres are made up of attractive woodland. We produce traditionally reared suckled beef calves. We are part of the Countryside Stewardship Scheme, which promotes environmentally friendly farming and encourages wildlife habitat conservation. Numerous species can be found in the fields and woods, including badgers, foxes, buzzards and waterfowl. To preserve them from development the cottages and farm are covenanted to the National Trust. The quay at the end of Goongillings Farm provides a lovely spot for swimming, watersports and boating when the tide is in.

enquiries@goongillings.co.uk www.goongillings.co.uk/flower.htm

FOWEY *(S-C)*

CHURCH MEADOW 25

Penquite Farm
Golant PL23 1LB
Tel: 01726 833319

Split Level House: sleeps 6
£300-£800 pw

Cream team to welcome you on arrival

Organic Farmers & Growers

A spacious split-level house that has been tastefully furnished and decorated to a very high standard. There are wonderful views from the upstairs sitting room of the Fowey River Valley and surrounding open countryside. Patio doors open onto a paved balcony leading to the fenced garden, which has a large secluded lawn. Church Meadow is a five minute stroll from the peaceful riverside village of Golant with a traditional local pub, art gallery and children's play area. Penquite is a 150-acre organic farm with forty suckler cows and their calves. Bring your boots and enjoy the circular walk over the farm with its abundant wildlife, and help feed our friendly farm animals and collect the free-range eggs.

ruth@penquitefarm.co.uk www.penquitefarm.co.uk

FOWEY *(S-C)*

COACHES REST 26

Penquite Farm
Golant PL23 1LB
Tel: 01726 833319

Barn Conversion: sleeps 4
£200-£750 pw

Cream team to welcome you on arrival

Organic Farmers & Growers

Coaches Rest is a very spacious sympathetically restored barn conversion retaining all the traditional old beams. It has been tastefully furnished to a superior 5-star quality. Designed with a wet room (level entry shower with handrails) for wheelchair users, it is also ideal for people with restricted walking ability. There is a paved patio area with garden furniture and gas barbecue, and steps that lead up to a large fenced lawn with extensive views of the river with boats resting on their moorings. Penquite is a 150-acre organic farm with forty suckler cows and their calves. Nestling beside the farm is a beautiful 13th-century church in this peaceful riverside village with wonderful views of the river and open countryside.

ruth@penquitefarm.co.uk www.penquitefarm.co.uk

FOWEY (S-C)

OLD GRANARY 27

Penquite Farm
Golant PL23 1LB
Tel: 01726 833319

Converted Barn: sleeps 8-10
£400-£1370 pw

Cream team to welcome you on arrival

Organic Farmers & Growers

The Old Granary has been beautifully restored to a superior 5-star quality with traditional beams and lovely oak flooring. All the rooms have wonderful views over the Fowey Valley and the surrounding countryside, and from upstairs you can see the river with sailing and pleasure boats going up and down the estuary to visit other creeks and inlets. There is a large fenced garden, a gas barbecue and ample parking. Penquite is a 150-acre organic farm with forty suckler cows and their calves. Come and help feed our friendly farm animals and collect the free-range eggs – children just love it. Bring your boots and enjoy the circular walk over the farm with breathtaking views of the river, wildlife and open countryside.

ruth@penquitefarm.co.uk   www.penquitefarm.co.uk

HAYLE (B&B)

SEAWITCH COTTAGE 28

Chapel Road
Leedstown TR27 6BA
Tel: 01736 850917

Bed and Breakfast
Double, £70-£80 pn

Ingredients used are organic, locally sourced or home produced

Seawitch Cottage offers luxury, spacious accommodation and is ideally situated for exploring the beautiful environs of west Cornwall, being within six miles of both north and south coasts. All the ingredients used in our kitchen are locally sourced, sometimes home-grown and where possible organic. Our delicious breakfasts include homemade jams, freshly pressed fruit juices, eggs from our own hens, as well as free-range, organic meat from local farmers and fish from a nearby smoke house. Also available are homemade organic cakes, pasties and pies, which we supply to our local farm shop. These would be ideal for you to take with you on a picnic lunch.

seawitch.hearts@btinternet.com   www.seawitchcottage.com

HELSTON *(S-C)*

THE BARN COTTAGE 29

Tregellast Barton Farm
St Keverne TR12 6NX
Tel: 01326 280479

Converted Loft: sleeps 5
£200-£595 pw

Our own organic milk, cream, ice cream, etc

Soil Association

The Barn Cottage is the upper half of an old farm building which forms one side of the Croust house yard. Over the Bull Pen Gallery, it used to be the corn loft. Tregellast Barton has always been home to Channel Island cows. The farm has grown to 200 acres and has around a hundred milking Jersey cows. Both the land and the herd are certified organic. Farm produce includes organic milk, organic cream, organic ice cream, organic clotted cream fudge, apple juice, cider, pasties, mustards, chutneys, jams and marmalade. You can enjoy delicious homemade food and locally made organic beers at our licensed restaurant. There is a mile of easy walking in a charming valley of ponds, meadows and woods.

admin@roskillys.co.uk www.roskillys.co.uk/fc-thebarn.htm

HELSTON *(S-C)*

ELMTREE FARM HOUSE 30

Rosuick Organic Farm
St Martin TR12 6DZ
Tel: 01326 231302

Cottage: sleeps 6
£200-£600 pw

Farm shop and café sell home and local produce

Soil Association

Rosuick Organic Farm is situated in its own picturesque valley in an Area of Outstanding Natural Beauty. The farm has been in the Oates family since the 1700s, ours being the 6th generation to farm here. The cottages are all in their own private grounds, but with access to the tennis court and farm trail. Elmtree is a traditional cob and stone cottage with its own half acre of garden. It has a sunny aspect, looking out across the fields. We sell as much of our own home produce as possible at our farm shop, located on the edge of the farm. Spring water supply. Wonderful walking, both on the farm and the Goonhilly Downs. We have nine Bactrian camels, to be used for camel treks. Visitor centre and café.

oates@rosuick.co.uk www.rosuick.co.uk

HELSTON *(Camping)*

GEAR ORGANIC CAMPING 31

St Martin
Helston TR12 6DE
Tel: 01326 221364

Simply Camping (open May-Sept)
£8 per adult pn

Farm shop sells organic produce and
homemade food

Biodynamic Agricultural Association

The camping field is one and a half acres of level mown grass overlooking the Helford River. Our organic farm shop sells organic and local produce – fresh fruit and vegetables, apple juice, milk, ice cream, etc. Organic and local produce is also used in the homemade takeaway food, including hot pizzas, bread and cakes. Real Cornish pasties made on site daily. The farm slopes down to the beautiful Helford River off Falmouth Bay. Boats for hire at Helford and St Anthony to explore Frenchman's Creek and along the river. Beaches and small fishing ports within six miles. Wet weather activities in the area – Ships and Castles swimming pool in Falmouth, Paradise Park in Hayle, Flambards in Helston.

pathosking@btinternet.com

HELSTON *(Camping)*

GEAR ORGANIC CL SITE 32

St Martin
Helston TR12 6DE
Tel: 01326 221364

Caravan Site (open May-Sept)
£12 pn for 2 persons

Farm shop sells organic produce and
homemade food

Biodynamic Agricultural Association

The CL is a well maintained large orchard offering shelter, space, privacy and peace. Our organic farm shop sells organic and local produce – fresh fruit and vegetables, apple juice, milk, ice cream, etc. Organic and local produce is also used in the homemade takeaway food, including hot pizzas, bread and cakes. Real Cornish pasties made on site daily. The farm slopes down to the beautiful Helford River off Falmouth Bay. Boats for hire at Helford and St Anthony to explore Frenchman's Creek and points along the river. There are beaches and small fishing ports within six miles. Wet weather activities in the area – Paradise Park in Hayle, Flambards in Helston, Ships and Castles swimming pool in Falmouth.

pathosking@btinternet.com

HELSTON *(S-C)*

ROSUICK COTTAGE 33

Rosuick Organic Farm
St Martin TR12 6DZ
Tel: 01326 231302

Cottage: sleeps 6
£250-£650 pw

Farm shop and café sell home and local produce

Soil Association

Rosuick Organic Farm is situated in its own picturesque valley in an Area of Outstanding Natural Beauty. The farm has been in the Oates family since the 1700s, ours being the 6th generation to farm here. The cottages are all in their own private grounds, but with access to the tennis court and farm trail. Rosuick Cottage has just been refurbished. It is a very grand house with its own amazing two-acre garden. It has a sunny aspect, looking out across its own garden and the fields beyond. We sell as much of our own home produce as possible at our farm shop, located on the edge of the farm. Spring water supply. Wonderful walks on the farm and the Goonhilly Downs. We now have nine Bactrian camels.

oates@rosuick.co.uk www.rosuick.co.uk

HELSTON *(S-C)*

ROSUICK FARM HOUSE 34

Rosuick Organic Farm
St Martin TR12 6DZ
Tel: 01326 231302

Cottage: sleeps 10
£450-£975 pw

Farm shop and café sell home and local produce

Soil Association

Rosuick Organic Farm is situated in its own picturesque valley in an Area of Outstanding Natural Beauty. Rosuick Farm House is a beautiful traditional stone farmhouse, with a history reaching back to the Domesday Book. The main property of the valley, it has 15th-century doors and many character features, and nestles in its country surroundings. There is access from the farmhouse to the tennis court and farm trail. We sell as much of our own home produce as possible at our farm shop, which is located on the edge of the farm. Spring water supply. Wonderful walking on the farm and the Goonhilly Downs. We have nine Bactrian camels, which are to be used for camel treks. Visitor centre and café.

oates@rosuick.co.uk www.rosuick.co.uk

HELSTON *(S-C)*

TREGITHEW FARM 35

Manaccan
Helston TR12 6HX
Tel: 01326 231382

Self-Catering: sleeps 2
Prices on request

Organic produce is available locally

Soil Association

Self-catering accommodation with a large garden in a peaceful location, close to Frenchman's Creek and the Helford River. Part of a listed building, the Georgian house has many original features. Panelled sitting room with television, books and board games. Farmhouse kitchen with modern conveniences (electric cooker, fridge, washing machine, tumble drier, microwave). Stairs to first floor lead to the bedroom with a double bed and a night store heater, and a bathroom with a shower. Linen is provided if necessary and costs £5 extra per person. A passage door leads to the side garden. Plenty of parking space. Saturday to Saturday, arriving 3pm and departing 10am. Details and prices on request.

HELSTON *(S-C)*

THE WING 36

Tregellast Barton Farm
St Keverne TR12 6NX
Tel: 01326 280479

Converted Barn: sleeps 6
£200-£595 pw

Our own organic milk, cream, ice cream, etc

Soil Association

The Wing has been converted from an old barn which forms the south-facing wing of the farmhouse. It has its own entrance and a small lawn outside. Tregellast Barton has always been home to Channel Island cows. The farm has grown to 200 acres and has around a hundred milking Jersey cows. Both the land and the herd are certified organic. Farm produce includes organic milk, organic cream, organic ice cream, organic clotted cream fudge, apple juice, cider, pasties, mustards, chutneys, jams and marmalade. Enjoy delicious homemade food and locally made organic beers at our licensed tea room / restaurant. There is a mile of easy walking in a charming valley of ponds, meadows and woods.

admin@roskillys.co.uk www.roskillys.co.uk/fc-thewing.htm

LAUNCESTON *(S-C)*

EAST PENREST BARN 37

East Penrest Farm
Lezant PL15 9NR
Tel: 01579 370186

Converted Barn: sleeps 10, £400–£1,400 pw
Home cooked meals (by arrangement)

Where possible our own organic produce is used

Soil Association

East Penrest is a 120-acre organic beef and sheep farm in the lovely Inny Valley, on the fringes of the Tamar Valley Area of Outstanding Natural Beauty. Free range children are especially welcome. Home cooked meals by prior arrangement, with lots of fresh vegetables and potatoes or rice. Where possible I use our own organic produce, otherwise it is sourced locally from non-intensive environmentally friendly systems. Enjoy a plate of hot from the oven scones with clotted cream and homemade strawberry jam at teatime (£10 for eighteen scones). Main course and pudding for supper (£10 pp, minimum of six persons). Or a candlelit three course dinner in the farmhouse (£20 pp, four to six persons).

jrider@lineone.net www.organicfarmholiday.co.uk

LISKEARD *(B&B)*

BOTELET 38

Herodsfoot
Liskeard PL14 4RD
Tel: 01503 220225

Farmhouse Bed and Breakfast
£30–£40 pppn

At least 80% organic (we have been serving organic food for more than ten years)

Situated in sparsely populated south-east Cornwall between Liskeard, Lostwithiel and Fowey, people have stayed at Botelet since the 1930s. Delicious non-cooked breakfasts are prepared with organic, local and fair-trade produce and, in season, blueberries and raspberries from our organic kitchen garden. Explore 300 acres of traditional farmland, our family home since 1865. As part of the Countryside Stewardship Scheme, see conservation work on scheduled monument Bury Down Hill Fort, orchards, woodland walks and Cornish hedging. No fuss healthy lifestyle amidst history, art, natural beauty, peace, clean air, pure water, zero light pollution. Massage and reflexology treatments are also available.

stay@botelet.com www.botelet.com

LOOE *(B&B)*

BUTTERVILLA 39

Polbathic
Torpoint PL11 3EY
Tel: 01503 230315

Bed and Breakfast, £37.50-£47.50 pppn
Evening Meal, £30

Local seasonal produce, organic wherever
possible

Soil Association

Fifteen organic acres of exceptionally beautiful countryside two miles from the Cornish coast. Comfortable large double ensuite rooms with modern conveniences and eco-friendly solar heated power showers. Local seasonal produce for breakfasts and evening meals, home-grown organic or sourced from organic suppliers whenever possible. We grow a range of fresh fruit and vegetables in our extensive kitchen garden. We care for our land in a sustainable, natural, eco-friendly way and have an abundance of wildlife to help you feel close to nature. Buttervilla has no farm animals, so guests can roam freely in the delightful grounds. The environment is clean, pure and influenced by sweet Atlantic breezes.

info@buttervilla.com   www.buttervilla.com

LOOE *(B&B)*

HALL BARTON FARM 40

Pelynt
Looe PL13 2JR
Tel: 01503 220203

Farmhouse Bed and Breakfast
Ensuite, £26 pppn

All food is organic and local subject to
availability

Soil Association

Hall Barton Farm has been in our family for over sixty years. It is a fully working organic farm, certified organic since 2000. Our sheep, cattle and deer are all farmed to organic standards. The animals are raised on our own home-grown organic crops. We grow crops such as wheat, oats and beans and pride ourselves on this self-sufficiency. We provide you with a healthy organic breakfast to set you up for the day. Hall Barton Farm is the perfect base to see all of Cornwall during your stay. It is only ten minutes drive to the historic fishing ports of Looe and Polperro and the surrounding sandy beaches, and less than thirty minutes drive to the Eden Project. We would prefer contact by phone for bookings.

giles@farmergiles.org

LOOE *(Camping)*

KEVERAL FARM 41

Nr Seaton
Looe PL13 1PA
Tel: 01503 250135

Camping, from £3 per adult pn
Yurts and Tipis, from £5 per adult pn

Organic produce sometimes available in season

Soil Association

Keveral Farm is a community of sixteen adults and ten children. We have been organic for over thirty years. Camping is in our orchard, and is quiet, sheltered and car-free. Tipis and yurts available for hire. There is a hot shower. Our visitors' barn (kitchen facilities and indoor space) can be used for an extra charge. The farm is very safe and secure. It is only fifteen minutes walk from the beach and the seaside village of Seaton. The walk to the beach is through the woods, along an ancient footpath. Many other scenic coastal and woodland walks are nearby, including the coast footpath and the Seaton Valley Countryside Park. Situated on the south-east coast, the farm is four miles from the fishing port of Looe.

oak@keveral.org www.keveral.org

LOOE *(B&B)*

LESQUITE B&B 42

Lansallos
Looe PL13 2QE
Tel: 01503 220315

Farmhouse Bed and Breakfast
Double £30-£32 pppn, Single £45 pn

Includes organic farm produce, homemade preserves

Soil Association

An attractive farmhouse, of 17th century origin, on a working organic farm in a peaceful wooded valley between Polperro and Fowey, which can be reached by picturesque ferry crossing. Lesquite nestles at the end of our farm drive in the midst of beautiful countryside. We offer bed and breakfast for up to six persons in the renovated farmhouse. Full Cornish breakfast of fresh fruit or yogurt, cereals or muesli, and traditional cooked fare including our own hens' eggs, toast and homemade preserves. The breakfast room has french doors onto a patio overlooking the garden. New for 2008 are our garden apartments, all on ground level, independent from the farmhouse with wheelchair users in mind.

stay@lesquite.co.uk www.lesquite.co.uk

LOOE *(S-C)* LITTLE COTTAGE 43

Lesquite
Lansallos PL13 2QE
Tel: 01503 220315

Cottage: sleeps 2, £200-£450 pw

Organic farm produce may be available

Soil Association

Little Cottage is a tastefully and sympathetically converted wagon house and stable, adjacent to Lesquite farmhouse. The accommodation, which is all on ground level, includes a sitting room with french doors opening onto its own patio looking out onto lawns, the woods and the pond. Wake up to the sound of birds singing. Contemplate the absolute tranquillity that our setting bestows on you. Take a walk and feed the waterfowl on our pond. Our stream, which feeds the pond, is a tributary of the Fowey River, and our pond is home to mallard and moorhen. You may even be lucky enough to see the turquoise flash of a very shy kingfisher. Woodland walks and the Cornwall Coast Path are nearby.

tolputt@lesquite-polperro.fsnet.co.uk   www.lesquite-polperro.fsnet.co.uk

LOOE *(S-C)* MEADOW BANK 44

West Kellow Farm
Lansallos PL13 2QL
Tel: 01503 272089

Cottage: sleeps 4, £250-£590 pw
Breakfast (on request)

Organic produce used whenever possible

In Conversion

An attractive stone cottage on a 160-acre organic beef farm in an Area of Outstanding Natural Beauty. Recently converted, it retains much of its original charm, with exposed wooden beams and galleried accommodation. Breakfast for guests of the cottage can be provided in the farmhouse for an additional cost (details on request). The hearty cooked Cornish breakfast is prepared on the farmhouse Aga. Homemade bread and preserves. Organic produce used whenever possible. The farm buildings are set in a peaceful location in a large garden with two ponds and panoramic countryside views. You can explore the garden, the wildlife ponds and surrounding farm (children must be accompanied).

westkellow@aol.com   www.westkellow.co.uk

LOOE *(S-C)*

VALLEY VIEW 45

West Kellow Farm
Lansallos PL13 2QL
Tel: 01503 272089

Cottage: sleeps 2, £200-£380 pw
Breakfast (on request)

Organic produce used whenever possible

In Conversion

A delightful stone cottage on a 160-acre organic beef farm in an Area of Outstanding Natural Beauty. The farm overlooks the beautiful and tranquil Cornish countryside only one mile from Polperro. Breakfast for guests of the cottage can be provided in the farmhouse for an additional cost (details on request). The hearty cooked Cornish breakfast is prepared on the farmhouse Aga. Homemade bread and preserves. Organic produce is used whenever possible. The farm buildings are set in a peaceful location in a large garden with two ponds and panoramic countryside views. You are welcome to explore the garden, the wildlife ponds and the surrounding farm (all children must be accompanied).

westkellow@aol.com www.westkellow.co.uk

LOOE *(B&B)*

WEST KELLOW FARM 46

Lansallos
Looe PL13 2QL
Tel: 01503 272089

Bed and Breakfast
£25 pppn

Organic produce used whenever possible

In Conversion

Victorian farmhouse on a 160-acre organic beef farm in an Area of Outstanding Natural Beauty. Set in a peaceful location in a large garden with two ponds and panoramic views of unspoilt countryside. On arrival, sample a cream tea in the conservatory. Enjoy a hearty cooked Cornish breakfast prepared on the farmhouse Aga. Homemade bread and preserves. Organic produce used whenever possible. Explore the garden and surrounding farm. The more adventurous may walk down the valley to the unspoilt fishing village of Polperro, about a mile away (where you can also join the famous coastal path). Then take a horse drawn bus down the quaint narrow streets to the picturesque fishing harbour.

westkellow@aol.com www.westkellow.co.uk

MORWENSTOW *(B&B)*

EAST WOOLLEY FARM 47

Woolley
Morwenstow EX23 9PP
Tel: 01288 331525

Farmhouse Bed and Breakfast
From £26 pppn

Local and organic food used whenever
possible

Organic Farmers & Growers

A mixed organic farm located in the quiet hamlet of Woolley in the parish of Morwenstow on the North Cornish coast. Guest rooms are self-contained in a converted barn. A traditional English breakfast, or something lighter if you prefer, is served in the farmhouse, and local and organic produce is used where possible. Eggs are from our own hens, the delicious bacon and sausages from our local butcher. You are welcome to sit and relax in the conservatory or laze in the garden. Guests are invited to view the farm and meet the animals. We have also made a nature walk for guests across our fields and through our woodland. The beaches at Duckpool and Welcombe are only a short distance away.

julia@eastwoolleyfarm.plus.com www.eastwoolleyfarm.co.uk

PENZANCE *(Camping)*

BOTREA 48

Botrea Farm
Newbridge TR20 8PP
Tel: 01736 788926

Tipis and Yurts
Courses

Seasonal organic vegetables and organic
meat (beef, chicken, pork, lamb)

Soil Association

Botrea is a working organic farm in an Area of Outstanding Natural Beauty in wonderful West Penwith. Over the summer we are planning to offer courses on a range of subjects – bow making, natural dyeing and spinning, willow weaving, flint knapping, green woodworking, bush craft, tipi and yurt construction, yoga, tai chi, etc. We will update our website with more courses once details have been confirmed. Accommodation will be in one of our tipis or yurts, made to the highest quality from locally sourced sustainable materials. You can buy seasonal vegetables and meat from our own farm and neighbouring farms, subject to availability. Fresh fish is available from nearby Newlyn harbour.

info@botrea.co.uk www.botrea.co.uk

PENZANCE *(Camping)*

PLAN-IT EARTH   49

Chyena
Sancreed TR20 8QS
Tel: 01736 810660

Plan-It Earth Yurt Holidays
Plan-it Earth Family Eco-Camps

Organic meat and vegetables available nearby

Two different eco holidays, both set on an 'Old Macdonald's Farm'-style smallholding with sheep, pigs, geese and chickens. Farmed on organic lines, the holding is in an idyllic location outside Penzance, surrounded by numerous golden sandy beaches. Plan-It Earth Yurt Holidays offer a choice of two yurts (sleeping 2-6), which are luxurious, cosy and comfortable, complete with sheepskins, lanterns, woodburners, and outside camp fires. Plan-it Earth Family Eco-Camps (two weekends in May) are designed to provide your family with an exciting and thought-provoking weekend of low-impact living. Workshops include bushcraft, wildlife walks, hedgerow herbalism and storytelling at nearby ancient sites.

enquiries@plan-itearth.org.uk www.plan-itearth.org.uk

PENDEEN, PENZANCE *(S-C)*

POLMINA   50

Bosigran Farm
Pendeen TR20 8YX
Tel: 01326 555555

Converted Barn (ref 1222): sleeps 2+cot
£282-£588 pw

Rare-breed lamb (subject to availability)

Soil Association

Found at the end of a bumpy track, this charming barn conversion overlooks the wild Penwith moorland and the Atlantic Ocean. Part of a working organic National Trust farm (beef, sheep, poultry) it has been thoughtfully restored under the watchful eye of the Trust. On the first floor and reached by exterior granite steps, this delightful, compact, open plan apartment is unique. Antique pine furniture, stripped floorboards and whitewashed walls enhance the attractive décor. Set within its own grounds, Polmina offers total seclusion. It is perfect for couples seeking peace and tranquillity close to the sea, and ideally located for coastal walking. Short breaks are available from October to March.

enquiries@classic.co.uk www.classic.co.uk/cottage.aspx?year=2007&code=1222

PENZANCE *(B&B)*

TREZELAH FARMHOUSE 51

Trezelah
Badger's Cross TR20 8XD
Tel: 01736 874388

Bed and Breakfast, £35-£50 pppn
Cottage: sleeps 2, £202-£492 pw

We endeavour to use fresh Cornish organic produce where possible

In a former farmyard setting, Trezelah Farmhouse, together with its attached Old Carthouse, forms part of the tiny rural hamlet of Trezelah. We offer a delicious breakfast of fresh fruits, natural ewes' milk yogurt, bacon and sausages from a rare-breed herd and free-range organic eggs (all locally sourced) plus seeded breads baked daily on the premises. An organic vegetable box is available on request for self-catering visitors, or they can take breakfast in the farmhouse by arrangement. Trezelah is built on high ground facing south above Mounts Bay and St Michael's Mount. Tucked away down a small lane leading off the country road, it's five minutes drive from Penzance and ten minutes from St Ives.

info@trezelah.co.uk www.trezelah.co.uk

PRAZE *(B&B)*

DRYM FARM 52

Drym
Praze TR14 0NU
Tel: 01209 831039

Farmhouse Bed and Breakfast
£35-£45 pppn

We use the best ingredients we can find (about 80% organic)

Drym Farm, built in 1705, is a fine Grade II listed house set in a sunny and secluded valley. It has over 2 acres of gardens stocked with exotic plants, roses, camellias and ancient apple trees. The simple and stylish guest rooms offer lovely views of the gardens and countryside. Breakfasts offer a wide choice, including organic and free-range produce, and we try to use local suppliers wherever possible. Drym is a tiny hamlet of a few houses spread along a typically Cornish deep flower lined lane. Although rural and peaceful, Drym Farm is ideally positioned between the north and south coasts. Wonderful beaches, galleries, restaurants (St Ives, Penzance, Marazion, Porthleven, Helston) within ten miles.

drymfarm@hotmail.co.uk www.drymfarm.co.uk

REDRUTH *(S-C)*

BYRE COTT 53

Higher Laity Farm
Portreath TR16 4HY
Tel: 01209 842317

Cottage: sleeps 4, £280-£690 pw

Organic farm produce (beef, lamb, pork, eggs, cauliflower in season), local organic veg

Soil Association

This ground floor, level access cottage (formerly the milking parlour for the farm's pedigree Holstein herd) is full of character and offers a truly delightful holiday retreat. Our working farm is just a mile from the old mining port of Portreath. We have an organic suckler herd of South Devon cattle, all naturally reared on our 60 acres of grassland. Organic pigs, sheep and chickens can also be seen on the farm. We are ideally placed for walkers, with the recently upgraded Mineral Tramways Coast to Coast Path and the nearby beach at Portreath on the South West Coast Path. Higher Laity Farm is also close to the spectacular north coast, with its breathtaking scenery and abundant bird and wildlife.

info@higherlaityfarm.co.uk www.higherlaityfarm.co.uk

REDRUTH *(S-C)*

THE LOFT 54

Higher Laity Farm
Portreath TR16 4HY
Tel: 01209 842317

Loft: sleeps 4
£270-£660 pw

Organic farm produce (beef, lamb, pork, cauliflower in season, eggs), local organic veg

Soil Association

Approached by granite steps, the accommodation (with exposed wooden beams) is on the first floor. Views over superb open countryside can be enjoyed from this delightful cottage. Our working farm is just a mile from the old mining port of Portreath. We have an organic suckler herd of South Devon cattle, naturally reared on our 60 acres of grassland. Organic pigs, sheep and chickens can also be seen on the farm. Ideally placed for walkers, with the recently upgraded Mineral Tramways Coast to Coast Path and the nearby beach at Portreath on the South West Coast Path. Higher Laity Farm is also close to the spectacular north coast, with its breathtaking scenery and abundant bird and wildlife.

info@higherlaityfarm.co.uk www.higherlaityfarm.co.uk/cottages/loft.asp

REDRUTH *(S-C)* TROTTERS 55

Higher Laity Farm
Portreath TR16 4HY
Tel: 01209 842317

Converted Barn: sleeps 4-6
£300-£730 pw

Organic farm produce (beef, lamb, pork, eggs, cauliflower in season), local organic veg

Soil Association

Formerly the farm's pig farrowing house, this stylish and superbly equipped ground floor barn has been converted to provide a charming, spacious holiday home. Our working farm is situated just a mile from the old mining port of Portreath. We have an organic suckler herd of South Devon cattle, all naturally reared on our 60 acres of grassland. Organic pigs, sheep and chickens can also be seen on the farm. We are ideally placed for walkers, with the recently upgraded Mineral Tramways Coast to Coast Path and the nearby beach at Portreath on the South West Coast Path. Higher Laity Farm is also close to the spectacular north coast, with its breathtaking scenery and abundant bird and wildlife.

info@higherlaityfarm.co.uk www.higherlaityfarm.co.uk/cottages/trotters.asp

SALTASH *(B&B)* LANTALLACK FARM 56

Landrake
Saltash PL12 5AE
Tel: 01752 851281

Farmhouse Bed and Breakfast
£45-£50 pppn

Organic milk, yogurt, meat, eggs, fruit, vegetables

Lovely Georgian farm with breathtaking views. ETC 5 diamond Gold Award. Delicious breakfast of fresh fruit salad, organic yogurt, Lantallack orchard apple juice, local organic sausages, Cornish smoked bacon, free-range eggs, homemade bread, or smoked haddock en cocotte straight from the Aga. All produce – including milk, meat, bread, eggs (from our own free-range hens) and vegetables – is sourced organically. We are not officially registered organic, but pesticides or fertilizers have not been used on the land for 20 years. We produce our own lamb. Other locally reared meat comes from our local butcher. Our outdoor solar-heated swimming pool is open May to Sept. Art courses through the year.

nickywalker44@tiscali.co.uk www.lantallack.co.uk

SALTASH *(B&B)*

SMEATON FARM 57

Pillaton
Saltash PL12 6RZ
Tel: 01579 351833

Farmhouse Bed and Breakfast, from £30
pppn Evening Meal, from £15 (pre-book)

Home produced organic food is always used
whenever available

Soil Association

Smeaton is a 450-acre working organic farm situated within the Duchy of Cornwall. A choice
of breakfasts includes Full English, Continental, or fresh local fish, taken in our cosy breakfast
room. Guests can enjoy the beautiful gardens here at the farm whilst enjoying a true Cornish
cream tea. If you require an organic evening meal (complimentary glass of wine included),
this can be pre-booked. Home produced organic food is always used whenever available,
including beef, pork, lamb, free-range eggs and seasonal vegetables. The Aberdeen Angus beef
cattle, Dorset Horn sheep, and Saddleback and Tamworth pigs can always be seen around the
farm. Farm fresh organic meats are available for sale.

info@smeatonfarm.co.uk www.smeatonfarm.co.uk

ST AUSTELL *(B&B)*

PENVERGATE 58

Penvergate Farm
Gorran PL26 6LX
Tel: 01726 842768

Bed and Breakfast
£25-£30 pppn

90% organic, includes own organic produce

Soil Association

A 15th-century house and organic farm situated just five minutes walk from the local beach.
Although modernised, it retains much of its character with thick cob walls and beamed
ceilings. The house is set in extensive grounds with an organic fruit orchard, small streams,
garden and children's play area. All the rooms overlook the orchard and streams. At
Penvergate Farm we raise organic rare breed Large Black Pigs, traditional Herefords, and
most rare breeds of chickens and ducks (all free-range), giving the most wonderful eggs for
your breakfast, or to take home. We also use our own sausage and bacon in the full English
breakfast. Cornish cream teas served in our idyllic country garden.

penvergate@hotmail.com www.penvergateorganicfarm.co.uk

ST AUSTELL *(B&B)*

MOUNT PLEASANT FARM   59

Gorran High Lanes
St Austell PL26 6LR
Tel: 01726 843918

Bed and Breakfast, £24-£30 pppn
Supper, £14 (book in advance)

80%-90% organic breakfasts and suppers

An organic smallholding set in a peaceful rural location with fine views over traditional stone walled fields to the sea beyond. We are environmentally friendly and have been awarded the Green Tourism Gold Award. We are developing half an acre of organic vegetable plots and now growing our own organic food. Delicious organic breakfasts served with eggs from their own hens. Substantial and wholesome homemade vegetarian / vegan suppers available with prior notice. Provenance local and organic. You are welcome to wander in the garden and meet the ducks and hens. Spectacular cliffs and the beautiful south Cornish coastline, with some of the finest sandy beaches in Cornwall, just a mile away.

jill@mpfarm.aquiss.com   www.vegetarian-cornwall.co.uk

ST IVES *(B&B)*

BOSWEDNACK MANOR   60

Zennor
St Ives TR26 3DD
Tel: 01736 794183

Vegetarian Bed and Breakfast
Open April-Sept, £21-£28 pppn

Exclusively organic food if requested in advance

Spacious granite farmhouse set in 3 acres of eco-friendly meadows, vegetable, fruit and flower gardens. We are one mile west of Zennor and surrounded by an ancient, unspoiled landscape of moorland, stone walled fields and magnificent coastal cliffs and coves. Fine views from all the guest rooms. Solar-powered panels provide much of the hot water. Our delicious breakfast is vegetarian and around 50% of the fare is organic (100% organic on request). Homemade, home-grown blackcurrant jam is usually available. We also offer guided wildlife walks. If you prefer to explore on your own there are free walk sheets of circular routes from Boswednack, with notes on local archaeology, wild flowers and birds.

boswednack@ravenfield.co.uk   www.boswednackmanor.co.uk

ST IVES *(B&B)*

THE ORGANIC PANDA 61

1 Pednolver Terrace
St Ives TR26 2EL
Tel: 01736 793890

Bed and Breakfast, £40-£70 pppn
Packed Lunch (order night before)

Organic breakfast and complimentary cakes
or biscuits

The Organic Panda is situated in the vibrant community of St Ives. Our bed and breakfast has stunning views overlooking the harbour and the sea. With its use of natural materials and eco-friendly products the Organic Panda offers beautiful, spacious, contemporary accommodation. Enjoy breakfast at our ten-seater rustic table. All our food is fresh, organic, and locally sourced where possible. Choose your delicious breakfast (meat, fish, vegetarian, vegan) from an extensive menu. Dietary requirements are welcomed and catered for, including gluten-free, sugar-free, diary-free, but never taste-free. We bake all our own bread (wholemeal, gluten-free, yeast-free), as well as specialist cakes and biscuits.

info@organicpanda.co.uk www.organicpanda.co.uk

TINTAGEL *(B&B)*

MICHAEL HOUSE 62

Trelake Lane
Treknow PL34 0EW
Tel: 01840 770592

Vegetarian Guest House, B&B £22-£30 pppn
Evening Meal, 3 course £17.50

60%-80% of the food we offer is organic or
home-grown

Vegetarian and vegan guest house offering delicious food and a peaceful atmosphere. The house is just over a mile from Tintagel in the pretty hamlet of Treknow. It looks down towards the sea over rolling fields and the valley leading to Trebarwith Strand, whose stunning beach is five minutes drive away (fifteen minutes on foot). As well as delicious and extensive breakfasts we offer 3 course evening meals to guests by arrangement. These are on a set menu basis and draw inspiration from traditional and world cuisine. Colour and flavour are paramount. We aim to use the best local, fairly-traded, home produced and / or organic produce that we can obtain. We are licensed. Michael House is open all year.

info@michael-house.co.uk www.michael-house.co.uk

TRURO (S-C)

ARRALLAS FARM COTTAGE   63

Arrallas Farm
Ladock TR2 4NP
Tel: 01872 510032

Cottage: sleeps 6-8, £325-£1,075 pw

Short Breaks (out of season)

Fresh unpasteurised milk available by arrangement

Soil Association

The cottage is the west wing of a partly Georgian Grade II listed farmhouse on a 300-acre Duchy of Cornwall organic dairy farm. We have 180 cows and a viewing area from which to watch the milking. We sell our milk through OMSCO, and our milk regularly gets used to produce Yeo Valley cheese and sometimes to make organic Cornish brie. We are happy to show our guests around the farm. Visitors might enjoy helping give the young calves their milk or collecting the eggs from our friendly chickens. Below the farm is a large area of mixed woodland, a great place for wildlife enthusiasts. Lots of walks in the area. The farm is twenty minutes from the sea. An organic vegetable box can be ordered.

aliceebush@aol.com   www.arrallasfarmholidays.co.uk

TRURO (S-C)

ARRALLAS STABLES   64

Arrallas Farm
Ladock TR2 4NP
Tel: 01872 510032

Cottage: sleeps 6, £325-£1,000 pw
Short Breaks (out of season)

Fresh unpasteurised milk available by arrangement

Soil Association

A stylish single storey property with high ceilings and a slate floor on a 300-acre Duchy of Cornwall organic dairy farm. We have 180 cows and a viewing area from which to watch the milking. We sell our milk through OMSCO, and our milk regularly gets used to produce Yeo Valley cheese and sometimes to make organic Cornish brie. We are happy to show our guests around the farm. Visitors might enjoy helping give the young calves their milk or collecting the eggs from our friendly chickens. Below the farm is a large area of mixed woodland, a great place for wildlife enthusiasts. Lots of walks in the area. The farm is only twenty minutes drive from the sea. An organic vegetable box can be ordered.

aliceebush@aol.com   www.arrallasfarmholidays.co.uk

TRURO *(S-C)*

CALLESTOCK COURTYARD 65

Little Callestock Farm
Zelah TR4 9HB
Tel: 01872 540445

Apartments: sleep 2 £270-£485 pw

Organic milk, scones, jam, clotted cream, eggs

Organic Farmers & Growers

Set in a truly rural location, these charming barns have been lovingly restored to an excellent standard (4 stars). These properties have four-posters, whirlpool baths, woodburning stoves, exposed stonework, wooden floors and beautiful pine beams. Little Callestock is an organic dairy farm with a herd of sixty Jersey cows. Our organic produce includes milk, homemade scones, jam, clotted cream, and eggs. A welcome tray with an organic clotted cream tea is provided on arrival. Ramble through the farm and surrounding tranquil countryside. Use our bikes and explore pretty unspoilt country lanes. Visit Truro, the Eden Project, and superb sandy beaches. Come and find out why our guests keep returning.

liznick@littlecallestockfarm.co.uk www.callestockcourtyard.com

TRURO *(S-C)*

MILLERS 66

Kennall Vale Mills
Ponsanooth TR3 7HL
Tel: 01209 861168

Cottage: sleeps 4, £310-£580 per week
Short breaks, 2 person discounts available

Organic welcome tray plus organic fruit from the forest garden when available

Granite stone cottage in a secluded woodland valley setting next to the River Kennall. There are riverside seating areas and gardens around an attractive mill leat. The cottage also has its own private courtyard. Organic welcome tray includes homemade Cornish ginger biscuits. Complimentary organic fruit bowl. Visitors can walk in our private nature reserve, which features a wildlife conservation lake and bluebell woodland. We are part of the forest garden network set up by the Agroforestry Research Trust. Tours are available of our newly established organic forest garden project. We are registered as a WWOOF host for volunteers. There's a well stocked organic shop and café in the nearby village.

natasha@austin-uk.co.uk www.kennallvale.co.uk

TRURO *(S-C)*

OFFICE 67

Kennall Vale Mills
Ponsanooth TR3 7HL
Tel: 01209 861168

Cotttage: sleeps 2
£250-£400 pw

Organic welcome tray plus organic fruit
from the forest garden when available

Granite stone cottage in a secluded woodland valley setting next to the River Kennall. It has its own private riverside seating area and small garden (the cottage is not recommended for young children). Organic welcome tray includes homemade Cornish ginger biscuits. Complimentary organic fruit bowl. Visitors can walk in our private nature reserve, which features a wildlife conservation lake and bluebell woodland. We are part of the forest garden network set up by the Agroforestry Research Trust. Tours are available of our newly established organic forest garden project. We are registered as a WWOOF host for volunteers. There's a well stocked organic shop and café in the nearby village of Four Lanes.

natasha@austin-uk.co.uk   www.kennallvale.co.uk

TRURO *(S-C)*

ORCHARD COTTAGE 68

Little Callestock Farm
Zelah TR4 9HB
Tel: 01872 540445

Converted Barn: sleeps 4
£295-£520 pw

Organic milk, scones, jam, clotted cream, eggs

Organic Farmers & Growers

Pretty detached barn conversion set in its own private garden. Renovated to a high standard (3-star property) it offers year-round family holidays and breaks. Large garden with patio and garden furniture. Barbecue available. Little Callestock is an organic dairy farm with a herd of sixty Jersey cows. Our organic produce includes milk, homemade scones, jam, clotted cream, butter and eggs. A welcome tray with an organic clotted cream tea is provided on arrival. Ramble through the farm and surrounding tranquil countryside. Use our bikes and explore pretty unspoilt country lanes. Visit the cathedral city of Truro, the Eden Project, and superb sandy beaches. Come and find out why our guests keep returning.

liznick@littlecallestockfarm.co.uk www.callestockcourtyard.com

TRURO *(S-C)*

STABLES 69

Kennall Vale Mills
Ponsanooth TR3 7HL
Tel: 01209 861168

Cottage: sleeps 4+1, £300-£580 per week
Short breaks, 2 person discounts available

Organic welcome tray plus organic fruit
from the forest garden when available

Granite stone cottage in a secluded woodland valley setting. It is set back a little from the river and has its own private garden with cobbled paths and steps leading down to a mill leat (the cottage is not recommended for under fives). Organic welcome tray includes homemade Cornish biscuits. Complimentary organic fruit bowl. Visitors can walk in our private nature reserve, featuring a wildlife conservation lake and bluebell woodland. We are part of the forest garden network set up by the Agroforestry Research Trust. Tours available of our newly established organic forest garden project. We are registered as a WWOOF host. Well stocked organic shop and café in the nearby village.

natasha@austin-uk.co.uk www.kennallvale.co.uk

ZELAH, TRURO *(S-C)*

WHEAL BUSY 70

Little Callestock Farm
Zelah TR4 9HB
Tel: 01872 540445

Converted Barn: sleeps 3
£315-£610 pw

Organic milk, scones, jam, clotted cream,
eggs

Organic Farmers & Growers

A detached barn conversion (our 5-star property), Wheal Busy is on the edge of the courtyard. The living area has a lovely oak floor and a woodburning stove. The gallery bedroom is accessed via a beautiful claret spiral staircase. Little Callestock is an organic dairy farm with a herd of sixty Jersey cows. Organic produce includes milk, homemade scones, jam, clotted cream, butter and eggs. A welcome tray with an organic clotted cream tea is provided on arrival. Ramble through the farm and surrounding tranquil countryside. Use our bikes and explore pretty unspoilt country lanes. Visit the cathedral city of Truro, the Eden Project, and superb sandy beaches. Come and find out why our guests keep returning.

liznick@littlecallestockfarm.co.uk www.callestockcourtyard.com/whealbusy.html

WEST PENWITH *(B&B)*

KEIGWIN FARMHOUSE 71

Morvah
West Penwith TR19 7TS
Tel: 01736 786425

Vegetarian Bed and Breakfast
£28 pppn

80%-95% organic (local or home-grown / homemade)

The house is about 300 years old, set in 2 acres of gardens and a field overlooking the Atlantic near the small village of Morvah. I provide an organic vegetarian breakfast with fruit, yogurt, cereal, toasts and croissants and homemade marmalade, with a cooked vegetarian breakfast if required. A large organic potager provides us with plenty of vegetables, herbs and salads. We are Wholesome Food Association producers. We get eggs from our own organically reared ducks, and from nearby hens. Enjoy homemade scones or a cake and a pot of tea on your arrival. A sandy / rocky beach and the South West Coast Path are just a few minutes' walk away. Six miles from St Ives, on the B3306.

g.wyatt-smith@virgin.net www.yewtreegallery.com/gardens.htm

AMBLESIDE *(B&B)*

COTE HOW 72

Rydal
Ambleside LA22 9LW
Tel: 015394 32765

Bed and Breakfast
From £45 pppn (min 2 nights stay)

All food is freshly prepared using only organic ingredients

Soil Association

Centrally located within the Lake District National Park, Cote How is a 16th-century country guest house and tearoom offering luxury accommodation and organic food. We are Soil Association licensed for our breakfast and tearoom to provide our visitors with the best organic, seasonal, local and wholesome food available. Packed lunches on request. Enjoy a homemade organic cream tea whilst contributing to local conservation projects. We bake all our own scones, cakes and bread, and make our own preserves and chutneys using organic produce. Set in 4 acres and close to Rydal Water, Cote How is within easy reach of Ambleside and Grasmere. Green Tourism Business Scheme Gold Award.

info@cotehow.co.uk www.cotehow.co.uk

AMBLESIDE *(Hotel)*

MOSS GROVE HOTEL 73

Grasmere
Ambleside LA22 9SW
Tel: 015394 35251

Small Hotel, £65-£120 pppn
Mediterranean buffet-style breakfast

Buffet breakfast in the country kitchen
(70%-95% organic)

Centrally located in the village of Grasmere, within the Lake District National Park. The hotel features beautiful bathroom suites with spa baths, showers and underfloor heating, mostly superking-size beds (handmade from reclaimed timbers or natural leather), high-speed internet access and flat screen TVs in all rooms, an extensive Mediterranean buffet breakfast serving only organic, local and fair trade food. The organic ethos includes recycling wherever possible, redecoration with organic clay paints, oak hardwood flooring, furnishings predominantly free from man-made fibres and chemicals, cotton and wool used for all soft furnishings, natural duck down duvets and pillows, and filtered water throughout.

enquiries@mossgrove.com www.mossgrove.com

AMBLESIDE *(B&B)*

NAB COTTAGE 74

Rydal
Ambleside LA22 9SD
Tel: 015394 35311

B&B (Oct-July), £27-£30 pppn
Dinner, 3 course £18 (by arrangement)

We make our own bread, and use organic produce wherever possible

Nab Cottage is between Grasmere and Ambleside in the heart of the Lake District, with beautiful views over the lake. It dates from the 16th century and stands alone near the shores of Rydal Water, surrounded by mountains. Many original features remain – beams, flagged floors, spice cupboard, mullioned windows, open fire. Enjoy our homemade bread and a long breakfast. The atmosphere is easy-going, and guests can enjoy spending time inside. Outside, the views and the walks are stunning. Excellent low level routes and longer treks directly from the cottage. Packed lunches, dinner or lighter snacks by arrangement using fresh, organic and fairtrade ingredients. Massage, Reiki, Shiatsu available.

tim@nabcottage.com www.nabcottage.com

AMBLESIDE *(B&B)*

YEWFIELD 75

Hawkshead Hill
Hawkshead LA22 0PR
Tel: 015394 36765

Vegetarian Bed and Breakfast, £35-£45 pppn

We have a vegetarian restaurant in Ambleside

Breakfast is between 70% and 90% organic

A peaceful retreat in the heart of the English Lake District. We offer a wholefood continental buffet including fresh fruits, muesli, cereals, home baked bread, yogurt, preserves, coffee and teas and a full cooked breakfast. There are over 30 acres of land around the house, including native woodland, rough fell pasture, a small tarn and a stream. The grazed pasture is managed carefully, giving priority to ecological considerations (part of the Environmentally Sensitive Areas scheme). Newly developed ornamental areas closer to the house include orchards, organic vegetable gardens, a herb patio and a mixed border. A nature trail through the land and gardens guides you round the grounds.

derek.yewfield@btinternet.com www.yewfield.co.uk

BROUGHTON IN FURNESS *(S-C)*

HIGH WALLABARROW 76

High Wallabarrow Farm
Ulpha LA20 6EA
Tel: 01229 715011

Barn: sleeps 4-5, £250-£450 per week

Camping Barn, £8 pppn

Free-range eggs, Hebridean lamb, Galloway beef may be available

A beautiful sheltered corner of Dunnerdale amongst native oakwoods and flower-rich meadows in a sweeping bend of the River Duddon. Adjoining the farmhouse, the accommodation overlooks the garden, beck, rocky crags and the farmyard. The woodlands, garden and vegetable beds at Wallabarrow are all managed organically. Visitors are free to roam over 450 acres of farm woodland and pastures. Free-range eggs, Hebridean lamb, Galloway beef, and organically grown fruit and vegetables may be available to buy. A camping barn sleeping twelve (available from May 2008, £8 pppn) is situated in the farmyard, but safely enclosed with a newly planted organic orchard and lovely lakeland views.

info@wallabarrow.co.uk www.wallabarrow.co.uk

BRAMPTON *(B&B)*

SLACK HOUSE FARM 77

Gilsland
Brampton CA8 7DB
Tel: 016977 47351

Farmhouse Bed and Breakfast, £28-£35 pppn; Packed Lunch £6, Evening Meal £15

Home or locally produced (at least 95% organic)

Soil Association

A 45-hectare working organic dairy and sheep farm in open, unspoilt countryside. Beautiful, peaceful surroundings. Magnificent views in all seasons. The house overlooks Birdoswald Roman Fort and Hadrian's Wall. An ideal location for a tranquil holiday. Group rates available. Enjoy home cooking of wholesome meals, freshly prepared from home or locally produced organic food (at least 95% organic). Fairtrade tea, coffee, fruit, etc. Sample our Birdoswald Organic Farmhouse Cheese. The farm is managed within the Country Stewardship Scheme to enhance the wildlife habitat. Enjoy the diversity of wildlife on our conservation farm walk. On-farm accommodation for horses, and routes to ride.

slackhousefarm@lineone.net www.slackhousefarm.co.uk

CARLISLE *(S-C)*

LOW LUCKENS 78

Low Luckens Farm
Roweltown CA6 6LJ
Tel: 016977 48186

Self-Catering: sleeps 9+3, £12-£15 pppn
Full Centre £100 pn, £375 pw

Organic produce can be purchased from the farm when available

Soil Association

The Organic Resource Centre is housed in a traditional farm building at Low Luckens Farm. Set in beautiful countryside close to the Scottish Borders and Hadrian's Wall. Part of the Soil Association's Farm Network, the farm produces organic beef, lamb, pork and vegetables. The centre provides simple, clean and inexpensive self-catering accommodation for groups and families who enjoy the countryside, or want to become actively involved in farm or conservation. It is also excellent for walkers and cyclists. An extensive Countryside Stewardship agreement covers the farm's 220 acres, including riverside and woodland footpaths. Organic produce can be purchased from the farm when available.

lowluckensorc@hotmail.com www.lowluckensfarm.co.uk

GRANGE-OVER-SANDS *(B&B)*

HOWBARROW B&B 79

Cartmel
Grange-over-Sands LA11 7SS
Tel: 015395 36330

Bed and Organic Breakfast, £57.50 room pn
Dinner, 4 course £19.50 (by arrangement)

100% organic food

Soil Association

Howbarrow is an organic smallholding with panoramic views of the Lake District and the Cumbrian coast. The 16th-century family farmhouse has slate floors and oak beams. Full organic breakfast and evening meals by arrangement. 100% of the food provided is organic, much of which is produced on the farm. Farm produce includes meat, vegetables, herbs and soft fruit. The land is in an environmentally sensitive area, and is managed under a scheme to enhance the wildlife and landscape features. 44 varieties of birdlife have been recorded, as well as deer, badgers and bats. Part of the Soil Association's Open Farm Network, Howbarrow also has a farm shop, a display area and a farm walk.

enquiries@howbarroworganic.co.uk www.howbarroworganic.co.uk

GRASMERE *(Hotel)*

LANCRIGG HOTEL 80

Easedale
Grasmere LA22 9QN
Tel: 015394 35317

Dinner Bed and Breakfast, from £70 pppn
Organic Vegetarian Restaurant

Delicious organic vegetarian food, organic wines and beers

Biodynamic Agricultural Association

The hotel is set in the picturesque valley of Easedale in the heart of the Lake District, half a mile from the village of Grasmere. It provides comfortable and relaxing accommodation and makes a wonderful escape from a busy world. There are wonderful walks from the door. The house has many connections with past and present writers, poets, artists and musicians. The Green Valley Organic Restaurant at Lancrigg is open daily for breakfast, lunch, tea, evening meals. The food is freshly prepared and the imaginative menu has been designed by experienced chefs and a qualified nutritionist. Special diets are well catered for. Most of the dishes have a vegan alternative. Booking advisable for evening meals.

info@lancrigg.co.uk www.lancrigg.co.uk

ASHBOURNE (S-C)

ANCESTRAL BARN   81

Church Farm
Stanshope DE6 2AD
Tel: 01335 310243

5-star Ancestral Barn: sleeps 6

£483-£876 pw

Home produced meat, free-range eggs, our own honey, bread

Organic Farmers & Growers

Fabulous award-winning 5-star 200 year old Grade II listed barn on our organic farm. We are situated on top of Halldale, which meanders down to Dovedale in the Peak District National Park. Come and enjoy seeing our lambs being born in the spring and our wild flower meadows in the summer, and cosy open fires in the winter to snooze by. Locally produced foods can be delivered to your barn door. Just ask Sue at Church Farm door for our organic beef and lamb. Proud holders of the District Environmental Quality Mark for our accommodation and organic farming practices (use of locally grown or locally produced products, use of environmentally friendly products, conservation of landscape).

sue@fowler89.fsnet.co.uk www.dovedalecottages.co.uk/ancestralbarn

ASHBOURNE (S-C)

BEECHENHILL COTTAGE 82

Beechenhill Farm
Ilam DE6 2BD
Tel: 01335 310274

Cottage: sleeps 2, £180-£390 pw

Seasonal range of locally produced ready meals and puddings

Soil Association

Romantic small cottage hideaway on an organic dairy farm. Ready meals are available to buy, made with produce from local farms managed under environmentally sensitive systems. Tiny, warm and peaceful, the beautifully decorated stone cottage is in its own walled garden with not another house in sight. Relax by the real fire for cosy evenings. Virtually allergy-free, so no pets. The farmhouse garden has garden games, a Swedish-style hot tub (book in advance), sculptures, and stunning views. The farm trail is a lovely way to spend an hour or so. Beechenhill Haybarn is an ideal venue for parties and events. The farm and tourism business have achieved the Peak District Environmental Quality Mark.

beechenhill@btinternet.com www.beechenhill.co.uk/cottage.htm

ASHBOURNE *(B&B)*   BEECHENHILL FARM   83

Ilam
Ashbourne DE6 2BD
Tel: 01335 310274

Farmhouse Bed and Breakfast
£34-£40 pppn

Local and organic produce where possible

Soil Association

Working organic dairy farm (Peak District Environmental Quality Mark) situated in a beautiful area of the Peak District National Park. The long, low, ivy-clad, traditional farmhouse, built from local limestone, has been added to since the 1500s. Wonderful views over the lovely garden and fields with grazing cows. Farmhouse breakfasts are prepared with local and organic produce where possible. Fruit, cereals, homemade organic yogurt, our famous porridge, homemade bread toasted with homemade jam and honey from the farm, feature alongside a delicious traditional farmhouse breakfast. Farm walks, garden games, table tennis, Swedish-style hot tub. Events and parties welcome at the Haybarn.

beechenhill@btinternet.com www.beechenhill.co.uk

ASHBOURNE *(S-C)*   CHURCH FARM COTTAGE 84

Church Farm
Stanshope DE6 2AD
Tel: 01335 310243

Grade II Listed Cottage: sleeps 4
£393-£676 pw

Home produced meat, free-range eggs, our own honey, bread

Organic Farmers & Growers

Discover our lovingly restored, Grade II listed pretty 16th-century country cottage on our organic farm. Situated on top of Halldale, which meanders down to Dovedale in the Peak District National Park. Come and enjoy seeing our lambs being born in the spring, our wild flower meadows in the summer, and cosy open fires to snooze by in the winter. Locally produced foods can be delivered to the cottage door. Just ask Sue at Church Farm door for our organic beef and lamb. We are proud holders of the Peak District Environmental Quality Mark for supporting environment practices such as conservation of landscape, use of locally grown / produced products, use of environmentally friendly products.

sue@fowler89.fsnet.co.uk www.dovedalecottages.co.uk/farmcottage

ASHBOURNE *(S-C)*

DALE BOTTOM COTTAGE 85

Church Farm
Stanshope DE6 2AD
Tel: 01335 310243

Cottage: sleeps 2-6
£583-£1057 pw

Home produced meat, free-range eggs, our own honey, bread

Organic Farmers & Growers

Dale Bottom Cottage is situated in the hamlet of Hopedale in a little enclave on its own, with the cottage's front and the delightful cottage garden soaking up the sun. Its stone walls are smothered in clematis, and there's a medley of colour from roses and sweet peas which clamber up the wall beside the front door. From whichever direction you approach, you can't ignore the display of English cottage garden flowers at their best, containing such as dancing dahlias, dianthus, cosmos and helianthus. Locally produced foods can be delivered to your door. Just ask Sue at Church Farm door for our organic beef and lamb. Also ask Sue for our free-range eggs or a jar of our delicately flavoured honey.

sue@fowler89.fsnet.co.uk   www.dovedalecottages.co.uk/dalebottom

ASHBOURNE *(S-C)*

NEW HOUSE FARM 86

Kniveton
Ashbourne DE6 1JL
Tel: 01335 342429

Cottage: sleeps 4, £50 pn, £200-£300 pw
Caravans £10-£20 pn, Camping £2 pppn

Farm shop (organic, free-range, fairtrade foods)

Organic Farmers & Growers

New House is a two hundred year old farmhouse on a 41-acre working organic farm. Our traditional family farm produces beef, lamb, eggs, fruit and vegetables. Organic, free-range and fairtrade foods, including vegetables, bread, eggs, sausages, chicken, beef and lamb, are available at the farm shop. We have a small animals farmyard for children. There are guided farm walks during the summer. The location has historical and archaeological features (leyline, Bronze Age burials, quarry, lead mine) suitable for field trips and research. Experimental permaculture and conservation areas. Working conservation holidays. Courses in permaculture. Good walking area with wild flowers and lovely views.

bob@newhousefarm.co.uk   www.newhousefarm.co.uk

ASHBOURNE *(B&B)* PARK VIEW FARM 87

Bullhurst Lane
Weston Underwood DE6 4PA
Tel: 01335 360352

Farmhouse Bed and Breakfast
Double, £80-£85 pn

Organic and locally produced where possible

Organic Farmers & Growers

Enjoy country house hospitality in our elegant farmhouse, set in large gardens overlooking the National Trust's magnificent Kedleston Park. Park View is a working sheep farm, managed organically. Sheep graze peacefully in the fields beyond the farmhouse, which dates back to 1860. Beautiful four-poster ensuite rooms, crisp white sheets, flowers and books. The delightful dining room and drawing room overlook the south-facing vine covered terrace. Delicious breakfasts cooked on the Aga. Eggs collected each morning from the hens who wander from their house to the garden and clover-filled fields beyond. Fresh fruits from the farm are made into a delicious compote for breakfast. We bake our own bread.

enquiries@parkviewfarm.co.uk www.parkviewfarm.co.uk

ASHBOURNE *(S-C)* THE CHOP HOUSE 88

Windlehill Farm
Sutton-on-the-Hill DE6 5JH
Tel: 01283 732377

Converted Barn: sleeps 6, £280-£520 pw
Short Breaks (out of season)

Organic produce available locally

Organic Farmers & Growers

The Chop House has been carefully converted from the farm corn shed. It features original beams and has pleasant views of the farmyard, duck pond and surrounding countryside. There has been a farm on this site since at least the 16th century. Set in tranquil countryside, the 10-acre working organic smallholding specialises in traditional and rare breeds of livestock. We keep pure breed Poll Dorset Sheep and Kerry Cattle, which are milked on the family organic farm next door, as well as pedigree beagles. We have a fully accessible meeting room which caters for up to fifteen people. Spinning and weaving and other courses run by local specialists are available. Please contact us for more information.

windlehill@btinternet.com www.windlehill.btinternet.co.uk

ASHBOURNE *(S-C)*

COTTAGE BY THE POND 89

Beechenhill Farm
Ilam DE6 2BD
Tel: 01335 310274

Cottage: sleeps 6, £260-£690 pw

Seasonal range of locally produced ready meals and puddings

Soil Association

Beautifully decorated cottage (converted from the old milking barn) on an organic dairy farm near Dovedale. It is virtually allergy-free, so no pets, and designed to be accessible to everybody, including those with wheelchairs. The large sitting room has a patio window which looks due south over a little courtyard, a walled pond and rolling farmland. Savour the distinctive foods of the area – a delicious range of locally made ready meals and puddings is available to buy from the farmhouse. The seasonal range includes Dovedale Traditional Beef, Peak Feast vegetarian dishes, and traditional Peak Puddings. The farm and tourism business have achieved the Peak District Environmental Quality Mark.

beechenhill@btinternet.com www.beechenhill.co.uk/cottagebypond.htm

ASHBOURNE *(S-C)*

THE HAYLOFT 90

Windlehill Farm
Sutton-on-the-Hill DE6 5JH
Tel: 01283 732377

Apartment: sleeps 2, £160-£250 pw
Short Breaks (out of season)

Organic produce available locally

Organic Farmers & Growers

The Hayloft is a first floor apartment over the old stable. It features original beams and pleasant views of the farmyard, duck pond and surrounding countryside. There has been a farm on this site since at least the 16th century. Set in tranquil countryside, this 10-acre working organic smallholding specialises in traditional and rare breeds of livestock. We keep pure breed Poll Dorset Sheep and Kerry Cattle, which are milked on the family organic farm next door, as well as pedigree beagles. We have a fully accessible meeting room which caters for groups of up to fifteen people. Spinning and weaving and other courses run by local specialists are also available. Please contact us for more information.

windlehill@btinternet.com www.windlehill.btinternet.co.uk

HOPE VALLEY *(B&B)*

STONECROFT 91

Edale
Hope Valley S33 7ZA
Tel: 01433 670262

Bed and Breakfast, double from £65 pn

Packed lunches and picnic baskets to order

Organic, fairtrade, or locally sourced when possible (at least 70% organic)

A charming period country residence in the beautiful and historic hamlet of Edale in the Derbyshire Peak District. At Stonecroft we are passionate about good food, and this means it must be natural, of top quality and full of flavour; and because of this we follow an organic policy as much as possible. We use local food producers in preference to imported goods, which have an adverse affect on the environment, as well as fairtrade and natural products. Even the body lotions, hand creams and soaps that you will find in your bedrooms are made especially for us in Derbyshire from natural ingredients. We also use environmentally friendly products and use local recycling facilities as much as is practical.

stonecroftedale@btconnect.com www.stonecroftguesthouse.co.uk

MATLOCK *(B&B)*

HEARTHSTONE FARM 92

Hearthstone Lane
Riber DE4 5JW
Tel: 01629 534304

Farmhouse Bed and Breakfast
Double £65 pn, Single £45 pn

We use our own organic produce wherever possible

Organic Farmers & Growers

Hearthstone Farm is a traditional working family farm producing organic beef, pork and lamb, plus bacon, gammon and sausage made from organic pork (sold through our on-farm outlet). Nestling at the edge of the Peak District, our 16th-century stone farmhouse is the perfect location for a relaxing break in some of Britain's most breathtaking countryside. Situated on the edge of the village, the farm offers a comfortable environment from which to explore the surrounding area. We pride ourselves on the quality of our breakfasts, using our own organic produce wherever possible. Guests are welcome to go out onto the farm, and we are delighted to answer any questions about our farming methods.

enquiries@hearthstonefarm.co.uk www.hearthstonefarm.co.uk

ASHBURTON *(B&B)*

CUDDYFORD 93

Rew Road
Broadpark TQ13 7EN
Tel: 01364 653325

Vegetarian Bed and Breakfast, £20-£25 pppn
Optional Evening Meal, £12-£15

Organically grown home produce

Family-run vegetarian guest house in a rural setting amongst peaceful rolling landscape within Dartmoor National Park. Wholesome cooking is prepared using organically grown fruit and vegetables, free-range eggs, honey from our own hives, and home baked bread. Home pressed apple juice. River and woodland walks nearby, where a wide range of lichen, ferns, primroses and sage can be found, as well as a variety of birds such as the redstart, flycatcher and wood wren. Near Grimspound (a Bronze Age settlement with tumuli), stone circles and dolmens. We are ideally situated for exploring the heather-covered moors and the Dart Valley, with easy access to the South Devon coast.

a.vevers@csl.gov.uk

BAMPTON *(B&B)*

HARTON FARM 94

Oakford
Bampton EX16 9HH
Tel: 01398 351209

Farmhouse Bed and Breakfast, £20 pppn
Evening Meal, £12

Vegetables home-grown and pesticide-free,
meat home produced without additives

This stone-built 17th-century farmhouse faces south in one of the hidden valleys above the River Exe on the southern edge of Exmoor. The farm covers 53 acres. The ancient hedgerows and banks of the farm are a typical Devon feature. We specialise in producing our own naturally grown lamb, pork and beef, and many varieties of vegetables and unusual herbs. Hearty, wholesome home cooking using vegetables, herbs and fruit from our own kitchen gardens, and home produced meat. Enjoy the wildlife and the landscape by walking the farm trail. Explore areas of flower-rich pasture, and the pretty wooded valley and streamside. We have been awarded the Green Tourism Business Scheme Gold Award.

lindy@hartonfarm.co.uk www.hartonfarm.co.uk

BARNSTAPLE *(B&B)*

BOWDEN FARM 95

Muddiford
Barnstaple EX31 4HR
Tel: 01271 850502

Farmhouse Bed and Breakfast
£40-£50 pppn

Mostly local, homemade and / or organic
produce

Soil Association

Bed and Breakfast in a Grade II listed house, originally built in the 16th century. Revive your senses at our wonderful 82-acre organic farm in North Devon. We have three ensuite bedrooms. Guests have sole use of a large sitting room and dining room with inglenook fireplaces and woodburning stoves. Take in the panorama, with stunning views over Saunton Sands to the sea beyond. Breathe fresh sea air, and feast on a delicious breakfast, which consists of as much local, homemade and / or organic produce as possible. Guests are welcome to wander around the farm. Rare breeds and wildlife galore. The beaches are about eight miles to the west of the farm, and Exmoor about six miles to the east.

stay@bowdenfarm.com www.bowdenfarm.com

BARNSTAPLE *(Camping)*

PARKHILL FARM 96

Shirwell
Barnstaple EX31 4JN
Tel: 01271 850323

Caravan: sleeps 6, £20-£25 pn
Camping, £8 per unit

Organic lamb is sometimes available from
the farm

Soil Association

Parkhill Farm is a level field with outstanding views, but with shelter from hedges. We are a quiet site on an organic beef and sheep farm. We also have free-range chickens. Our holiday caravan is situated in a private and quiet garden area surrounded by trees. Enjoy our farm walks. There are spectacular views across the countryside, including Exmoor. This is a wonderful place to come on holiday, with a great mixture of beaches and countryside. There are more than enough places to visit and things to do to keep even the most active person perfectly happy. Close to both Arlington Court and the Broomhill Sculpture Gardens. Barnstaple town centre is two and a half miles away. Coastal resorts nearby.

ray.toms@virgin.net

BIDEFORD *(S-C)*

THE BARN 97

Old Pound House, Woolsery
Bideford EX39 5QA
Tel: 01237 431589

Converted Barn: sleeps 2-4
£225-£375 pw

Home-grown organically produced
vegetables in season

The small converted barn is separated from our house by a drive and a large herb bed. A single dwelling beside a single track road, the barn backs onto a small field full of wild flowers in summer. We are surrounded by 13 acres of fields with a large wildlife pond. All our vegetables are organic (available to purchase in season) and are grown on our land. Herbs are free. The house and barn are situated about half a mile outside the rural village of Woolfardisworthy (Woolsery) between Bideford and Bude. The village has a pub and a general store and post office. An outside tennis court is available by the new village hall. Many sand and stone beaches nearby, and lovely walks both coastal and inland.

oldpoundhouse@ntlworld.com

BOVEY TRACEY *(S-C)*

STICKWICK FARM 98

Frost Farm
Hennock TQ13 9PP
Tel: 01626 833266

Cottage, Farmhouse, Manor House
Sleep 5, 7, 12, from £215 pw

Our farm shop sells a small variety of produce

Organic Farmers & Growers

Stickwick is a 140-acre working organic farm, splendidly sited between Dartmoor and the sea. The cosy cottage, character farmhouse and grand Georgian manor house (dating from the 1780s and listed Grade II) are renovated in keeping with the period and retain many original features. Discover the seasons of the year, as early spring sunshine warms the earth, primroses, catkins, bluebells and campions burst forth. Pack your wellingtons, bring binoculars and follow the nature trail with bird and wildlife hide – or just relax in the spacious garden. You can buy fresh farm eggs, organic vegetables (in season), homemade cakes, scones, local honey and local ice cream from the farm shop.

linda@frostfarm.co.uk www.frostfarm.co.uk

BRAUNTON *(S-C)*

CAEN BYRE 99

Little Comfort Farm, Braunton
Barnstaple EX33 2NJ
Tel: 01271 812414

Cottage: sleeps 4-5
£337-£828 pw

Organic sausages, bacon, pork, lamb, beef,
eggs, jam, apple juice

Soil Association

Working organic family farm in an exceptionally secluded, peaceful valley through which the little River Caen flows. Caen Byre is a spacious two bedroom detached cottage with a large entrance porch. Converted from a traditional stone farm building, it is set in its own lovely garden. Enjoy a homemade Devonshire cream tea on arrival, prepared with organic and local produce. We supply our own organic sausages, bacon, pork, lamb, beef and eggs, as well as homemade meals using our own meat. Feed the animals and collect the eggs. Explore the Devon Wildlife Trust private nature trail. Coarse fishing on our tranquil well stocked lake. Fifteen minutes from secluded coves, miles of golden sand, super surfing.

info@littlecomfortfarm.co.uk www.littlecomfortfarm.co.uk

BRAUNTON *(S-C)*

CAEN END 100

Little Comfort Farm, Braunton
Barnstaple EX33 2NJ
Tel: 01271 812414

Cottage: sleeps 6
£385-£946 pw

Organic sausages, bacon, pork, lamb, beef,
eggs, jam, apple juice

Soil Association

Working organic family farm in a secluded, peaceful valley through which the little River Caen flows. Caen End is a completely self-contained three bedroom single storey wing of the farmhouse, with level access and its own terrace and lawn running down to the river. Enjoy a homemade Devonshire cream tea on arrival, prepared with organic and local produce. We supply our own organic sausages, bacon, pork, lamb, beef and eggs, as well as homemade meals using our own meat. Feed the animals and collect the eggs. Explore the Devon Wildlife Trust private nature trail. Coarse fishing on our tranquil well stocked lake. The farm is fifteen minutes from secluded coves, miles of golden sand, super surfing.

info@littlecomfortfarm.co.uk www.littlecomfortfarm.co.uk

BRAUNTON (S-C)

THE GRANARY 101

Little Comfort Farm, Braunton
Barnstaple EX33 2NJ
Tel: 01271 812414

Cottage: sleeps 4
£321-£789 pw

Organic sausages, bacon, pork, lamb, beef,
eggs, jam, apple juice

Soil Association

Working organic family farm in a secluded valley through which the little River Caen flows. The Granary is a spacious two bedroom single storey cottage with level access from the parking area. Converted from a traditional stone farm building, it is set in its own lovely garden. Enjoy a homemade Devonshire cream tea on arrival, prepared with organic and local produce. We supply our own organic sausages, bacon, pork, lamb, beef and eggs, as well as homemade meals using our own meat. Feed the animals. Collect the eggs. Explore the Devon Wildlife Trust private nature trail. Coarse fishing on our well stocked lake. Fifteen minutes from secluded coves, miles of golden sand, and super surfing.

info@littlecomfortfarm.co.uk   www.littlecomfortfarm.co.uk

BRAUNTON (S-C)

MILL HOUSE 102

Little Comfort Farm, Braunton
Barnstaple EX33 2NJ
Tel: 01271 812414

Cottage: sleeps 10
£602-£1,557 pw

Organic sausages, bacon, pork, lamb, beef,
eggs, jam, apple juice

Soil Association

Working organic family farm in an exceptionally secluded, peaceful valley through which the little River Caen flows. The Mill House is a spacious five bedroom cottage on two levels. Converted from a traditional stone farm building, it is set in its own lovely garden. Enjoy a homemade Devonshire cream tea on arrival, prepared with organic and local produce. We supply our own organic sausages, bacon, pork, lamb, beef and eggs, as well as homemade meals using our own meat. Feed the animals and collect the eggs. Explore the Devon Wildlife Trust private nature trail. Coarse fishing on our tranquil well stocked lake. The farm is fifteen minutes from secluded coves, miles of golden sand, super surfing.

info@littlecomfortfarm.co.uk   www.littlecomfortfarm.co.uk

BRAUNTON *(S-C)*

WOODLARK   103

Little Comfort Farm, Braunton
Barnstaple EX33 2NJ
Tel: 01271 812414

Cottage: sleeps 4
£289-£716 pw

Organic sausages, bacon, pork, lamb, beef,
eggs, jam, apple juice

Soil Association

Working organic family farm in an exceptionally secluded, peaceful valley through which the little River Caen flows. Woodlark is a two bedroom 'upside down' cottage, with lovely views from its first floor living room over the gardens. Outside is a lawned area with terrace. Enjoy a homemade Devonshire cream tea on arrival, prepared with organic and local produce. We supply our own organic sausages, bacon, pork, lamb, beef and eggs, as well as homemade meals using our own meat. Feed the animals and collect the eggs. Explore the Devon Wildlife Trust private nature trail. Coarse fishing on our tranquil well stocked lake. The farm Is fifteen minutes from secluded coves, miles of golden sand, super surfing.

info@littlecomfortfarm.co.uk www.littlecomfortfarm.co.uk

BUCKFASTLEIGH *(S-C)*

BOWDEN LODGE   104

Bowden Farm
Buckfastleigh TQ11 0JG
Tel: 01364 643955

Cottage: sleeps 4
£205-£512 pw

Home reared beef, lamb, free-range eggs

Soil Association

Bowden Farm is set in some of Devon's most striking countryside. It has panoramic views from Widecombe on the foothills of Dartmoor, right around to Dawlish, Teignmouth, Torquay, and Brixham on the South Devon coastline. Bowden Lodge is a recently converted self-contained unit adjoining the farmhouse. Situated on a working organic farm, visitors are welcome to take a guided tour of the farm to meet the animals. These include cattle, sheep, chickens and miniature Shetland ponies. There are some fantastic walks adjoining the farm and within the Dartmoor National Park. Pony trekking, climbing, canoeing, swimming, fishing, cycling, letterboxing are some of the activities available in the area.

cowsnsheepnponies@bowdenfarm.org.uk www.holidaydevon.org.uk

BUCKFASTLEIGH (S-C)

MOORVIEW 105

Bowden Farm
Buckfastleigh TQ11 0JG
Tel: 01364 643955

Caravan: sleeps 6
£150-£360 pw

Home reared beef, lamb, free-range eggs

Soil Association

Bowden Farm is set in some of Devon's most striking countryside. It has panoramic views from Widecombe on the foothills of Dartmoor, right around to Dawlish, Teignmouth, Torquay and Brixham on the South Devon coastline. Moorview is a luxury caravan set in its own individual plot. It is fully equipped, double glazed, with heaters in every room. The veranda and lounge area enjoy spectacular views over the surrounding countryside. Situated on a working organic farm, visitors are welcome to take a guided tour of the farm to meet the animals. These include cattle, sheep, chickens and miniature Shetland ponies. There are fantastic walks adjoining the farm and also within Dartmoor National Park.

cowsnsheepnponies@bowdenfarm.org.uk www.holidaydevon.org.uk

COLYTON (S-C)

HIGHER WISCOMBE 106

Higher Wiscombe
Southleigh EX24 6JF
Tel: 01404 871360

Barn Conversions: sleep 6-20
£440-£4,450 pw

Organic produce available at many close local outlets, also farms and markets

Three luxury conversions developed from old stone barns, with underfloor heating throughout, luxury bathrooms, and oak and granite kitchens with range cookers. Extensive information is given regarding local producers, detailing which provide organic food. We can also provide a variety of catering options for you. The courtyard setting is down a three-quarter mile drive in the centre of the extensive grounds of the owners' 19th century farmhouse, and enjoys panoramic rural views over open unspoilt countryside. Guests can explore our 52-acre grounds. We do not allow any chemicals of any kind inside or outside the farm. We have been awarded the Gold standard by the Green Tourism Business Scheme.

alistair@higherwiscombe.com www.higherwiscombe.com

CREDITON *(B&B)*

ASHRIDGE FARM 107

Sandford
Crediton EX17 4EN
Tel: 01363 774292

Farmhouse Bed and Breakfast
From £25 pppn

Local organic produce used in the breakfast

Soil Association

Set in the beautiful mid Devon countryside, Ashridge Farm is a 200-acre working organic farm with cattle, sheep, pigs, chickens and cereals. You will stay in a warm friendly barn conversion with home cooking. All rooms are on the ground floor with ensuite facilities and underfloor heating (one room has a mobility M2 certificate). Farm holidays are great fun on Ashridge. Guests can help feed the chickens and collect the eggs for breakfast, and feed the lambs. There's a large lawn where children can play safely, and there are 200 acres to roam with wildlife in abundance. Ideal for a holiday or a short break. The north and south Devon coasts, Dartmoor and Exmoor are all within an hour's drive from the farm.

jill@ashridgefarm.co.uk www.ashridgefarm.co.uk

CULLOMPTON *(B&B)*

UPTON FARM 108

Plymtree
Cullompton EX15 1RA
Tel: 01884 33097

Farmhouse Bed and Breakfast
Double, £60 pn

Local, free-range, organic (around 50% organic)

Organic Farmers & Growers

We welcome you to this lovely 17th-century house nestling in the heart of Devon's peaceful Culm Valley. In a tranquil parkland setting, the farmhouse is charmingly furnished with a wealth of beams and an inglenook fireplace. The emphasis is on comfort and a high standard of ensuite accommodation. A delicious home cooked breakfast (around 50% organic, or more on request) is served around a large elegant table in the delightful surroundings of our oak-panelled dining room. The 180-acre organic farm is home to an abundance of birds and wildlife inhabiting the parkland surrounding the garden. Coarse fishing in two lakes (both with lodges) set in the beautiful surroundings. Our great love is training race horses.

DARTMOUTH (B&B)

FIR MOUNT HOUSE 109

Higher Contour Road
Kingswear TQ6 0DE
Tel: 01803 752943

Bed and Breakfast, £40-£45 pppn
Manna from Devon Cookery School

Mainly local and organic food used in all our cooking

Victorian period home in the lovely village of Kingswear, with wonderful views of the River Dart and the surrounding South Hams countryside. Start the day with one of our fabulous breakfasts – organic breads, jams and marmalades, homemade granola, fresh fruits and yogurt with freshly squeezed juices, eggs from our own hens, scrummy bacon and sausages from our friends' organically reared rare-breed pigs. We offer an evening meal of the very finest locally sourced organic meat, fish and vegetables, followed by truly luscious puddings. We also run the Manna from Devon Cookery School, providing relaxed courses concentrating on the great seasonal local food that is on our doorstep.

enquiries@mannafromdevon.com www.mannafromdevon.com

DARTMOUTH (S-C)

HONEYSUCKLE 110

Dittisham Farm
Capton TQ6 0JE
Tel: 07768 625333

Bungalow: sleeps 2-5, £239-£459 per week
Reduced tariff for parties of two people

Organic Berkshire rare breed pork, Red Ruby beef, sausages, organic eggs, honey

Soil Association

A two bedroom bungalow on an organic farm in the unspoilt hamlet of Capton, between Dartmouth and Dittisham (both 3 miles). Here live prize-winning rare breed organic Berkshire pigs, Red Ruby cattle, poultry, bees and Poppy the labrador. The accommodation has been refurbished in a 'farm and country' style. The layout has been designed to appeal to couples of any age, a family with up to three children (travel cot available), or up to four adults. South-facing sun trap area with sun loungers, barbecue and picnic table. Our 20-acre farm is on the edge of the hamlet with some lovely walks. There's an undulating walk around the land, from the far side of which are spectacular views on a clear day.

sue@self-cater.co.uk www.self-cater.co.uk/DittishamFarmHolidayLet

DAWLISH *(S-C)*

DUCKALLER FARM   111

Port Road
Dawlish EX7 0NX
Tel: 01626 863132

Holiday Home: sleeps 6
£185-£440 pw

Organic pork, sausages and bacon plus a
limited range of seasonal vegetables

Soil Association

Situated in its own garden and bordering open fields, the accommodation is a well equipped six berth holiday home with main facilities throughout. It is comprised of a double bedroom, a twin bedroom and a small double bed in the lounge area. A large and private decking area, with views across open countryside, makes an ideal place to relax and unwind. Duckaller Farm is a small organic farm of around 90 acres, primarily growing organic vegetables for local distribution. The farm walk follows a combination of arable margins designed to enhance the habitat for farmland birds. Approached by a private road, Duckaller Farm is well located for exploring the surrounding area and nearby beaches.

holidays@duckallerfarm.co.uk www.duckallerfarm.co.uk

DAWLISH *(B&B)*

SMALLACOMBE FARM   112

Aller Valley
Dawlish EX7 0PS
Tel: 01626 862536

Bed and Breakfast, £26 pppn
Evening Meal (4 evenings pw)

There is plenty of home produced organic food

Soil Association

The farmhouse was built at the turn of the century. It has an attractive veranda and a garden for you to relax in. Your children can play freely with no fear of busy roads, as Smallacombe Farm is at the end of a lane. We are a 120-acre working farm with sheep and free-range chickens. Wildlife includes buzzards, kestrels, pheasants, badgers and the occasional deer. As a Soil Association certified organic farm there is plenty of home produced organic food. Breakfast includes our own organic sausages, bacon, eggs, etc. Although delightfully secluded and completely surrounded by country views, the farm is only two miles from the seaside town of Dawlish with its award-winning sandy beaches.

smallacombefarm@btopenworld.com www.smallacombe-farm-dawlish.co.uk

EXETER *(B&B)*

GREAT CUMMINS FARM   113

Tedburn St Mary
Exeter EX6 6BJ
Tel: 01647 61278

Farmhouse Bed and Breakfast
Double £55 pn, Single £40 pn

Mainly organic (100% organic by prior arrangement)

Soil Association

An exceptionally comfortable 4-star bed and breakfast in a 16th-century farmhouse with wonderful rural views. The delicious breakfast, cooked to order, is either wholly organic (by prior arrangement) or mainly organic using farm produce. Great Cummins is a small family-run organic farm in the glorious rolling hills of mid Devon. It comprises about 40 acres of permanent pasture, some 12 acres of woodland – hardwoods like oak and ash, most of which we planted when we came here ten years ago, an acre of (mainly cider) apple trees and an acre of land for growing vegetables. We sell our organic produce (fruit, vegetables, eggs, meat) direct to our customers via a box scheme and direct orders.

davidgaraway@yahoo.co.uk www.greatcumminsfarm.co.uk

EXETER *(Camping)*

HIGHFIELD FARM   114

Clyst Road
Topsham EX3 0BY
Tel: 01392 876388

Caravan and Camping Site
£5.50 pn per pitch + hook-up

Organic produce in season from the farm gate

Soil Association

Enjoy a truly green break on this family-run organic farm situated in the beautiful Clyst Valley. The family have been farming these 118 acres for the past three generations. Always farmed in a traditional manner, wild flower-rich hay meadows and hedgerows abound. There is a circular nature trail on the farm that runs down to the River Clyst (watch out for otters and other wildlife). You can buy organic free-range eggs and other organic produce in season from the farm gate. Electric hook-up is available for an additional £2 per night (the site has only cold water and no showers). Caravans, motorcaravans, tents welcome. The farm is just a short walk from the historic riverside town of Topsham.

ian@highfieldharvest.freeserve.co.uk

EXETER *(S-C)*

HUXLEY'S HOME 115

Bickham Farm
Kenn EX6 7XL
Tel: 01392 833833

Farmhouse: sleeps 5, £237-£561 pw

When available, pre-order a box of organic vegetables, fruit, bacon, sausages, lamb

Soil Association

Approached by a quiet country lane, this charming farmhouse enjoys peace and seclusion with far-reaching views over open countryside. The property is decorated and furnished to a high standard and retains much of its original charm and character. With some lovely walks adjoining the land and Dartmoor National Park within a short driving distance, walkers and nature lovers will be in their element. The farmhouse is situated on a 120-acre organic farm with sheep, pigs, Huxley the pet pig, turkeys, chickens and cattle. In the evenings, enjoy a guided tour around the farm. You will have the opportunity to pre-order a box of organic vegetables, fruit, bacon, sausages and lamb to await your arrival (when available).

roddy@rodandbens.com www.rodandbens.com

EXETER *(S-C)*

POLTIMORE COTTAGES 116

Poltimore
Nr Exeter EX4 0AA
Tel: 01647 433593

Cottage: sleeps 6, £237-£699 pw

Apartments: sleep 3-4, £185-£523 pw

We can organise an organic vegetable box to be delivered

Soil Association

A cottage adjoining two smart apartments in the grounds of the owners' 60-acre organic farm. Two shared enclosed gardens and a shared games barn. Old farm buildings are close by, but beyond are stunning views. This is the good life – totally peaceful, ducks in the yard, a Shetland pony, goats, some domestic animals, and a half-acre lake. Picturesque Poltimore is a mainly thatched and red-stone hamlet in farmland on the outskirts of Exeter. There's an organic farm shop in Thorverton. Darts Farm Village in Topsham (food hall, deli bar, restaurant) offers a wide range of local farm / organic / high quality produce. Otterton Mill (bakery, restaurant) uses locally sourced ingredients, organic if available.

help@helpfulholidays.com www.helpfulholidays.com/place.asp?placeid=125

EXETER *(S-C)*

POORMAN'S COT   117

Highdown Farm
Bradninch EX5 4LJ
Tel: 01392 881028

Cottage: sleeps 4, £250-£500 pw

Delivery service from Riverford Organic
Farm

Soil Association

Homely cottage, formerly a farm worker's cottage. The name derives from Poorman's Close, the name of a field which borders the cottages. The orchard contains varieties of old-fashioned fruit trees which are becoming rare in this part of the country. We have some laying hens, many of which are old-fashioned breeds. Organic eggs can be purchased from the farmhouse. Fresh organic food, including a seasonal variety of fruit and vegetables, can be delivered to your accommodation from Riverford Organic Farm. Our 450-acre family-run organic dairy farm is owned by the Duchy of Cornwall. Peacefully situated above the Culm Valley, the farm has breathtaking views of the countryside.

svallis@highdownfarm.co.uk   www.highdownfarm.co.uk/poormans.htm

EXETER *(B&B)*

RAFFLES   118

11 Blackall Road
Exeter EX4 4HD
Tel: 01392 270200

Bed and Breakfast, £33-£38 pppn

We offer around 75% organic produce

Centrally located in historic Exeter, Raffles offers excellent bed and breakfast accommodation. The Victorian town house is furnished with antiques and has been sympathetically restored. A full range of breakfast menus is served in the comfortable and spacious dining room. Where possible, much of the fare is organically produced. Guests have use of the well stocked garden. Exeter is one of the few cities to have free guided tours which allow you to experience the detail and history of this beautiful city. The National Parks of Dartmoor and Exmoor are within easy reach. Exeter also provides easy access to unspoiled coastal regions such as Sidmouth, Exmouth, Beer and Seaton.

raffleshtl@btinternet.com   www.raffles-exeter.co.uk

EXETER (B&B)

REKA DOM · 119

43 The Strand
Topsham EX3 0AY
Tel: 01392 873385

Bed and Breakfast
£37.50-£45 pppn

We aim to only provide organic food

Family-run Bed and Breakfast in an unusual 17th-century riverside property. Choice of three very different suites. Facing south, all rooms enjoy views over the beautiful Exe estuary towards Exmouth and the wooded Haldon hills. Our famously extensive breakfast includes homemade breads, jams and marmalades, and is served at your leisure in our unique Blue Room, in front of a log fire during winter months. Please note that our food is organic / free-range and locally sourced whenever possible. An excellent base for exploring Devon, Topsham itself offers river walks, wildlife, quiet spaces, independent shops, a Saturday market and a range of pubs and restaurants championing West Country produce.

beautifulhouse@hotmail.com   www.rekadom.co.uk

EXETER (S-C)

THE CIDER BARN · 120

Highdown Farm
Bradninch EX5 4LJ
Tel: 01392 881028

Converted Barn: sleeps 2
£225-£395 pw

Delivery service from Riverford Organic Farm

Soil Association

Many years ago, this thoughtfully and creatively restored barn was used as a place to press the apples from the farm's orchards to make cider. The orchard now contains varieties of old-fashioned fruit trees which are becoming rare in this part of the country. In the orchard you'll find some laying hens, many of which are old-fashioned breeds. Organic eggs can be purchased from the farmhouse. Fresh organic food, including a seasonal variety of fruit and vegetables, can be delivered to your accommodation from Riverford Organic Farm. Our 450-acre organic dairy farm is owned by the Duchy of Cornwall. Peacefully situated above the Culm Valley, it has breathtaking views of the Devon countryside.

svallis@highdownfarm.co.uk   www.highdownfarm.co.uk/ciderbarn.htm

EXETER *(S-C)*

THE HAYLOFT 121

Maddocks Farm
Kentisbeare EX15 2BU
Tel: 01647 433593

Cottage: sleeps 12, from £653 pw
Short Breaks (minimum stay 3 nights)

Seasonal produce (vegetables, salads, strawberries) when available

Soil Association

Spacious converted barn, attached to other uninhabited barns, across a courtyard from our partly 17th-century listed farmhouse. A welcome pack includes organic, local and fairtrade items plus a homemade organic chocolate banana loaf and six of our own organic eggs. Guests have their own large lawned garden with a patio. We have a 5-acre organic smallholding and specialise in salads, supplying various local shops and a pub with unusual spicy and herb salads. We also run a vegetable box scheme (Jun-Dec). You are welcome to walk around the farm and enjoy the lovely views across miles of countryside. Kentisbeare is an attractive village in the middle of the rolling farmland of the Lower Culm Valley.

help@helpfulholidays.com www.helpfulholidays.com

EXETER *(S-C)*

THE OLD FARMHOUSE 122

Highdown Farm
Bradninch EX5 4LJ
Tel: 01392 881028

House: sleeps 7, £375-£775 pw

Delivery service from Riverford Organic Farm

Soil Association

The Old Farmhouse dates back 400 years. Ideal for families sharing, it is a very spacious house with its own secure garden. The orchard contains varieties of old-fashioned fruit trees which are becoming rare in this part of the country. In the orchard you'll find some laying hens, many of which are old-fashioned breeds. Organic eggs can be purchased from the farm. Fresh organic food, including a seasonal variety of fruit and vegetables, can be delivered to your accommodation from Riverford Organic Farm. Highdown is a 450-acre family-run organic dairy farm owned by the Duchy of Cornwall. Peacefully situated high above the Culm Valley, it has breathtaking views of the beautiful Devonshire countryside.

svallis@highdownfarm.co.uk www.highdownfarm.co.uk/farmhouse.htm

GOODLEIGH *(S-C)*

THE HAVEN AT BAMPFIELD 123

Bampfield Farm
Goodleigh EX32 7NR
Tel: 01271 346566

Cottage: sleeps 4-6, £270-£780 pw
Short Breaks (minimum stay 2 nights)

Try our delicious home produced beef

Organic Farmers & Growers

A perfect location for a special break. The Haven is a charming 17th-century cottage on an organic dairy farm with stunning views of the sea, offering peace, tranquillity and fresh air. The farm nestles in rolling hills and overlooks the River Yeo, and is a favourite with young families and walkers. Enjoy a Devon cream tea on arrival. Collect the eggs and cook them for your breakfast. Watch the farmer, working hand in hand with the land and wildlife. Identify an abundance of wildlife and plants on the farm's nature trail. The lanes around the farm are scented with wild flowers – with their traditional high Devon hedges they have remained the same for centuries. Come and discover this unspoilt corner of North Devon.

lynda@bampfieldfarm.co.uk www.bampfieldfarm.co.uk/haven.htm

GOODLEIGH *(S-C)*

THE OLD GRANARY 124

Bampfield Farm
Goodleigh EX32 7NR
Tel: 01271 346566

Cottage: sleeps 2-8, £290-£920 pw
Short Breaks (minimum stay 2 nights)

Succulent Bampfield beef for you to eat

Organic Farmers & Growers

The Old Granary is a delightful cottage on an organic dairy farm with stunning views of the sea, offering peace, tranquillity and fresh air. The farm nestles in rolling hills and overlooks the River Yeo, and is a favourite with young families and walkers. Enjoy a Devon cream tea on arrival. Watch the cows come home for milking, and the farmer working the land and caring for the wildlife. If you try our organic beef you will definitely want to take some home. Identify an abundance of wildlife and plants on the farm's nature trail. The lanes around the farm are scented with wild flowers – with their traditional high Devon hedges they have remained the same for centuries. Come and discover this unspoilt corner of North Devon.

lynda@bampfieldfarm.co.uk www.bampfieldfarm.co.uk/granary.htm

GREAT TORRINGTON *(B&B)*   LOCKSBEAM FARM   125

Great Torrington
Torrington EX38 7EZ
Tel: 01805 623213

Farmhouse Bed and Breakfast
£27.50-£32.50 pppn

Homemade produce, local produce

In Conversion

Locksbeam is a family-run dairy farm with a herd of ninety dairy cows born and bred on the farm. We are currently in conversion with Organic Farmers & Growers, aiming to achieve full organic status by April 2008. Come and relax and unwind in a family-friendly bed and breakfast in our spacious farmhouse. Homemade cream tea on arrival. All rooms are ensuite. Family rooms are available. Delicious Aga-cooked full English breakfast in the large dining room, with homemade jam and marmalade. Much of the produce in the breakfast is from our local area. Packed lunches available by arrangement. Enjoy many beautiful country walks and panoramic views of the River Torridge and valley from Rise Point.

tracey@locksbeamfarm.co.uk www.locksbeamfarm.co.uk

HARTLAND *(S-C)*   LITTLE BARTON   126

Hartland
Bude EX39 6DY
Tel: 01237 441259

Farmhouse: sleeps 10, £700-£1350 pw
Winter Breaks, from £300 (min 3 nights)

Organic produce, locally grown vegetables, local fish

Set in an Area of Outstanding Natural Beauty, Little Barton is a large Victorian farmhouse with panoramic sea views. Run on organic principles, the farmhouse is under a mile from the coastal path, Atlantic beaches and beautiful wild countryside. A variety of organic food is available locally and orders can be placed in advance. We have our own water supply. A wide range of wildlife lives on the land surrounding the house and the long access track is full of seasonal wildflowers. Situated in the far north-west of the county, Hartland is a thriving community with many craftspeople and a wholefood shop / café. The area is wonderful for swimming, surfing, walking, mountain boarding, bird-watching, etc.

enquiries@littlebartonhartland.co.uk www.littlebartonhartland.co.uk

HOLSWORTHY *(S-C)* THE OWL BARN 127

Berry Barns
Shebbear EX21 5RA
Tel: 01409 281859

Converted Barn: sleeps 6-10
£526-£1,101 pw

Sample our home-grown organic produce

Soil Association

Situated in the grounds of the owners' organic farm, this barn conversion stands detached in a tranquil rural setting. Home to Highland cattle and registered with the Soil Association, the farm produces organic vegetables and free-range eggs, which are available in season to visitors staying at the accommodation. The property has been built using mostly reclaimed timber and displays a wealth of beams. It has oak or flagstone floors to the ground floor and a fitted handmade oak kitchen. Close to Dartmoor National Park, the converted barn commands fine views over the surrounding countryside. The Owl Barn lies within easy reach of the North Devon coastline with its fine sandy beaches.

info@berrybarns.co.uk www.berrybarns.co.uk

HOLSWORTHY *(S-C)* THE SHIPPEN 128

Berry Barns
Shebbear EX21 5RA
Tel: 01409 281859

Converted Barn: sleeps 4-6
£386-£828 pw

Sample our home-grown organic produce

Soil Association

Situated in the grounds of the owners' organic farm, this barn conversion stands detached in a tranquil rural setting. Home to Highland cattle, the farm produces organic vegetables and free-range eggs, which are available in season to visitors staying at the property. The Shippen offers single storey accommodation. The property has been built using mostly reclaimed timber and displays a wealth of beams. It has oak or flagstone floors to the ground floor and a fitted handmade oak kitchen. Close to Dartmoor National Park, the accommodation commands fine views over the surrounding countryside. The Shippen lies within easy reach of the North Devon coastline with its fine sandy beaches.

info@berrybarns.co.uk www.berrybarns.co.uk

HONITON *(S-C)*

CLEW PARK 129

Upcott Farm
Broadhembury EX14 3LP
Tel: 01404 841444

Converted Barn: sleeps 6
£400-£1,050 pw

Superb organic market stall in Honiton
market twice weekly

Organic Farmers & Growers

Clew Park is one of four high quality cottages at Hembury Court. It is situated on a 240-acre organic farm at the edge of the Blackdown Hills in East Devon, a mile from the thatch village of Broadhembury. The four cottages, all with quality finishes of granite, oak and terracotta, are complemented by superb additional facilities. These include a large hot tub, fitness suite, games lawn, barbecue veranda and two large 'oak cruck' structures providing a communal sitting room and games room. When all four cottages are hired together, sleeping a maximum of seventeen, an additional kitchen is available, and the games room, which also has oak tables and chairs, makes a stunning setting for celebrations.

persey@upcottfarm.fsnet.co.uk www.hembury-court-barns.co.uk

HONITON *(S-C)*

POCKETS 130

Upcott Farm
Broadhembury EX14 3LP
Tel: 01404 841444

Converted Barn: sleeps 2
£239-£440 pw

Superb organic market stall in Honiton
market twice weekly

Organic Farmers & Growers

Pockets is one of four high quality cottages found at Hembury Court. It is situated on a 240-acre organic farm at the edge of the Blackdown Hills in East Devon, a mile from the thatch village of Broadhembury. The four cottages, all with quality finishes of granite, oak and terracotta, are complemented by superb additional facilities. These include a large hot tub, fitness suite, games lawn, barbecue veranda and two large 'oak cruck' structures providing a communal sitting room and games room. When all four cottages are hired together, sleeping a maximum of seventeen, an additional kitchen is available, and the games room, which also has oak tables and chairs, makes a stunning setting for celebrations.

persey@upcottfarm.fsnet.co.uk www.hembury-court-barns.co.uk

HONITON *(S-C)*

POPPY'S   131

Upcott Farm
Broadhembury EX14 3LP
Tel: 01404 841444

Converted Barn: sleeps 4
£310-£865 pw

Superb organic market stall in Honiton
market twice weekly

Organic Farmers & Growers

Poppy's is one of four high quality cottages found at Hembury Court. It is situated on a 240-acre organic farm at the edge of the Blackdown Hills in East Devon, a mile from the thatch village of Broadhembury. The four cottages, all with quality finishes of granite, oak and terracotta, are complemented by superb additional facilities. These include a large hot tub, fitness suite, games lawn, barbecue veranda and two large 'oak cruck' structures providing a communal sitting room and games room. When all four cottages are hired together, sleeping a maximum of seventeen, an additional kitchen is available, and the games room, which also has oak tables and chairs, makes a stunning setting for celebrations.

persey@upcottfarm.fsnet.co.uk www.hembury-court-barns.co.uk

HONITON *(S-C)*

SMART'S HOUSE   132

Upcott Farm
Broadhembury EX14 3LP
Tel: 01404 841444

Converted Barn: sleeps 5
£355-£950 pw

Superb organic market stall in Honiton
market twice weekly

Organic Farmers & Growers

One of four high quality cottages found at Hembury Court. It is situated on a 240-acre organic farm at the edge of the Blackdown Hills in East Devon, a mile from the thatch village of Broadhembury. The four cottages, all with quality finishes of granite, oak and terracotta, are complemented by superb additional facilities. These include a large hot tub, fitness suite, games lawn, barbecue veranda and two large 'oak cruck' structures providing a communal sitting room and games room. When all four cottages are hired together, sleeping a maximum of seventeen, an additional kitchen is available, and the games room, which also has oak tables and chairs, makes a stunning setting for celebrations.

persey@upcottfarm.fsnet.co.uk www.hembury-court-barns.co.uk

IVYBRIDGE *(B&B)*

HILLHEAD FARM 133

Ugborough
Ivybridge PL21 0HQ
Tel: 01752 892674

Farmhouse Bed and Breakfast
£25-£30 pppn, single supplement £5

Locally sourced, homemade, much of it organic

Soil Association

A traditional working beef and sheep farm, Hillhead Farm is surrounded by tranquil fields, yet is only five minutes stroll from the village of Ugborough. There are lovely views over the peaceful South Hams countryside. We grow organic vegetables on a field scale as part of a co-operative of like-minded local farmers. Our produce goes to supply a thriving box scheme. Our own garden is organic and we grow vegetables, herbs and soft fruit. We also have a flock of about twenty hens which are truly free-range. Enjoy delicious farmhouse breakfasts in the sunny conservatory, using local produce and homemade organic bread and preserves. We have been awarded the South Hams Green Tourism Silver award.

info@hillhead-farm.co.uk www.hillhead-farm.co.uk

KINGSBRIDGE *(S-C)*

CRANNACOMBE FARM 134

Hazelwood
Loddiswell TQ7 4DX
Tel: 01647 433593

Farmhouse: sleeps 9, from £369 pw
Cider House: sleeps 8, from £361 pw

Our own apple based products, organic food shop three miles away

Soil Association

17th-century farmhouse on a working family farm (80 acres, including apple orchards and sheep). Set in a beautiful unspoilt valley in a designated Area of Outstanding Natural Beauty. Producers of farm-pressed organic apple juices and skilfully blended organic cider from old varieties of apples. Hand-selected organic apples are used to make the delicious apple juice and apple with grape fruit. The 3 acres of organic orchards are certified by the Soil Association. Half a mile of the River Avon runs through the farm, where you can picnic, paddle and swim. Wildlife abounds around the farm, and there are lovely walks. Kingsbridge is just five miles away, and there are many sandy beaches nearby.

help@helpfulholidays.com www.helpfulholidays.com/property.asp?ref=1200a

KINGSBRIDGE *(S-C)*

GARDEN ROOMS 135

Lower Coombe Royal
Kingsbridge TQ7 4AD
Tel: 01548 852880

Self-Catering Retreat: sleeps 2+
£530-£1,030 pw

Organic welcome hamper supplied

Lower Coombe Royal is set in its own private valley in the heart of the South Hams. The one bedroom 5-star self-catering accommodation opens straight out onto the gardens and its own Italianate terrace. It has been as organically prepared as possible, with the bed made from sustainable wood, a mattress made of entirely organic fibres, organic towels and towelling robes, linens and toiletries. An organic welcome hamper is supplied, with home-grown vegetables and fruit when in season. We have eight acres of organic and historic gardens and a growing organic vegetable patch. Plans for the near future include a freshwater swimming pond, chickens to provide eggs and bees to make our own honey.

susi@lowercoomberoyal.co.uk www.lowercoomberoyal.co.uk

KINGSBRIDGE *(B&B)*

HAZELWOOD HOUSE 136

Loddiswell
Kingsbridge TQ7 4EB
Tel: 01548 821232

Bed and Breakfast, £47-£75 pppn
Lunch from £10, Dinner £18-£30

Delicious food using local produce (around 80% organic)

Hazelwood House, set in lush South Devon countryside, reflects this beautiful setting in the food it serves. Every attempt is made to use the fresh, locally grown, organic produce for which Devon is so well known. Hazelwood has its own water supply. The accommodation is unpretentious and comfortable, with fifteen bedrooms (seven of them ensuite). Situated in 67 acres of woodland, meadows and orchards in a wild, unspoilt river valley, it is the perfect place to relax, reflect, and refuel. At Hazelwood we put the earth first. The resulting unspoiled natural beauty of the valley provides a haven for a wide range of wildlife, with otters, badgers, deer and foxes among its residents.

info@hazelwoodhouse.com www.hazelwoodhouse.com

LYNMOUTH *(B&B)*

NORTH WALK HOUSE   137

Lynton
Lynmouth EX35 6HJ
Tel: 01598 753372

Bed and Breakfast, from £40 pppn
Evening Meal, 4 course from £22.95

We pride ourselves on using only the
freshest local organic produce

North Walk House is a former gentleman's residence. Built in 1850, it has fabulous views over the Welsh coast, Countisbury and Foreland Point. We serve amazing breakfasts with lots of fresh fruit, free-range eggs and local organic produce. Choose your home-cooked evening meal from a blackboard menu, featuring locally caught seafood and organic produce from Hindon Farm. The extensive gardens provide the ability to study the flora and fauna of the National Park. North Walk House specialises in walking holidays, offering details of a range of self-guided walks for the novice and the experienced. We have immediate access to the South West Coast Path, which passes the front of the house.

walk@northwalkhouse.co.uk www.northwalkhouse.co.uk

MANATON *(B&B)*

EASDON COTTAGE   138

Long Lane
Manaton TQ13 9XB
Tel: 01647 221389

Vegetarian B&B, from £60 per room pn
Evening Meal (by arrangement)

At least 95% organic food all year round

Beautiful location, peaceful surroundings, comfort, relaxation, and a warm welcome are all to be found at Easdon Cottage – a classic stone house on the edge of Dartmoor with historic roots back beyond the 17th century. Bed and breakfast accommodation is a cosy ensuite double / twin room. A vegetarian or vegan breakfast is prepared using organically produced food wherever possible, including home-grown in season. Packed lunches are from £5 per person. Evening meal by prior arrangement. At different times of the year the countryside is rich with native species of wildlife and wild flowers. Artists and photographers find much to inspire them. Good walking, riding, bicycling country.

easdondown@btopenworld.com

MANATON *(S-C)*

THE BARN 139

Long Lane
Manaton TQ13 9XB
Tel: 01647 221389

Barn: sleeps 2-3, £215-£375 per week.
Winter Breaks, from £135 (min 3 nights)

Organic food available locally, home-grown
in season

Nestling into the hill and on the edge of the bridlepath leading on to Easdon Tor, the barn, with its thick granite walls, provides a comfortable hideaway in the landscape. The setting, on the east side of Dartmoor, is remote and tranquil. A short flight of steps leads up through a stable door into the main open plan accommodation, with views over the surrounding countryside and moorland. An area of garden is available to sit and enjoy the views, or for meals outside. You can buy organic food locally, and home-grown vegetables may be available in season for purchase from the owners' nearby garden. Spring water. Good walking and wildlife watching with excellent views in the surrounding area.

easdondown@btopenworld.com

OKEHAMPTON *(S-C)*

EVERSFIELD COACH HOUSE 140

Ellacott Barton
Bratton Clovelly EX20 4JF
Tel: 01837 871480

Cottage: sleeps 8
From £250 pw

Organic breakfast pack includes our own
bacon and sausages

Soil Association

Luxury self-catered accommodation on an 850-acre organic estate. The Coach House is set in an attractive courtyard of old stone buildings next to the manor house. Outside, guests can enjoy soaking up the sun in their own sheltered private courtyard. At the rear of the house there is easy access onto a public footpath, which winds across lovely farmland to the village pub. Eversfield breeds and rears Aberdeen Angus cattle, Large Black pigs and Romney sheep in a truly organic and traditional way. Organic produce (meat, poultry, eggs, vegetables, fruit, salad) is available for guests to purchase from the farm, subject to availability. An organic breakfast can be provided in Eversfield Lodge with prior notice.

bookings@eversfieldlodge.co.uk www.eversfieldlodge.co.uk

OKEHAMPTON *(B&B)*

EVERSFIELD LODGE 141

Ellacott Barton
Bratton Clovelly EX20 4LB
Tel: 01837 871480

Country House Bed and Breakfast
From £65 per room pn

Organic where possible, homemade, local
and regional

Soil Association

Nestling on the edge of Dartmoor, Eversfield Lodge forms part of an 850-acre organic working farm producing award-winning meat. We offer luxury ensuite accommodation for up to sixteen people, and provide a full English organic breakfast served in the elegant dining room with glorious views towards Dartmoor. Organic orange juice, locally made organic apple juice, award-winning Eversfield organic bacon and sausages, eggs from our own chickens, local organic marmalade, jams and honey, a selection of toast, croissants and pastries, fresh fruit and yogurts, West Country milk and butter. Complimentary hot and cold drinks and homemade cakes. Dinner option is available for house parties.

bookings@eversfieldlodge.co.uk www.eversfieldlodge.co.uk

OKEHAMPTON *(Hotel)*

PERCY'S COUNTRY HOTEL 142

Coombeshead Estate
Virginstow EX21 5EA
Tel: 01409 211236

Small Hotel (contact for prices)
Restaurant (breakfast, lunch, dinner)

Contemporary country cooking, delicious
home-produced organic breakfast

Soil Association

Located in one of England's three designated areas of tranquillity, the tasteful and eco-friendly hotel offers superbly appointed rooms. The cuisine delivers exceptional country cooking. The award-winning dishes – food created on the estate with zero food miles – burst with colour and flavour and include organic pork and lamb reared on the estate together with organic vegetables, herbs and salads from the well stocked vegetable garden. Stroll around the gardens, woodland and peaceful lakes to experience the outstanding beauty of the 130-acre organic estate. The 60,000 tree plantation, comprising mixed broadleaves and edible shrubs, goes a long way to making Percy's a carbon neutral hotel.

info@percys.co.uk www.percys.co.uk

OTTERY ST MARY *(S-C)*

THE HAY HOUSE 143

Blacklake Farm, East Hill
Ottery St Mary EX11 1QA
Tel: 01404 812122

Holiday House: sleeps 6
£350-£850 pw

Organic farm produce is available (fresh or frozen)

Soil Association

Blacklake Farm is set on the upper slopes of East Hill. We have converted and restored the old hay house and adjacent dairy to make an exclusive holiday home. The conversion has been done with traditional building materials throughout, such as lime plaster and lime-based paint. Being the only holiday house on the farm, the Hay House offers peace and privacy, with only the ebb and flow of traditional farm life to punctuate the day. The farmland is varied – a mix of permanent old pasture, deciduous woodland and old apple orchards. We are a Soil Association Organic Demonstration Farm and welcome opportunities to talk to people about our organic farming experience. The coast is three miles away.

catherine@blacklakefarm.com   www.blacklakefarm.com

PAIGNTON *(B&B)*

WEST BLAGDON 144

Blagdon Barton
Paignton TQ4 7PU
Tel: 01803 665599

Vegetarian Bed and Breakfast, from £25 pppn
Evening Meal (by arrangement)

We can offer 100% organic if required

An organic smallholding on the edge of Torbay – the 'English Riviera'. It is contained in a small medieval hamlet, yet is secluded and surrounded by views of fields and hills. We have a small menagerie of animals including goats and ducks, and children are welcome to feed and pet them. We have two double rooms with views of the garden – one ensuite and the other with a private, but separate, bathroom. Food is vegetarian and we can offer 100% organic if required. Some of the food will be home-grown. In addition to bed and breakfast we also offer an evening meal by arrangement. We run art retreat weekends for those who would enjoy a restful and creative diversion from the rigours of modern living.

ronigail@aol.com

PLYMOUTH *(B&B)*

BERKELEY'S OF ST JAMES 145

4 St James Place East
The Hoe PL1 3AS
Tel: 01752 221654

Guest House
Double B&B, £55-£60 pn

Organic / free-range where possible (40%-60% organic)

Berkeley's of St James is an elegant Victorian guest house situated in a secluded square on Plymouth Hoe. Quiet, exclusive, and furnished to a very high standard, it is tucked away from the main thoroughfare in pleasant and relaxing surroundings. We offer a substantial traditional full English breakfast with a choice of menu. Fresh fruit and fish. Organic and free-range produce is used wherever possible (average 40%-60% organic food during the year). Vegetarians are welcome. We are within easy walking distance of the sea front, the historic Barbican, the theatre and the pavilions. Plymouth is an ideal base for touring Dartmoor, Devon and Cornwall, and is within travelling distance of the Eden Project.

enquiry@onthehoe.co.uk www.onthehoe.co.uk

PLYMOUTH *(S-C)*

CORNER COTTAGE 146

Carswell Farm
Holbeton PL8 1HH
Tel: 01752 830020

Cottage: sleeps 8, £450-£1,500 pw
Organic breakfast hamper (to order)

Organic meat, local organic fruit and vegetables

Soil Association

We are organic dairy farmers on the South Devon coast. The farm is deep in unspoilt countryside in the heart of the South Hams, and overlooks the sea. Our farm cottages are situated along secluded farm lanes a few minutes walk from the coast and Wadham beach. Taste delicious organic milk fresh from our cows when you arrive. Try our award-winning organic lamb and beef (Carswell is the birthplace of The Well Hung Meat Company). Organic Devon breakfast hamper to order. Because we are organic you will see an exceptional quantity and variety of wildlife, including some resident barn owls. Beautiful coves and beaches are nearby, with acres of sand at low tide and some dramatic coastal walks.

enquiries@carswellcottages.com www.carswellcottages.com/cornercottage

PLYMOUTH *(S-C)*   EFFORD HOUSE   147

Flete Estate,
Haye Farm PL8 1JZ
Tel: 01752 830234

Country House: sleeps 12
£740-£2,050 pw

Home produced organic beef and lamb
delivered to the cottage

Soil Association

A beautifully proportioned detached country house set in its own grounds and bordered by mature woodlands. It is one of several properties on our 1,000-acre organic farm, part of the Flete Estate. We are in an Area of Outstanding Natural Beauty by the River Erme estuary, a designated SSSI on the South Devon coast with six miles of drives for walking and bird watching and access to beaches and coastal paths. The estate offers beef and lamb produced on the home farm to our cottage guests. Riverford organic farm shop and café is three miles away, and it's fifteen miles to their farm and field kitchen. Nearby Modbury, the UK's first plastic bag-free town, is a great supporter of organic and local produce traders.

cottages@flete.co.uk www.flete.co.uk

PLYMOUTH *(S-C)*   FLETE MILL COTTAGE   148

Flete Estate,
Haye Farm PL8 1JZ
Tel: 01752 830234

Cottage: sleeps 5
£580-£1,350 pw

Home produced organic beef and lamb
delivered to the cottage

Soil Association

Flete Mill Cottage, one mile along a four mile private drive, has been completely restored and exquisitely renovated. It is one of several properties on our 1,000-acre organic farm, part of the Flete Estate. We are in an Area of Outstanding Natural Beauty by the River Erme estuary, a SSSI on the South Devon coast with six miles of drives for walking and bird watching and access to beaches and coastal paths. The estate offers beef and lamb produced on the home farm to our cottage guests. Riverford organic farm shop and café is three miles away, and it's fifteen miles to their farm and field kitchen. Nearby Modbury, the UK's first plastic bag-free town, is a great supporter of organic and local produce traders.

cottages@flete.co.uk www.flete.co.uk

PLYMOUTH *(S-C)*

LAMBSIDE HOUSE 149

Carswell Farm
Holbeton PL8 1HH
Tel: 01752 830020

Georgian House: sleeps 11+3, £640-£2200 pw

Organic breakfast hamper (to order); Organic meat, local organic fruit and vegetables

Soil Association

We are organic dairy farmers on the South Devon coast. The farm is deep in unspoilt countryside in the heart of the South Hams, and overlooks the sea. Our farm cottages are situated along secluded farm lanes a few minutes walk from the coast and Wadham beach. Taste delicious organic milk fresh from our cows when you arrive. Try our award-winning organic lamb and beef (Carswell is the birthplace of The Well Hung Meat Company). Organic Devon breakfast hamper to order. Because we are organic you will see an exceptional quantity and variety of wildlife, including some resident barn owls. Beautiful coves and beaches are nearby, with acres of sand at low tide and some dramatic coastal walks.

enquiries@carswellcottages.com www.carswellcottages.com/lambsidehouse

PLYMOUTH *(S-C)*

NEPEANS COTTAGE 150

Flete Estate,
Haye Farm PL8 1JZ
Tel: 01752 830234

Cottage: sleeps 8, £700-£1655 pw

Home produced organic beef and lamb delivered to the cottage

Soil Association

This fairytale cottage, with stunning views across the estuary, is hidden in a small clearing deep in the woods. It is one of several properties on our 1,000-acre organic farm, part of the Flete Estate. We are in an Area of Outstanding Natural Beauty by the River Erme estuary, a SSSI on the South Devon coast with six miles of drives for walking and bird watching and access to beaches and coastal paths. The estate offers beef and lamb produced on the home farm to our cottage guests. Riverford organic farm shop and café is three miles away, and it's fifteen miles to their farm and field kitchen. Nearby Modbury, the UK's first plastic bag-free town, is a great supporter of organic and local produce traders.

cottages@flete.co.uk www.flete.co.uk

PLYMOUTH (S-C)

SHEPHERD'S COTTAGE   151

Carswell Farm
Holbeton PL8 1HH
Tel: 01752 830020

Cottage: sleeps 6, £280-£960 pw

Organic breakfast hamper (to order); Organic meat, local organic fruit and vegetables

Soil Association

We are organic dairy farmers on the South Devon coast. The farm is deep in unspoilt countryside in the heart of the South Hams, and overlooks the sea. Our farm cottages are situated along secluded farm lanes a few minutes walk from the coast and Wadham beach. Taste delicious organic milk fresh from our cows when you arrive. Try our award-winning organic lamb and beef (Carswell is the birthplace of The Well Hung Meat Company). Organic Devon breakfast hamper to order. Because we are organic you will see an exceptional quantity and variety of wildlife, including some resident barn owls. Beautiful coves and beaches are nearby, with acres of sand at low tide and some dramatic coastal walks.

enquiries@carswellcottages.com www.carswellcottages.com/shepherdscottage

PLYMOUTH (S-C)

SPRING COTTAGE   152

Carswell Farm
Holbeton PL8 1HH
Tel: 01752 830020

Cottage: sleeps 6, £280-£960 pw

Organic breakfast hamper (to order); Organic meat, local organic fruit and vegetables

Soil Association

We are organic dairy farmers on the South Devon coast. The farm is deep in unspoilt countryside in the heart of the South Hams, and overlooks the sea. Our farm cottages are situated along secluded farm lanes a few minutes walk from the coast and Wadham beach. Taste delicious organic milk fresh from our cows when you arrive. Try our award-winning organic lamb and beef (Carswell is the birthplace of The Well Hung Meat Company). Organic Devon breakfast hamper to order. Because we are organic you will see an exceptional quantity and variety of wildlife, including some resident barn owls. Beautiful coves and beaches are nearby, with acres of sand at low tide and some dramatic coastal walks.

enquiries@carswellcottages.com www.carswellcottages.com/springcottage

PLYMOUTH *(S-C)*

THE BOSUN'S COTTAGE 153

Flete Estate
Haye Farm PL8 1JZ
Tel: 01752 830234

Cottage: sleep 7, £580-£1,550 pw

Home produced organic beef and lamb
delivered to the cottage

Soil Association

The Bosun's Cottage is surrounded by its own garden with tranquil views over the valley and woods beyond. It is one of several properties on our 1,000-acre organic farm, part of the Flete Estate. We are in an Area of Outstanding Natural Beauty by the River Erme estuary, a SSSI on the South Devon coast with six miles of drives for walking and bird watching and access to beaches and coastal paths. The estate offers beef and lamb produced on the home farm to our cottage guests. Riverford organic farm shop and café is three miles away, and it's fifteen miles to their farm and field kitchen. Nearby Modbury, the UK's first plastic bag-free town, is a great supporter of organic and local produce traders.

cottages@flete.co.uk www.flete.co.uk

PLYMOUTH *(S-C)*

COASTGUARDS COTTS 154

Coastguards Cottages, Flete Estate
Haye Farm PL8 1JZ
Tel: 01752 830234

Cottages: sleep 6, £600-£1,600 pw

Home produced organic beef and lamb
delivered to the cottage

Soil Association

Three cottages perched above Coastguards Beach with spectacular ever-changing views. There are several other individual properties on our 1,000-acre organic farm, part of the Flete Estate. We are in an Area of Outstanding Natural Beauty by the River Erme estuary, a designated SSSI on the South Devon coast with six miles of drives for walking and bird watching and access to beaches and coastal paths. The estate offers beef and lamb produced on the home farm to our cottage guests. Riverford organic farm shop and café is three miles away, and it's fifteen miles to their farm and field kitchen. Nearby Modbury, the UK's first plastic bag-free town, is a great supporter of organic and local produce traders.

cottages@flete.co.uk www.flete.co.uk

PLYMOUTH *(S-C)*

THE MEWS 155

Carswell Farm
Holbeton PL8 1HH
Tel: 01752 830020

Converted Barn: sleeps 2+1, £220-£545 pw

Organic breakfast hamper (to order); Organic meat, local organic fruit and vegetables

Soil Association

We are organic dairy farmers on the South Devon coast. The farm is deep in unspoilt countryside in the heart of the South Hams, and overlooks the sea. Our farm cottages are situated along secluded farm lanes a few minutes walk from the coast and Wadham beach. Taste delicious organic milk fresh from our cows when you arrive. Try our award-winning organic lamb and beef (Carswell is the birthplace of The Well Hung Meat Company). Organic Devon breakfast hamper to order. Because we are organic you will see an exceptional quantity and variety of wildlife, including some resident barn owls. Beautiful coves and beaches are nearby, with acres of sand at low tide and some dramatic coastal walks.

enquiries@carswellcottages.com   www.carswellcottages.com/themews

POSTBRIDGE *(S-C)*

LOWER MERRIPIT 156

Lower Merripit Cottage,
Lower Merripit Farm, Postbridge PL20 6TJ
Tel: 01822 880301

Farm Cottage: sleeps 8
£325-£775 pw

Organic free-range eggs available

16th-century stone cottage on an ancient farmstead located in the heart of Dartmoor. Wood stoves, inglenook fireplace, water pumped from our spring-fed well. Organic smallholding with traditional flower meadows, free-range organic hens, extensive tree planting programme, and protected areas for rare flora and fauna. Ecological cleaning and recycled products used. Neolithic-style roundhouse built on-farm to promote awareness of Dartmoor prehistory. Programme of workshops and music events, all catered for using organic and locally produced foods. Strong commitment to sustainable living and care of the land. Dartmoor Society Award 2006 for services to the community and the environment.

info@seventhwavemusic.co.uk   www.seventhwavemusic.co.uk/cottage.html

SALCOMBE *(B&B)*

THRESHOLD 157

20A Longfield Drive
Salcombe TQ8 8NT
Tel: 01548 842877

Bed and Breakfast
£25-£40 pppn

Home baked organic bread, milk, soya,
spreads, yogurt, butter, free-range eggs

A warm welcome awaits you at our organic bed and breakfast accommodation. It is in a tranquil setting overlooking North Sands valley and farmland, just a short walk from Salcombe town centre and North Sands beach (down a footpath from our garden). Our luxury room has a king-size waterbed and ensuite / steam room with aromatherapy oils. Large choice of breakfast menu. Full English or vegetarian, including organic home baked bread, organic milk, butter, yogurt, preserves. Sausages and bacon from local farms. All drinks are organic, also on beverage trays in bedrooms. Good café selling organic food and drinks at East Portlemouth beach. Two restaurants / cafés in Kingsbridge provide organic meals.

info@salcombebedandbreak.co.uk www.salcombebedandbreak.co.uk

SOUTH MOLTON *(B&B)*

CATSHEYS 158

Romansleigh
South Molton EX36 4JW
Tel: 01769 550580

Bed and Breakfast, £55-£60 pppn

Breakfasts include home-grown, organic and locally sourced produce

A contemporary rural retreat set in 11 tranquil acres of organic gardens and woodland, a natural habitat for deer, badgers, foxes and birds. Spacious, light and airy, eclectically furnished double ensuite rooms, large comfortable beds, crisp linens, down duvets, and fresh flowers from the garden. All our food is prepared with fresh, organic (wherever possible) fruit and vegetables from the kitchen garden plus quality local produce. We make our own marmalade, bread and cereals. Swim in the solar-heated pool, relax in the garden, walk in the woods, explore Exmoor and Dartmoor, surf the dramatic North Devon coast, and visit many gardens and historic houses. Regret no children, no pets, no smoking.

rosie@catsheys.co.uk www.catsheys.co.uk

SOUTH MOLTON *(B&B)* — FERN TOR — 159

Meshaw
South Molton EX36 4NA
Tel: 01769 550339

Vegetarian Guest House, B&B £22-£32 pppn
Evening Meal, £11-£17

Vegetarian / vegan meals, home-grown
organic produce when available

Fern Tor's 5 acres of culm grassland along the Little Silver River has been awarded a Countryside Stewardship grant and is rich with wild flowers, particularly in spring. The remaining land is used for our many rescued animals and for growing organic fruit and vegetables. Jane is a Cordon Vert trained cook and will happily cater for special diets on request. Dining is at separate tables, and when the nights are long, by candlelight. Gourmet vegetarian or vegan meals are provided, using fairtrade and organic produce when available. This is an ideal centre for exploring the superb countryside of North and Mid-Devon and Exmoor. Many local walks. Awarded Best Vegetarian B&B 2006 by PeTA.

veg@ferntor.co.uk   www.ferntor.co.uk

SOUTH MOLTON *(B&B)* — GREAT STONE FARM — 160

Exeter Road
South Molton EX36 4HX
Tel: 01769 574461

Farmhouse Bed and Breakfast
£25-£35 pppn

Breakfast includes local and organic produce

Organic Farmers & Growers

Great Stone Farm is a working organic dairy farm situated in a quiet location just one and a half miles from the market town of South Molton. At Great Stone you can enjoy our 15th-century thatched farmhouse (Grade II listed) and large garden. Comfortable ensuite bedrooms. A full English, continental or vegetarian breakfast is served, using local and organic produce. South Molton is in one of the last remaining rural areas of Britain. Visit a honey farm where you can watch the bees working behind glass. The local countryside and villages are interesting too, with lovely country pubs for eating out. If you enjoy walking or visits to the beach, Exmoor and the North Devon coast are only a short drive away.

bgreatstone@aol.com   www.greatstonefarm.co.uk

TAVISTOCK *(B&B)*

HELE FARM B&B   161

Gulworthy
Tavistock PL19 8PA
Tel: 01822 833084

Farmhouse Bed and Breakfast
From £22.50 pppn

Mostly organic breakfast

Organic Farmers & Growers

Hele Farm is a 250-acre fully organic dairy farm in the Tamar Valley near Blanchdown Woods. Wildlife includes deer, foxes, badgers and partridge. The architecturally listed slate-hung farmhouse (circa 1780) retains stone floors, bread ovens, wood panelling, and old farming artifacts. There is a large garden with a registered wych elm tree, and an organic vegetable garden. The farm has put an area into Country Stewardship, which has helped the moorhen and butterfly populations. The breakfast is mostly organic, and non-organic items are all sourced locally. Situated near wild Dartmoor, there are many organised walking and bird-watching trips. Welcoming tea and log fires on your return.

rosemary@dartmoorbb.co.uk www.dartmoorbb.co.uk

TAVISTOCK *(S-C)*

MINER'S DRY   162

Hele Farm
Gulworthy PL19 8PA
Tel: 01822 833084

Self-Catering: sleeps 2
£35-£45 pn (minimum stay 2 nights)

Organic Farmers & Growers

Miner's Dry is a well equipped one bedroom self-catering unit. The accommodation consists of a bedroom with an ensuite shower room, and a kitchen / dining / sitting room with a feature stone fireplace and a woodburner. This property would suit those looking for a quiet retreat surrounded by local wildlife and birds. Self-catering is for a minimum of two nights stay, charged on a daily basis with all services included in the price. Hele Farm is a 250-acre fully organic dairy farm situated in the Tamar Valley near Blanchdown Woods. The farm has put an area into Country Stewardship, which has helped the moorhen and butterfly populations. Wildlife includes deer, foxes, badgers and partridge.

rosemary@dartmoorbb.co.uk www.dartmoorbb.co.uk

TAVISTOCK *(S-C)*

THE OLD ROOT HOUSE 163

Hele Farm
Gulworthy PL19 8PA
Tel: 01822 833084

Self-Catering: sleeps 4
£35-£45 pn (minimum stay 2 nights)

Organic Farmers & Growers

Hele Farm has a well equipped, spacious one bedroom self-catering unit in the Old Root House. The lounge was the former 'root house', where potatoes and vegetables were stored in the winter. Self-catering can be for any length of stay, and is charged on a daily basis with all services included in the price. The farm is a 250-acre fully organic dairy farm in the Tamar Valley near Blanchdown Woods. Wildlife includes deer, foxes, badgers and partridge. There is a large garden with a registered wych elm tree, and an organic vegetable garden. The farm has put an area into Country Stewardship, which has helped the moorhen and butterfly populations. Dartmoor National Park is within easy reach.

rosemary@dartmoorbb.co.uk www.dartmoorbb.co.uk

TIVERTON *(S-C)*

MIDDLEWICK BARTON 164

Nomansland
Tiverton EX16 8NP
Tel: 01884 861693

Apartment: sleeps 2, £295-£369 pw
Short Breaks, from £145

Organic and natural food store and café
(Griffin's Yard) in South Molton

Soil Association

A spacious, newly converted, one bedroom luxury ground floor self-catering apartment in a character Georgian farmhouse on a working organic farm. Get away from the pressures of everyday life on our idyllic organic farm, situated in the heart of rural Devon in beautiful unspoilt countryside. Explore over 200 acres of secluded farmland with hilltop views, wooded valleys, streams, and a wonderful variety of plant and wildlife. Take advantage of the excellent local facilities for walking, riding and cycling. Sample the best of local Devonian eating establishments. Discover this undiscovered part of Devon for yourself. We are open all year. Short breaks (three or four nights) available out of season.

middlewick.barton@tiscali.co.uk www.middlewick-barton-devon.co.uk

TIVERTON *(S-C)*

THE COOMBE FARM TRUST 165

Middle Coombe Farm
Uplowman EX16 7QQ
Tel: 01884 821176

House: sleeps 16, from £875 pw/wkend
Barn: holds 70 for events, £650 per wkend

Seasonal organic vegetables and beef

Soil Association

Beautiful Grade II* listed 16th/17th-century cob and thatched farmhouse set in its own sheltered valley. Licensed for weddings. Surrounded by a gatehouse, barns (including a thatched cider barn), gardens and 400 acres of organic farm and mixed woodland with an extensive footpath network. Mountain bikes for loan. Solar-heated swimming pool. 5.5kw solar photovoltaic generator. The woodland is sustainably managed. The farm produces organic beef, willow, comfrey plant feed, seasonal vegetables. We have replanted our organic orchard with traditional apple varieties and undertaken extensive pasture management, hedge laying, planting schemes, with noticeable positive impact on flora and fauna.

timal@gn.apc.org

TOTNES *(B&B)*

DART VILLAS B&B 166

3 Dart Villas
Totnes Down Hill TQ9 5ET
Tel: 01803 865895

Vegetarian Bed and Breakfast
Double from £55 pn, Single from £35 pn

We like to provide good quality organic food (at least 95% organic)

Dart Villas organic vegetarian bed and breakfast is situated up on the hill overlooking the River Dart and the town. It has lovely views of the town and the surrounding countryside. All our food and drinks are organic where possible, including locally made organic bread, eggs, butter, yogurt and milk, fresh organic fruits and fruit spreads. We believe organic food is healthier for you and the environment, and it tastes better too. We operate an environmental policy as far as washing sheets and towels is concerned, and use all biodegradable cleaning products. It is only a five minute walk to the interesting and unique town of Totnes, with its individual shops, restaurants and cafés to suite all tastes.

mounivk@yahoo.co.uk www.dartvillasbb.co.uk

TOTNES *(B&B)*

NORWEGIAN WOOD 167

Berry Pomeroy
Totnes TQ9 6LE
Tel: 01803 867462

Bed and Breakfast
Double £60 pn, Single £40 pn
95% organic, locally sourced where possible

Beautifully converted Devon long barn, full of colour and atmosphere, in a stunning location overlooking the edge of Dartmoor. Relaxing, restful, refreshing. Start the day with a healthy organic traditional English meat, vegan, lacto-vegetarian, wheat-free, raw food or other customised breakfast to suit your dietary needs. Organic beverages in double and twin with filtered water. Our food is certified organic and locally sourced where possible (average 95% organic). We adhere to the Soil Association's open book certification for small businesses. We are a non-smoking, ecologically sensitive, environmentally friendly household. Children welcome. In-house nutritional therapy / iridology treatments available.

heather@norwegianwood.eclipse.co.uk www.organicbedandbreakfast.info

UMBERLEIGH *(S-C)*

BARTON COURT 168

Barton Farm
Burrington EX37 9JQ
Tel: 01237 479146

Barn (ref BCOUR): sleeps 10
£430-£1,135 pw

Soil Association

Barton Farm is a 175-acre organic farm with sheep, cattle, cereals and an abundance of wildlife. The farm is situated on the edge of the small village of Burrington in rural north Devon. Barton Court has recently been converted from an old stone barn. The holiday cottage has a large well equipped kitchen with a range cooker, sitting room with woodburning stove, spacious dining room with patio doors onto the patio and lawn area. The private garden is ideal for sunny afternoons and evening barbecues. The village has a historic church, a village inn and a shop. Set on the top of rolling Devon hills the village is midway between the old market towns of Barnstaple and Crediton, South Molton and Torrington.

www.holidaycottages.co.uk

UMBERLEIGH *(B&B)*

BURRINGTON BARTON   169

Burrington
Umberleigh EX37 9JQ
Tel: 01769 520216

Farmhouse Bed and Breakfast
From £30 pppn

The full English breakfast is made with local produce

Soil Association

Burrington Barton is a 175-acre mixed working organic farm. Relax in the peaceful surroundings of the ancient farmhouse and awake to the crow of the cockerel and the sound of bird song. Enjoy a full English breakfast made with local produce. Alongside sheep, cattle and cereals the land hosts an abundance of wildlife such as badgers, foxes, squirrels, roe and red deer. The woodlands and the water meadows are also a tranquil home to a variety of plant and bird life. On the edge of the small village of Burrington, this is a good base for exploring Dartmoor, Exmoor and the beautiful North Devon coast. Near Eggesford Forest, woodland walks, the Tarka Trail and Tarka Line, local pannier markets.

bartonfarm@yahoo.com   www.burrington-barton.co.uk

YELVERTON *(B&B)*

LAMMERGEIER   170

Yennadon
Dousland PL20 6NA
Tel: 01822 855837

Bed and Breakfast, from £25 pppn
Evening Meal (by arrangement)

We offer a high percentage of organic produce to our visitors

Lammergeier is a detached individual residence with beautiful views and pleasant gardens. Enjoy good quality home-cooked food at our family-run traditional Bed and Breakfast. We offer a high percentage of organic produce to our visitors, almost all sourced locally, as well as our own free-range eggs. The generous wholesome breakfast is served in our lovely Victorian conservatory overlooking the garden. Packed lunches and evening meals are available by special arrangement. Situated in one of Dartmoor's picturesque and peaceful locations, there is direct access from Lammergeier to open moorland. Burrator Reservoir, a local beauty spot within walking distance, is surrounded by some of Devon's finest tors.

yvonne.parkinson@virgin.net   http://freespace.virgin.net/yvonne.parkinson

BEAMINSTER *(S-C)*

CHILDHAY MANOR 171

Childhay Manor Cottage
Blackdown DT8 3LQ
Tel: 01460 432004

Cottage: sleeps 6, £450-£850 pw
Short Breaks, from £300 (out of season)

Organic lamb, pork, chicken, beef, local organic vegetables

Soil Association

Childhay Manor Cottage is situated in the deepest depths of West Dorset, nestled in beautiful rolling hills and high hedges on a working organic farm. It is a self-contained part of the main manor house, which dates back to the 13th century. Childhay offers the ideal base for a family holiday, enjoying picturesque views across open farmland with an abundant mixture of flora and fauna around the organic fields. Organic lamb, pork, chicken and beef are available for guests to purchase from the farm. Organic vegetable boxes are available from Riverford Farm. West Dorset is almost entirely designated as an Area of Outstanding Natural Beauty, and the coast is a natural World Heritage Site.

kate@childhaymanor.com www.childhaymanorcottage.co.uk

BRIDPORT *(B&B)*

BECKLANDS FARM 172

Whitchurch Canonicorum
Bridport DT6 6RG
Tel: 01297 560298

B&B, £30 pppn (£35 pppn single night)
Packed lunches (by arrangement)

Fully organic English breakfast, tea or coffee and cake on arrival

Soil Association

Becklands' thatched farmhouse lies in an Area of Outstanding Natural Beauty two and a half miles from Charmouth beach. Organic linen and eco-friendly paints have been used throughout. A bedhead and the dining table have been made from Becklands' ash. Our 100% organic breakfast includes the farm's eggs, beef sausages and homemade preserves. The 12-hectare farm has been managed organically since 1973. Visitors are welcome to collect eggs, help move cattle etc. Becklands' organic produce is sold in the small farm shop. Self-guided map walks (map and guide at farm shop). One-night bookings are taken from September to June (£35 pppn). Minimum two nights stay July and August.

becklandsorganicfarm@btopenworld.com www.becklandsorganicfarm.co.uk

BRIDPORT *(S-C)*

MILL COTTAGES 173

Powerstock Mill Farm
West Milton DT6 3SL
Tel: 08700 781 100

Cottages ref. DKD, DKC: sleep 2-5+
From £265 pw

Soil Association

Two cosy beamed cottages, each with their own garden, next to a pretty stream (toddlers beware). They have been carefully refurbished, retaining much original character, and stand opposite the owners' home on the edge of their organic dairy farm. Facilities include natural spring water, shared use of 60 acres of organic farmland, coarse fishing (by arrangement). B&B available for visitors' guests at the owners' farmhouse (by arrangement). In a designated Area of Outstanding Natural Beauty, the cottages are ideal for people who enjoy the delights of the countryside. Wonderful walks from the door amid the magnificent scenery of a secluded valley. There's a pebble beach at West Bay, about four miles away.

www.english-country-cottages.co.uk

BRIDPORT *(B&B)*

MONKTON WYLD COURT 174

Monkton Wyld
Bridport DT6 6DQ
Tel: 01297 560342

Bed and Breakfast, £22-£26 pppn
Breakfast, Lunch, Supper (by arrangement)

Home cooked organic vegetarian food, some grown in our own garden

Holistic education centre set in beautiful countryside near Lyme Regis. We run courses on permaculture, yoga, arts, crafts, voice, movement and family weeks. We also welcome B&B visitors when possible. All our food is vegetarian and we are proud that we provide mainly organic food. We use small local businesses to purchase food, and our one-acre walled kitchen garden provides some of our fruit, vegetables and salads. Our kitchen garden is not certified organic, but has been cultivated on organic principles since 1940. Located in a beautiful Dorset valley three miles from the sea, the 11-acre estate includes a small dairy and chicken farm, terraced lawns, woods and a stream. Camping from £5.50 per night.

bookings@monktonwyldcourt.org   www.monktonwyldcourt.org/bb.php

BRIDPORT *(B&B)*

POWERSTOCK MILL FARM 175

West Milton
Bridport DT6 3SL
Tel: 01308 485213

Farmhouse B&B, £30 pppn
Minimum 3 nights stay

Mostly organic home produce

Soil Association

Powerstock Mill Farm is a comfortable old farmhouse by a meandering stream in a small valley in south-west Dorset. It is situated between two idyllic villages in a designated Area of Outstanding Natural Beauty. The present farmhouse is over a hundred years old, and there has been a mill on the site since before the Domesday Book. The farm consists of dairy cows, chickens, calves, lambs, and a duck pond. Visit the unspoilt village of Powerstock, with its stone cottages and Norman church. There are many beautiful coastal and country walks in the area, and the remains of several iron age forts to explore. The farm is about four miles from the pebble beach at West Bay and the World Heritage Coast.

DORCHESTER *(B&B)*

COWDEN HOUSE 176

Fry's Lane
Godmanstone DT2 7AG
Tel: 01300 341377

Vegetarian Bed and Breakfast, £25-£32 pppn
Evening Meal, 3 course £16.50

As much local organic produce as possible

Cowden House offers spacious accommodation for up to six guests. Set in its own 3 acres in the beautiful Cerne Valley, on the edge of the tiny unspoilt village of Godmanstone. All the guest rooms have lovely views. The emphasis of the house is peace and quiet. Catering is vegetarian, using as much local produce as possible, sourced from an organic dairy farm and an organic market garden in the village. Breakfast is plentiful, and evening meals (including complimentary drinks) are available on request. From the house you can walk up a farm lane and off into the hills. All around are views of rolling downland hills and wide skies. Therapies are available (£25-£30), with fully qualified therapists.

www.cowdenhouse.co.uk

DORCHESTER *(S-C)*

STABLE COTTAGE 177

Manor Farm, Lower Road
Toller Porcorum DT2 0DH
Tel: 01300 321413

Cottage: sleeps 2-4, £180-£400 pw
Short Breaks (October-March)

Our own organic milk, local organic produce

Soil Association

A converted stable adjoining the farmhouse on a family-run organic dairy farm. Cosy and well equipped, the cottage has two bedrooms and its own private garden. It is situated in the village of Toller Porcorum in an area renowned for wildlife. Toller is a lovely village off the beaten track, surrounded by heavenly West Dorset countryside, including the farm itself and Dorset Wildlife Trust's reserves at Kingcombe and Powerstock. There are many local walks to enjoy without the use of a car. Midway between Bridport and Dorchester, the cottage is only twenty minutes drive (with stunning views) to the Heritage coast. Perfect for nature and beach lovers. If you want a great holiday with a very small ecological footprint, this is it.

janetchaffey@hotmail.co.uk

DORCHESTER *(S-C)*

SUNNYSIDE FARM 178

Lower Kingcombe
Toller Porcorum DT2 0EQ
Tel: 01300 321537

Cottage: sleeps 2-4, £350-£595 pw
Organic Supper, £8.50 per head

Organic home produce may be available to buy

Soil Association

Beautifully converted from an old cow byre, The Old Barn is on a working organic farm situated in an Area of Outstanding Natural Beauty. Home produced beef and lamb (subject to availability) can be purchased during your stay. A night off? Supper on arrival? We will cook you an organic casserole with a bottle of wine between two for £8.50 per head. We can also supply a breakfast basket of organic or local ingredients. Sunnyside Organic Farm is set in the Kingcombe Valley, famous for its wild flower meadows, amid 600 acres of the Dorset Wildlife Trust. There are many local walks for you to enjoy in the area without having to use your car. The holiday cottage is only six miles from the sea.

sunnyside.farm@tiscali.co.uk   www.sunnysideorganicfarm.co.uk

DORCHESTER *(B&B)*

THE KINGCOMBE CENTRE 179

Toller Porcorum
Dorchester DT2 0EQ
Tel: 01300 320684

Holidays, Courses, Bed and Breakfast
Contact for more information

As much organic and organically grown as
possible

Kingcombe is a study centre offering holidays, courses, bed and breakfast, and guided walks. Situated in converted farm buildings at the heart of Lower Kingcombe beside the River Hooke, the centre is on 4 acres of riverside pasture and is surrounded by the Kingcombe Meadows Nature Reserve. The food we cook for our guests is seasonal, organic if possible and local. The garden is run along organic lines and we grow a substantial amount of our own fruit and vegetables. We have a small flock of sheep, so produce our own lamb. Pork and beef is sourced from farms along the Lower Kingcombe Valley. The milk and cream come from a nearby organic dairy farm from cows grazing in this valley and the next.

kingcombe@hotmail.co.uk www.kingcombe-centre.demon.co.uk

GILLINGHAM *(B&B)*

ANSTYROSE COTTAGE 180

Wyke Road
Gillingham SP8 4NH
Tel: 01747 825379

Bed and Breakfast
From £25 pppn

Mainly organic (at least 95%) and local
where possible

Charming 18th-century detached cottage with a working pottery in a beautiful cottage garden. Situated on the western outskirts of Gillingham, a small rural town in North Dorset. Keen gardener and professional potter offers very comfortable accommodation (one twin room and one single room) with full continental breakfast. Mostly organic and local where possible, breakfast includes cereal, juice, toast and marmalade or honey, ham, cheese, hard boiled eggs. Eco-friendly accessories. The cottage is a couple of minutes walk to fields and the same to a small pub with good food, ten minutes walk to the town centre and twenty minutes walk to the station. Gillingham is on the North Dorset Cycleway.

kazworks@waitrose.com www.kazworks.co.uk

SHAFTESBURY *(S-C)*

HARTGROVE FARM 181

Hartgrove
Shaftesbury SP7 0JY
Tel: 01747 811830

Cottages: sleep 2-5
£305-£850 pw

Small farm shop

Hartgrove is a family-run organic farm in glorious Dorset countryside. The village nestles below the majestic Cranborne Chase. Stroll the valley paths or drink in the views from the top of the Downs. It is absolutely beautiful. The four award-winning cottages are furnished and equipped to a very high standard. Old beams, log fires, full central heating. Tennis court. Games barn. Free local swimming. Help feed our friendly farm animals (goats, sheep, pigs, geese, chickens), collect eggs, bottle feed a lamb, or watch the milking. Visit the local farmers' markets and buy fresh organic produce. Pretty thatched villages have excellent pubs serving food. Shaftesbury is four miles away. Disabled guests welcome.

cottages@hartgrovefarm.co.uk www.hartgrovefarm.co.uk

WEST BEXINGTON *(S-C)*

GRANARY LODGE 182

Tamarisk Farm Cottages
Beach Road DT2 9DF
Tel: 01308 897784

Cottage: sleeps 7
£420-£960 pw

Our own organic produce for sale

Soil Association

Granary Lodge is a disabled-friendly (M1) stone-built bungalow. Tamarisk Farm slopes down to Chesil beach in the tiny village of Bexington. Our organic market garden has 6 acres of vegetables and fruit in season. Organic wheat and rye are grown and milled on the farm as organic wholemeal stoneground flour. Organic beef, lamb, mutton joints, sausages available in individual packs or freezer boxes to take home. Conservation is a major interest on the farm. The whole coastline is now of World Heritage status. The Dorset Wildlife Trust has designated extensive areas as SSSI and SNCI. In the Stewardship Scheme we have flower-rich meadows, repair forest marble walls, and plant hedges and trees.

holidays@tamariskfarm.com www.tamariskfarm.com/holidays/?p=granary

WEST BEXINGTON *(S-C)*   MIMOSA COTTAGE   183

Tamarisk Farm Cottages
Beach Road DT2 9DF
Tel: 01308 897784

Cottage: sleeps 4
£365 to £840 pw

Our own organic produce for sale

Soil Association

Mimosa is a large comfortable cottage (M3i disabled access). Tamarisk Farm slopes down to Chesil beach in the tiny village of Bexington. Our organic market garden has 6 acres of vegetables and fruit in season. Organic wheat and rye are grown and milled on the farm as organic wholemeal stoneground flour. Organic beef, lamb, mutton joints, sausages available in individual packs or freezer boxes to take home. Conservation is a major interest on the farm. The whole coastline is now of World Heritage status. The Dorset Wildlife Trust has designated extensive areas as SSSI and SNCI. In the Stewardship Scheme we have flower-rich meadows, repair forest marble walls, plant hedges and trees.

holidays@tamariskfarm.com   www.tamariskfarm.com/holidays/?p=mimosa

WEST BEXINGTON *(S-C)*   FOSSIL AND CROSS   184

Tamarisk Farm Cottages
Beach Road DT2 9DF
Tel: 01308 897784

Cottage: sleeps 4
£255-£590 pw

Our own organic produce for sale

Soil Association

The Fossil and the Cross is 800 metres from the sea. Tamarisk Farm slopes down to Chesil beach in the tiny village of Bexington. Our organic market garden has 6 acres of vegetables and fruit in season. Organic wheat and rye are grown and milled on the farm as organic wholemeal stoneground flour. Organic beef, lamb, mutton joints, sausages are available in individual packs or freezer boxes to take home. Conservation is a major interest on the farm. The whole coastline is now of World Heritage status. The Dorset Wildlife Trust has designated extensive areas as SSSI and SNCI. In the Stewardship Scheme we have flower-rich meadows, repair forest marble walls, and plant hedges and trees.

holidays@tamariskfarm.com www.tamariskfarm.com/holidays/?p=fossil

WEST BEXINGTON *(S-C)*

THE MOAT 185

Tamarisk Farm Cottages
Beach Road DT2 9DF
Tel: 01308 897784

Cottage: sleeps 5
£290-£650 pw

Our own organic produce for sale

Soil Association

The Moat looks straight down the village road towards the sea. Tamarisk Farm slopes down to Chesil beach in the tiny village of Bexington. Our organic market garden has 6 acres of vegetables and fruit in season. Organic wheat and rye are grown and milled on the farm as organic wholemeal stoneground flour. Organic beef, lamb, mutton joints, sausages available in individual packs or freezer boxes to take home. Conservation is a major interest on the farm. The whole coastline is now of World Heritage status. The Dorset Wildlife Trust has designated extensive areas as SSSI and SNCI. In the Stewardship Scheme we have flower-rich meadows, repair forest marble walls, and plant hedges and trees.

holidays@tamariskfarm.com www.tamariskfarm.com/holidays/?p=moat

WEST BEXINGTON *(S-C)*

TWO WINGS 186

Tamarisk Farm Cottages
Beach Road DT2 9DF
Tel: 01308 897784

Cottage: sleeps 6
£305-£695 pw

Our own organic produce for sale

Soil Association

Two Wings is a character cottage built in the 1930s. Tamarisk Farm slopes down to Chesil beach in the tiny village of Bexington. Our organic market garden has 6 acres of vegetables and fruit in season. Organic wheat and rye are grown and milled on the farm as organic wholemeal stoneground flour. Organic beef, lamb, mutton joints, sausages are available in individual packs or freezer boxes to take home. Conservation is a major interest on the farm. The whole coastline is now of World Heritage status. The Dorset Wildlife Trust has designated extensive areas as SSSI and SNCI. In the Stewardship Scheme we have flower-rich meadows, repair forest marble walls, and plant hedges and trees.

holidays@tamariskfarm.com www.tamariskfarm.com/holidays/?p=wings

WEST BEXINGTON *(S-C)*

WHISPERING PINES 187

Tamarisk Farm Cottages
Beach Road DT2 9DF
Tel: 01308 897784

Cottage: sleeps 5
£255-£590 pw

Our own organic produce for sale

Soil Association

Whispering Pines is a cottage bungalow of local stone, 800m from the sea. Tamarisk Farm slopes down to Chesil beach in the tiny village of Bexington. Our organic market garden has 6 acres of vegetables and fruit in season. Organic wheat and rye are grown and milled on the farm as organic wholemeal stoneground flour. Organic beef, lamb, mutton joints, sausages available in individual packs or freezer boxes to take home. Conservation is a major interest on the farm. The whole coastline is of World Heritage status. The Dorset Wildlife Trust has designated extensive areas as SSSI and SNCI. In the Stewardship Scheme we have flower-rich meadows, repair forest marble walls, and plant hedges and trees.

holidays@tamariskfarm.com www.tamariskfarm.com/holidays/?p=whispering

WEYMOUTH *(S-C)*

BRIDE COTTAGE 188

Gorwell Farm
Abbotsbury DT3 4JX
Tel: 01305 871401

Cottage: sleeps 4
From £225 pw

Organic beef, lamb and pork available to buy, plus ready meals

Soil Association

Oak beams and a hayloft roof add to the atmosphere of this cosy little cottage. Carefully converted, it retains many original features. Doors from the living room lead to a small, private garden. Gorwell is a family-run organic farm. We can help with meals as we have our own frozen beef, lamb and pork, and frozen ready meals are also available for you to buy. The farm is ideally positioned in its own secret wooded valley. Birds, wildlife, wildflowers in abundance. Nesting boxes and feeding posts with cameras for wildlife tourists. There is easy access to a wonderful network of footpaths from the farm, including the South West Coast Path and the MacMillan Way. Gorwell is just two miles from Chesil Beach.

mary@gorwellfarm.co.uk www.gorwellfarm.co.uk/bride.asp

WEYMOUTH *(Camping)*

EAST FLEET FARM — 189

Chickerell
Weymouth DT3 4DW
Tel: 01305 785768

Touring Park, £10-£19 pn
£3 extra for electric hook-up

Organic milk (shop), organic beef (bar meals)

Soil Association

The touring park is situated at the heart of our 300-acre organic dairy farm. We are delighted to have been chosen to receive a David Bellamy Gold Award for five consecutive years, naming us one of the most environmentally friendly parks in the UK. We offer a unique location on the shores of the Fleet Lagoon, overlooking Chesil Beach and the sea. Relax and unwind in the truly peaceful Dorset countryside. The Old Barn fully licensed family bar opens at Easter for the summer. This converted 19th-century grain barn has stunning views over the Fleet. Bar meals served (our own organic beef is on the menu). Local beers on sale. Peak season can get busy, so best avoided for those looking for tranquillity.

enquiries@eastfleet.co.uk www.eastfleet.co.uk

WEYMOUTH *(S-C)*

GORWELL GRANARY — 190

Gorwell Farm
Abbotsbury DT3 4JX
Tel: 01305 871401

Converted Barn: sleeps 8
From £300 pw

Organic beef, lamb and pork available to buy, plus ready meals

Soil Association

A spacious barn with beautiful wooden ceilings and oak beams, two miles from Chesil Beach. With views of amazing sunsets down the valley, the south-west-facing garden is the perfect place to relax and enjoy a drink or an evening barbecue. Gorwell is a family-run organic farm. We can help with meals as we have our own frozen beef, lamb and pork, and frozen ready meals are also available for you to buy. The farm nestles in its own secret wooded valley. Birds, wildlife and wildflowers in abundance. Nesting boxes and feeding posts with cameras for wildlife tourists. There is easy access to a wonderful network of footpaths from the farm, including the South West Coast Path and the MacMillan Way.

mary@gorwellfarm.co.uk www.gorwellfarm.co.uk/granary.asp

WEYMOUTH *(S-C)*

GREYMARE COTTAGE 191

Gorwell Farm
Abbotsbury DT3 4JX
Tel: 01305 871401

Cottage: sleeps 4+2
From £250 pw

Organic beef, lamb and pork available to buy, plus ready meals

Soil Association

An attractive stone-built Victorian semi-detached cottage. The conservatory overlooks the large garden, and the sitting room faces south with views overlooking the hills. Gorwell is a family-run organic farm. We can help with meals as we have our own frozen beef, lamb and pork, and frozen ready meals are also available for you to buy. The farm is ideally positioned in its own secret wooded valley. Birds, wildlife and wildflowers in abundance. Nesting boxes and feeding posts with cameras for wildlife tourists. There is easy access to a wonderful network of footpaths from the farm, including the South West Coast Path and the MacMillan Way. Gorwell is just two miles from West Dorset's Chesil Beach.

mary@gorwellfarm.co.uk   www.gorwellfarm.co.uk/greymare.asp

WEYMOUTH *(S-C)*

MEAD COTTAGE 192

Gorwell Farm
Abbotsbury DT3 4JX
Tel: 01305 871401

Cottage: sleeps 8
From £250 pw

Organic beef, lamb and pork available to buy, plus ready meals

Soil Association

The cottage has recently been completely refurbished to a high standard. The dining room will seat ten for meals, and the living room is comfortable with a log burner in the fireplace and patio doors to the garden. Gorwell is a family-run organic farm. We can help with meals as we have our own frozen beef, lamb and pork, and frozen ready meals are also available for you to buy. The farm nestles in its own secret wooded valley. Birds, wildlife and wildflowers in abundance. Nesting boxes and feeding posts with cameras for wildlife tourists. Easy access to a wonderful network of footpaths from the farm, including the South West Coast Path and the MacMillan Way. Gorwell is two miles from Chesil Beach.

mary@gorwellfarm.co.uk   www.gorwellfarm.co.uk/mead.asp

WEYMOUTH *(S-C)*

SPINDLE COTTAGE   193

Gorwell Farm
Abbotsbury DT3 4JX
Tel: 01305 871401

Cottage: sleeps 6
From £275 pw

Organic beef, lamb and pork available to buy,
plus ready meals

Soil Association

The original features of this former barn have been retained wherever possible, and a fireplace has been added to keep you cosy in cooler weather. Patio doors lead onto the garden with plenty of space all on one level. Gorwell is a family-run organic farm. We can help with meals as we have our own frozen beef, lamb and pork, and frozen ready meals are also available for you to buy. The farm nestles in its own secret wooded valley. Birds, wildlife, wildflowers in abundance. Nesting boxes and feeding posts with cameras for wildlife tourists. Easy access to a wonderful network of footpaths, including the South West Coast Path and the MacMillan Way. Gorwell Farm is just two miles from Chesil Beach.

mary@gorwellfarm.co.uk www.gorwellfarm.co.uk/spindle.asp

WEYMOUTH *(S-C)*

SUNDIAL COTTAGE   194

Gorwell Farm
Abbotsbury DT3 4JX
Tel: 01305 871401

Cottage: sleeps 5
From £250 pw

Organic beef, lamb and pork available to buy,
plus ready meals

Soil Association

Sundial is a cosy Victorian semi-detached farm cottage with its own fenced garden. The sitting / dining room is south-facing and retains the original features of a cottage of its period. Gorwell is a family-run organic farm. We can help with meals as we have our own frozen beef, lamb and pork, and frozen ready meals are also available for you to buy. The farm nestles in its own secret wooded valley. Birds, wildlife and wildflowers in abundance. Nesting boxes and feeding posts with cameras for wildlife tourists. There is access to a wonderful network of footpaths, including the South West Coast Path and the MacMillan Way, which both cross our farm. Gorwell is two miles from Chesil Beach in West Dorset.

mary@gorwellfarm.co.uk www.gorwellfarm.co.uk/sundial.asp

WEYMOUTH (S-C)

THE CARTSHED 195

Church Lane
Osmington DT3 6EW
Tel: 01305 833690

Cottage: sleeps 6+cot, £340-£780 pw
Camping (August only)

Organic beef, lamb, pork, eggs, vegetables,
milk, bread from Eweleaze Farmshop

Soil Association

The Cartshed is a delightful converted stone barn in an Area of Outstanding Natural Beauty. It is located on a very quiet no through road in the pretty village of Osmington. Renovated to a very high standard, its traditional features include a large open fireplace, beamed ceilings, and polished wood and flagstone floors. There are gardens to the front and rear, with a patio area and barbecue. Located a mile off the coast, the cottage is within easy reach of the beaches at Osmington Mills and Ringstead, as well as having the facility for private parking at Eweleaze Farm for access to our own private beach at Redcliff Point. Organic produce (beef, lamb, pork, eggs, vegetables, milk, bread) available from our farm shop.

peter@eweleaze.co.uk www.eweleaze.co.uk/cottage.htm

BISHOP AUCKLAND (B&B)

LOW CORNRIGGS FARM 196

Cowshill
Wearhead DL13 1AQ
Tel: 01388 537600

Farmhouse Bed and Breakfast, £27-£37 pppn
Dinner, £16.50 (book in advance)

Organic when possible, off the farm and local

A lovely old farmhouse, built over 200 years ago, with spectacular views over the top of Weardale in an AONB. We pride ourselves on good home cooked food, organic when possible or wild / local. Home-produced beef, wild salmon, trout, game, some vegetables grown in our garden or from our neighbour's organic farm. Most of our meals are traditional – food local to the North – and are served in the delightful dining room. We have the Pie Award for evening meals. Breakfast is taken in the conservatory. Homemade bread and jams. Silver award from the Green Tourism Business Scheme. Stunning scenery, waterfalls, open moorland, old green roads, hills, birds, flowers. Environmentally Sensitive Area.

enquiries@lowcornriggsfarm.fsnet.co.uk www.britnett.net/lowcornriggsfarm

TRIMDON STATION *(B&B)*

POLEMONIUM B&B 197

28 Sunnyside Terrace
Trimdon Grange TS29 6HF
Tel: 01429 881529

Bed and Breakfast, £24 pppn (under 3s free)
Packed Lunch £3, Evening Meal £8

All food organic / local / homemade on
organic nursery

Organic environmentally friendly bed and breakfast, with one double four-poster room and two singles. Organic soaps and shampoos. Room refreshments include organic biscuits. Fresh organic milk on request. Our own and local fresh organic produce, homemade bread and preserves for breakfast. Packed lunches and evening meals on request. Polemonium Plantery is a specialist organic and peat-free nursery, supplying hardy perennials, shrubs and trees. Weekend courses on organic / wildlife gardening (£100 pp). Organic nappy washing service, organic baby dressing gowns, cot / high chair provided, children's activity basket. Good access for cyclists, walkers, and from public transport.

bandb@polemonium.co.uk www.polemonium.co.uk/bnb.html

COLCHESTER *(B&B)*

HAMS FARM 198

Abberton Road
Fingringhoe CO5 7AL
Tel: 01206 735247

Bed and Breakfast, £30 pppn
Evening Meal, from £18 (by arrangement)

Our own organic produce and locally
sourced produce

Organic Farmers & Growers

Not a farmhouse, but a spacious bungalow with outstanding countryside views over the Pyfleet and Colne Estuary. It is set in quiet surroundings fifty yards from the road. Picnic lunches and evening meals are available with prior notice. Emma is a qualified cook, and uses our own organic farm produce and locally sourced produce in the homemade meals. Andrew works with 7 acres of apple orchard and 2 acres of vegetables, and also manages some acres of grass, woodland and ponds. The fruit and vegetables are sold by farm gate sales, and to local shops. Emma manages the vegetable stall and retail outlets. Our aim is to sell fresh organic farm produce at the best price to the consumer.

info@hamsfarm.com www.hamsfarm.com

BRISTOL *(B&B)*

FULL MOON HOTEL 199

1 North Street
Stokes Croft BS1 3PR
Tel: 0117 9245007

Bunk Bed Dormitory Style and Twin Rooms,
£16-£19 pppn

Organic and free-range food (restaurant
open 9am-9.30pm)

We are an eco-friendly independent backpacker hotel, suitable for like-minded travellers. We have an on-site pub / restaurant open to both guests and the public, providing quality fresh organic and local free-range food with beers, wines and spirits to match. Our linen and bedding is all organic, and where possible we do as much as we can to reduce our impact on the environment. Over 20% discount when paying for seven nights in advance. Getting here is easy. The city bus station is a one minute walk away. The bus station has regular links to and from Bristol international airport departing every hour. If you are arriving by train there is also a bus link between the two every hour.

info@fullmoonbristol.co.uk www.fullmoonbristol.co.uk

GLOUCESTER *(Camping)*

FOUR YURT ECO-CAMP 200

Abbey Home Farm
Cirencester GL7 5HF
Tel: 01285 640441

Yurts: sleep 18 in total
Mon-Thu £475, Fri-Mon £559, Fri-Fri £975

Organic Farm Shop and Café (open Tuesday-Saturday)

Soil Association

On the edge of a wood with lovely views. Suitable for holidays, friends or family gatherings, outdoor residential workshops, retreats. All cooking utensils and mattresses provided. Outside fireplace, gas ring and woodburner in the larger yurt. The four yurts sleep 18 maximum. Bookings taken for a full week (Fri-Fri), three day weekends (Fri-Mon), four day week (Mon-Fri). Use our large green oak meeting room simultaneously for workshops. In the award-winning farm shop you'll find organic food – fresh meat, eggs, milk, vegetables and soft fruit – all grown on the farm, plus general groceries and organic bed and table linen. Shop, eat and drink in the garden or the café and watch the vegetables grow.

info@theorganicfarmshop.co.uk www.theorganicfarmshop.co.uk/produce.htm

GLOUCESTER *(Camping)*　　HUT BY THE POND　　201

Burford Road
Cirencester GL7 5HF
Tel: 01285 640441

Hut by the Pond: sleeps 2, from £40 pn
Yurt: from £35 pn, Camp: adult £4, child £1

Organic Farm Shop and Café (open Tuesday
to Saturday)

Soil Association

The hut by the pond (adults only) is surrounded by trees at the water's edge – perfect for romance or retreat all year round. The yurt (sleeps 5, available Apr-Oct) is in a woodland glade, twenty minutes walk from the farm shop. All stays minimum two nights. The green field campsite is in a lovely spot next to the old oak wood. Quiet space, trees, walks, wildlife abound. Our farm shop and café is open Tuesday to Saturday. Lunches in the café change daily, closely following progress in the garden. We always have a good selection of fresh salads, a fresh soup of the day and a main dish of the day. The shop sells everything organic you can imagine, including lots of organic produce from the farm itself.

info@theorganicfarmshop.co.uk　www.theorganicfarmshop.co.uk/produce.htm

GLOUCESTER *(S-C)*　　LOWER WIGGOLD　　202

Abbey Home Farm
Cirencester GL7 5HF
Tel: 01285 640441

Cottage: sleeps 4+ £395-£600 (Fri-Fri)
Short Breaks (available in low season)

Organic Farm Shop and Café (open Tuesday-
Saturday)

Soil Association

A two bedroom semi-detached cottage with woodburner in the depths of the farm, far from the hustle and the bustle. Furnished with unusual old and reclaimed furniture from our travels. Beautiful organic bed linen to hire on request. Environmentally friendly cleaning products. Guests have sole use of a small south-facing garden to the side of the cottage, and the whole farm to roam. Twenty minutes walk away down our quiet lane is our award-winning 100% organic farm shop and café where you'll find organic food – fresh meat, eggs, milk, vegetables and soft fruit – all grown on the farm, plus general groceries and organic bed and table linen. Shop, eat and drink in the garden or the café. Watch the vegetables grow.

info@theorganicfarmshop.co.uk　www.theorganicfarmshop.co.uk/produce.htm

GLOUCESTER *(B&B)*

THE TRUE HEART 203

Frampton on Severn
Gloucester GL2 7ED
Tel: 01452 740504

Bed and Breakfast
From £35 pppn

All organic, locally sourced and homemade
where possible

A village pub until the 1960s, The True Heart has been transformed (ecologically, and with at least 75% of hot water solar-powered) into a homely bed and breakfast. Wonderful views of the Gloucester & Sharpness Canal, the River Severn (both within walking distance) and across to the Forest of Dean. Traditional breakfasts. All ingredients of the finest quality. Everything is local, homemade and organic where possible. Organic homemade jam for sale. Frampton on Severn is a Conservation Area within the glorious Severn Vale. It has reputedly the longest village green in England, where fairs and events are held throughout the year. Great walking and cycling country (wellies and cycles can be provided).

veronica@thetrueheart.co.uk www.thetrueheart.co.uk

LYDBROOK *(S-C)*

GREENWAY COTTAGE 204

Stowfield Road
Lower Lydbrook GL17 9NJ
Tel: 01594 860075

Cottage: sleeps 4, £450 per week
B&B and Short Breaks on application

Award-winning restaurant on the same
estate, all local food

The cottage is set in 3 acres of Lydbrook House estate just yards from the River Wye, with superb views from all the windows. The restaurant is in the converted Malt House extension on the estate. The food policy at the restaurant is to use only local produce. All the meats, fish, vegetables, dairy products, breads and puddings are from ingredients sourced in the South-West. Wherever possible they are also organic. Almost all the vegetables we use are grown organically in our own walled Georgian kitchen garden. We serve organic wines and locally made beers, cider and fruit juice. Visitors can also buy some of the fresh ingredients we use in the kitchen, such as organic vegetables, olives, olive oil and flour.

gardencafe@btinternet.com www.gardencafe.co.uk

LYDBROOK (S-C)

RAGMANS LANE FARM 205

Bishopwood
Lydbrook GL17 9PA
Tel: 01594 860244

Permaculture Courses
Bunkhouse: sleeps 18

The food will be mostly organic and vegetarian

Soil Association

Established 60-acre permaculture farm in the Forest of Dean, used as a teaching venue. Our courses include 'Cider and Apple Juice Weekend' (on which you will pick fruits from the organic orchard and then press them on a traditional farmhouse cider press), and 'Introduction to Permaculture'. The farm's Soil Association certified produce includes shiitake mushrooms, cider, and apple juice. Teaching room and bunkhouse available for hire for courses. Ample camping space with lovely views – close to the bunkhouse but far enough away to get some peace and quiet. The bunkhouse, and especially the campsite, are also available for recreational visitors as well as for courses (booking is essential).

info@ragmans.co.uk www.ragmans.co.uk

NEWENT (S-C)

HIGHLEADON COTTAGES 206

New House Farm
Highleadon GL18 1HQ
Tel: 01452 790209

Cottages: sleep 2-6
£175-£450 pw

Organic free-range eggs are available from the farm

Organic Farmers & Growers

Three self-catering cottages on a 330-acre working organic farm. Situated in the Leadon Vale on the northern edge of the Forest of Dean, the three well equipped units have been converted from a stable and a cart shed. Organic free-range eggs are available to buy from the farm. The farm abounds with wildlife. You can try your hand at badger watching or bird spotting. Buzzards regularly breed on the farm. The route of the now redundant Gloucester to Hereford canal runs through New House Farm. In places this has been reclaimed into the fields, but a long length is still evident and today used as a farm track. The cottages are ideally located for exploring the Malverns and the beautiful Cotswolds villages.

cjojan@aol.com

NEWNHAM ON SEVERN *(B&B)*

GROVE FARM B&B 207

Bullo Pill
Newnham On Severn GL14 1EA
Tel: 01594 516304

Farmhouse Bed and Breakfast, £30-£35 pppn
Packed Lunch, £3.50 (on request)

Locally sourced organic food wherever possible

Soil Association

A traditional farmhouse on an organic dairy and sheep farm. Grove Farm is quiet and secluded, with panoramic views over the Severn Vale towards the Cotswolds. The peace is broken only by the roaming guinea fowl. There are two double guest bedrooms. Guests have their own lounge with an open log fire in the oldest part of the farmhouse, full of exposed beams and a circular staircase. Garden and terrace for your use. Children are welcome. Wonderful walking on our doorstep, and your horse can come too. There is riding and walking access to the Royal Forest of Dean, with its many miles of waymarked trails. The Wye Valley and the Cotswolds are both nearby. There's an organic restaurant locally.

davidandpennyhill@btopenworld.com www.grovefarm-uk.com

STROUD *(B&B)*

ST ANNES 208

Gloucester Street
Painswick GL6 6QN
Tel: 01452 812879

Bed and Breakfast
Double £60 pn, Single £35-£40 pn

Organic, local free-range, homemade organic breads and jams

A Grade II listed, early 18th-century town house in the centre of beautiful Painswick. We offer one twin and two king-size double bedded rooms, all with ensuite or private bathroom. Relax by the open fire with a delicious Aga-cooked English breakfast, which includes organic porridge and other organic cereals, organic milk and butter, local free-range meats and eggs, organic fairtrade teas and coffee, homemade organic breads, and local or homemade organic jams and marmalade. Painswick offers several excellent options for dinner, all within just a few minutes walk. The village is on the scenic Cotswold Way. Walkers, cyclists and children are all welcome in our comfortable English family home.

greg.iris@btinternet.com www.st-annes-painswick.co.uk

SOUTHAMPTON *(B&B)*

BARN GUEST HOUSE 209

112 Lyndhurst Road
Ashurst SO40 7AU
Tel: 023 8029 2531

Vegetarian Guest House, B&B £28-£32 pppn
Evening Meal, £15

Wherever possible we use locally grown and
organic produce

We have two double ensuite bedrooms in our detached Edwardian house set within the New Forest National Park. The house has been refurbished with an environmental emphasis and it is now 80% solar powered from a large photovoltaic system. Our carbon footprint is around 30% of the UK household average. All our food is freshly prepared and is exclusively vegan. We use produce from our own small organic vegetable garden where possible, and although we don't claim to be 100% organic we generally use a high proportion of organic produce mixed with other local and / or fairtrade ingredients. We offer our guests a restful stay with easy access for walking, cycling and visits to the south coast.

info@veggiebarn.net www.veggiebarn.net

STOCKBRIDGE *(Camping)*

THE ANCHORAGE 210

Salisbury Road
Broughton SO20 8BX
Tel: 01794 301234

Camping, £5 pppn
WWOOF Host

Farm shop (fruit, vegetables, salads, eggs, etc)

Soil Association

A permaculture farm of 3.5 acres producing fruit, vegetables, salads, poultry and eggs. Organic farm produce and other organic products are for sale. We aim to provide an alternative to globalisation by supplying quality local food to the local community whilst minimising negative impact on the environment. The campsite is small and quiet – the perfect place to relax and observe the English countryside. The farm is situated below rolling chalk hills – a rich habitat for flora and fauna. Nature reserves (including a Site of Special Scientific Interest), chalk streams, bridleways, footpaths and historic churches are all within walking distance. Broughton is known as one of the best kept villages in Hampshire.

BROMYARD *(S-C)*   HANDLEY ORGANICS   211

Hardwick Hill
Bromyard HR7 4SX
Tel: 01885 482415

Caravan: sleeps 4
From £150 pw

Organic farm shop on site sells our own and other local produce

Soil Association

A luxury four berth single-sited caravan on a secluded organic farm in Herefordshire, with panoramic views of the Frome Valley. Well behaved dogs are welcome (maximum two dogs please). We have an organic farm shop on site selling our own and other local produce and, as we do markets two or three times a week, we can usually supply you with the full range of seasonal organic produce. We are open all year round. This is a working organic farm and you will be welcome to have a look around and see how and where we grow the organic produce which we sell. Local places to visit include Moors Meadow (a 7-acre organic garden) and Shortwood Organic Farm with its many family-friendly activities.

handleyorganics@btinternet.com www.handleyorganics.co.uk/caravan.aspx

BROMYARD *(S-C)*   WICTON FARM COTTAGE 212

Wicton Farm
Winslow HR7 4LR
Tel: 01747 828170

Cottage: sleeps 6-10
£810-£1,361 pw

Organic farm produce is available to buy

Soil Association

Very spacious Victorian farm cottage (sleeps up to ten guests) deep in the Herefordshire countryside, a mile and a half from the nearest road. The wisteria-clad cottage is situated on an organic farm, mainly dairy, but the owners also sell home-grown pork and lamb. Children can watch the cows being milked, help collect the farm eggs, or take part in one of the cookery workshops organised at the farm. There are lots of walks on the farm using the foot- and bridlepaths, or the disused railway line which runs the length of the farm. The large half-acre garden has an above-the-ground swimming pool for the summer months. A games room in an old oast house has a pool table, table tennis, darts, table football.

enq@hideaways.co.uk www.hideaways.co.uk/property.cfm/H185

HEREFORD *(S-C)*

HOLT FARM BARN 213

Rhydunnog Farm
Michaelchurch Escley HR2 0PS
Tel: 01747 828170

Converted Barn: sleeps 6-8, £581-£975 pw
Short Breaks (contact for prices)

Organic potatoes and vegetables grown on
the farm

Soil Association

Holt Farm lies in attractive, rolling hill country on the borders of Herefordshire and Monmouthshire. The farm has been in the family for generations, and is now farmed organically. The Grade II listed barn has been transformed into superb holiday accommodation, its original features contrasted with 21st-century luxury and comfort. An imaginative full height living and dining area is set between the two large glassed-in barn doors, with dining for up to 23 guests for special occasions. The barn has retained a wealth of original features – oak beams, glazed high trusses, spiral staircases, stone paved floor and a woodburner. For outdoor dining the barn also has a large paved patio with a lovely outlook.

enq@hideaways.co.uk www.hideaways.co.uk/holiday-cottage

HEREFORD *(S-C)*

HOLT FARM HOUSE 214

Rhydunnog Farm
Michaelchurch Escley HR2 0PS
Tel: 01747 828170

House: sleeps 6-7, £535-£897 pw
Short Breaks (contact for prices)

Organic potatoes and vegetables grown on
the farm

Soil Association

Dating from the 17th century, this Grade II listed building has recently been completely restored, retaining many of its original features. Full of an atmosphere of age and history, Holt Farm House has flagstone floors, a bread oven, and a stone spiral stair. There is an enclosed garden around the house with an orchard beyond. Holt Farm lies in attractive, rolling hill country on the borders of Herefordshire and Monmouthshire, at the end of a long private track. It is a wonderful, peaceful location, and has immediate access to superb walks and rides. The organic farm is situated at 900 feet, and a footpath rises behind to a hill with direct access to Offa's Dyke and the Black Mountains, affording extensive views.

enq@hideaways.co.uk www.hideaways.co.uk/holiday-cottage

HEREFORD *(S-C)*

HOLT FARM STABLE 215

Rhydunnog Farm
Michaelchurch Escley HR2 0PS
Tel: 01747 828170

Cottage: sleeps 2-4, £331-£548 pw
Short Breaks (contact for prices)

Organic potatoes and vegetables grown on
the farm

Soil Association

Holt Farm Stable is a recent conversion, resulting in a very bright and cosy hideaway to very high specifications. Attached to Holt Farm House, with which it can be jointly booked, Holt Farm Stable has its entrance from the courtyard with its own patio, garden and barbecue. Holt Farm, which is organically run, lies in attractive rolling hill country on the borders of Herefordshire and Monmouthshire. At the end of a long private track, it is a wonderful, peaceful location, and has immediate access to superb walks and rides. Situated at nine hundred feet, a footpath rises behind to a hill with direct access to Offa's Dyke and the Black Mountains, affording extensive views.

enq@hideaways.co.uk www.hideaways.co.uk/holiday-cottage

HAY-ON-WYE *(B&B)*

LOWER HOUSE 216

Cusop Dingle
Hay-on-Wye HR3 5RQ
Tel: 01497 820773

Bed and Breakfast, from £40 pppn
Occasional suppers

Organic eggs, milk, butter, yogurt, bread, and
most fruit and vegetables

Three double rooms in a beautiful old house set in its own secluded 7-acre valley, just over the border into Wales and one mile from the famous 'book town' of Hay-on-Wye. Exceptional garden and wood, orchard, wildlife pond, and wilderness (open by appointment from April to September). The house is in the Brecon Beacons National Park, on Offa's Dyke Footpath, close to the Black Mountains, and near the River Wye. Breakfasts are largely organic, locally sourced and fairtrade where possible. We use rare breed, free-range, additive-free pork. We are happy to provide occasional suppers by arrangement. We recycle as much as possible and use environmentally friendly cleaning products and toiletries.

nicky.daw@btinternet.com www.lowerhousegardenhay.co.uk

HAY-ON-WYE *(B&B)*

TY MYNYDD FARM 217

Llanigon
Hay-on-Wye HR3 5RJ
Tel: 01497 821593

Mountain Farmhouse Bed and Breakfast
Double, £35-£40 pppn

Breakfast is made with our own organic
produce when available

Organic Farmers & Growers

A small, family-run, working organic farm situated amidst the beautiful Black Mountains of Wales. From your room you can enjoy breathtaking panoramic views and stunning sunsets. The mountains offer a dramatic changeable aura to the vast space surrounding us here at Ty Mynydd (Welsh for 'Mountain House'). We serve a delicious organic breakfast using organic produce from our farm, and have a fresh mountain spring supplying our water. We run our home and farm on a chemical-free basis using only eco-friendly renewable and recycled products. We are currently undertaking an environment scheme, which helps us provide and maintain natural habitats for wildlife and vegetation.

nikibarber@tymynydd.co.uk   www.tymynydd.co.uk

HAY-ON-WYE *(B&B)*

WINDLE PARK FARM 218

Hardwicke
Hay-on-Wye HR3 5HA
Tel: 01497 831666

Farmhouse B&B, £20 pppn
Camping, £3 pppn

Organic food served and available for sale

Biodynamic Agricultural Association

This working organic farm rears rare breed stock, producing Hereford beef, Portland lamb and Tamworth pork, all reared outside. Bed and Breakfast is in the 17th-century cottage farmhouse, with one double bedroom and one single bedroom. Watercolour or pastel painting days can be arranged. There are walks in ancient oak woodlands for nature lovers. On the nearby hills the scenery is magnificent. On the western end of the village you can visit the site on which the ruins of Clifford Castle (built in the 11th century) stand. Although Windle Park Farm is in a delightfully secluded position, it's only ten minutes from the famous 'book town' of Hay-on-Wye. This is an ideal area for both walking and touring.

HEREFORD (B&B)

ASPEN HOUSE   219

Hoarwithy
Hereford HR2 6QP
Tel: 01432 840353

Bed and Breakfast, £35 pppn
Dinner, £25

Cosy dining room, real food and the
absolute best of local produce

Aspen House is much more than just a Bed and Breakfast. We are advocates of real food, and everything here is about the celebration of food. We stand against factory food and everything processed and, as members of the Slow Food movement, we champion artisan producers everywhere. We are tireless in our efforts to ensure that everything we prepare contains the finest ingredients sourced directly from local producers, growers and independent shops. Taste is paramount, and we cook everything from scratch using the best of what is available in season. Why not make food your focus, bring along some friends and savour the Aspen House private dining experience for yourselves?

sallyandrob@aspenhouse.net www.aspenhouse.net

HEREFORD (S-C)

HERMIT HOLIDAYS   220

The Hermitage
Canon Pyon HR4 8NR
Tel: 01432 760022

Cottages: sleep 2-6
£295-£645 pw

Optional vegetarian organic meals
(subject to pre-booking and availability)

4-star cottages and apartments with lovely views over organic gardens or woodlands. Ideally situated for a relaxing rural retreat. You'll find fresh flowers from the garden, spring water on tap, a chilled bottle of fairtrade organic wine, organic fresh coffee and teas. You're welcome to pick fresh herbs from the organic herb and vegetable gardens when you feel the urge to cook. Optional meals available (vegetarian and mostly organic). Japanese food is our speciality. Stroll around the 12 acres of organic gardens and breathe in the wonderful fresh country air. Approached via a half mile drive, the properties are surrounded by a 350-acre woodland with marked footpaths and home to buzzards, deer and badgers.

info@hermitholidays.co.uk www.hermitholidays.co.uk

HEREFORD (S-C)

THE OLD DAIRY 221

Winnal Common Farm
Winnal HR2 9BS
Tel: 01432 277283

Cottage: sleeps 5, £206-£400 pw
Short Breaks, 3 nights £127

Soil Association

A holiday cottage in the heart of the Herefordshire countryside. The Old Dairy is a tastefully converted milking parlour and dairy. It is situated in a beautiful rural location on a working organic farm and livery yard. We began the farm's organic conversion In 1999, and became fully organic in 2001. We keep a small herd of organic single sucklers, mostly Aberdeen Angus. Alongside this we run a livery yard and a small stud. Children will love playing football with our dogs, Ted and Pickles, and seeing the mares and foals as well as the cows and calves. The nearby village of Allensmore has a shop and a pub. We are five miles from the ancient cathedral city of Hereford. Dogs welcome. Horses by arrangement.

info@winnal.co.uk   www.winnal.co.uk

HEREFORD (S-C)

THE WAIN HOUSE 222

Rhydunnog Farm
Michaelchurch Escley HR2 0PS
Tel: 01747 828170

Cottage: sleeps 4, £413-£693 pw
Short Breaks (contact for prices)

Organic potatoes and vegetables grown on the farm

Soil Association

Opposite and across from Holt Farm Stable, The Wain House has been expertly converted from the old cart shed. All the accommodation is on the ground floor and offers level access for disabled visitors. As well as having access to the communal courtyard shared with the other cottages, it has its own attractively landscaped garden area at the rear. Holt Farm lies in rolling hill country on the borders of Herefordshire and Monmouthshire, at the end of a long private track. It is a wonderful, peaceful location, and has immediate access to superb walks and rides. The organic farm is situated at 900 feet, and a footpath rises behind to a hill with direct access to Offa's Dyke and the Black Mountains.

enq@hideaways.co.uk   www.hideaways.co.uk/holiday-cottage

KINGTON *(B&B)*

GREENCUISINE   223

Penrhos Court
Lyonshall HR5 3LH
Tel: 01544 230720

Food and Health Courses
Women's Health Courses

Natural, unrefined organic foods

Soil Association

At Penrhos Court, an old manor farm on the Welsh Borders, chef / nutritionist Daphne Lambert runs Greencuisine, a healing food centre. The courses are designed to enable participants to create a diet to give them optimal health and vitality. The courses include Women's Health, Food and Health, and Living Nutrition. The courses provide practical cookery in the kitchen preparing organic food, and groups are kept small to enable participants to have individual attention from our qualified practitioners. All courses are residential in individual ensuite rooms in a peaceful and inspiring environment and include course notes and recipes. The facilities are also available for other people to run their own courses.

daphne@greencuisine.org   www.greencuisine.org/courses

KINGTON *(Hotel)*

PENRHOS MANOR HOUSE 224

Lyonshall
Kington HR5 3LH
Tel: 01544 230720

Weddings, Conferences, Retreats
Seminars, Meetings

Fundamental to the philosophy of Penrhos is the use of fresh organic produce

Soil Association

A creative and inspiring setting for weddings, retreats, courses, team building events, business / corporate meetings. The group of medieval and Elizabethan timber-frame buildings makes a large square around a courtyard with a pond in the centre. Surrounded by 5 acres of homestead, it makes a unique venue for a company or individuals requiring space and total privacy away from day-to-day pressures, helping to build a team spirit which will enable the business to flourish. Penrhos is also the perfect setting for a green wedding. Your wedding becomes a house party for your family and friends with preparations the day before, the ceremony, the banquet, a party in the evening and breakfast the next morning.

info@penrhos.co.uk   www.hotel.penrhos.com

KINGTON (S-C)

SKYLARK AND BARN OWL 225

Penrhos Court
Lyonshall HR5 3LH
Tel: 01544 230720

Apartments: sleep 2-3

£250-£350 pw

Welcome organic food box on arrival, organic shop

Soil Association

Skylark and Barn Owl are two self-catering apartments in part of an 18th-century thrashing barn at Penrhos Court. The apartments have been sympathetically converted and maintain many of the original features. They are on three levels, with the kitchen and dining room on the ground floor, lounge and bathroom on the second, and a balcony bedroom on the third. The old manor farm is in a peaceful setting with beautiful views. There is an organic shop on site selling organic foods, superfoods, herbs and wines. Organic produce is also available locally. This is an excellent base from which to enjoy the untamed countryside of the borderlands. The area is delightful all year around, each season quite distinct.

info@penrhos.co.uk www.penrhos.co.uk/hotel/self_catering.html

LEDBURY (S-C)

CANON FROME COURT 226

Canon Frome
Ledbury HR8 2TD
Tel: 0870 765 0714

Apartment: sleeps 1-5
£27.50-£40 pn, £167-£242 pw

Small shop sells some organic, wholefood, fairtrade items

Georgian manor house overlooking a lake on a working farm in rural Herefordshire. The 40-acre community farm is farmed co-operatively and organically (though not certified). Stock includes cattle, sheep, goats, poultry, bees. We have a 2-acre walled kitchen garden growing vegetables and soft fruits, a large greenhouse, two polytunnels and a couple of orchards. Our arable land provides wheat for our flour, potatoes and further vegetables. The apartment, a recently converted space with a large kitchen / sitting room, is in the stable block. Whilst we provide a good deal of organic food for ourselves, unfortunately we only occasionally have enough surplus to sell from the shop to guests.

playroom@canonfromecourt.org.uk www.canonfromecourt.org.uk/guestaccom.html

LEOMINSTER *(B&B)*

LEEN FARM 227

The Leen
Pembridge HR6 9HN
Tel: 01544 388305

Farmhouse Bed and Breakfast
£25 pppn

Organic home produce includes milk, beef
and seasonal vegetables

Organic Farmers & Growers

A 500-acre traditional family farm, mentioned in the Domesday Book. Leen Farm is home to the oldest herd of Hereford cattle in the world, and a wildlife haven with butterflies, trout pools and award-winning nature reserves, including a marshland SSSI. Farms do not come this old without very careful management over a long period, backed by a great knowledge of the countryside and its flora and fauna. The farm is an ideal base for naturalists, historians, painters and photographers, and there is wonderful walking around the Black and White Villages of the Welsh Marches. Organic home produce includes milk, beef and seasonal vegetables. There are two good organic restaurants nearby.

tony@leenfarmorganics.co.uk www.leenfarmorganics.co.uk

LEOMINSTER *(B&B)*

LOWER BACHE HOUSE 228

Kimbolton
Leominster HR6 0ER
Tel: 01568 750304

Country House, B&B from £39.50 pppn
Evening Meal, £19.50-£24.50

Home and locally grown organic produce,
outsourcing committed to fairtrade
principles

Nestling in a tiny tranquil valley, this award-winning 17th-century farmhouse is an ideal haven for those seeking peace, quiet and beautiful countryside. We have three suites, each of which has its own bath or shower room and private sitting room. For our renowned cuisine we source from local organic suppliers as far as possible and our own organic kitchen garden. Our wine list is totally organic. Set in 14 acres of private nature reserve, lovingly nurtured to provide a diversity of habitats for wildlife, with traditional hay meadows, a stream, woodland, marshland, and gardens that complement the surrounding acres. Wildlife Action Gold Award and the Green Business award from Herefordshire Nature Trust.

leslie.wiles@care4free.net www.smoothhound.co.uk/hotels/lowerbache.html

LEOMINSTER *(S-C)*

BUZZARDS COTTAGES   229

Kingsland
Leominster HR6 9QE
Tel: 01568 708941

Cottages: sleep 2-6, £275-£475 pw
Camping, from £9 pn

Seasonal organic produce is available to buy

Biodynamic Agricultural Association

Our three self-contained cottages are spacious, comfortable, and attractively furnished with antique and modern furniture. The accommodation is equipped to a very high standard, and is located along a secluded country lane in the middle of 200 acres of farmland. Our award-winning, working organic and biodynamic smallholding produces fruit and vegetables. We have rare breed pigs, old breed sheep, hens and a goose. This practical and replicable lifestyle conserves, recycles and enriches. Seasonal organic produce is available to buy. There is an abundance of wildlife on our 16 acres of woodland, pasture land, orchards and ponds. B&B is occasionally available, from £35 per person per night.

holiday@thebuzzards.co.uk www.thebuzzards.co.uk

LEOMINSTER *(Camping)*

THE LEEN CARAVAN SITE 230

Leen Farm
Pembridge HR6 9HN
Tel: 01544 388305

Certified Location Caravan Site
£8 pn

Organic Farmers & Growers

Exclusive five pitch 'Certified Location' situated beside the River Arrow. We have a one acre, level, well drained, lawned site with well spaced pitches, all with electric hook-ups and water taps. The site is in the middle of our 500-acre organic farm, home to the oldest herd of Hereford cattle in the world, and a wildlife haven with butterflies, trout pools and award-winning nature reserves, including a marshland SSSI. Miles of tracks for quiet enjoyment of the countryside. Leen Farm is only a mile from the medieval village of Pembridge with its pubs, shops and visitor centre. There are two good organic restaurants nearby. Wonderful walking around the Black and White Villages of the Welsh Marches.

tony@leenfarmorganics.co.uk www.leenfarmorganics.co.uk

MONNINGTON-ON-WYE*(B&B)*   DAIRY HOUSE FARM   231

Monnington-on-Wye
Hereford HR4 7NL
Tel: 01981 500143

Farmhouse Bed and Breakfast, £30 pppn
Evening Meal (by arrangement)

Breakfast includes organic and local produce

Soil Association

A secluded farmhouse located between Hereford and Hay-on-Wye. It is beautifully furnished with oak floors and beams. The spacious rooms have lovely open views across our working organic farm to the surrounding hills. Delicious Aga-cooked breakfasts with homemade preserves and organic / local produce. Packed lunches. Evening meals by prior arrangement. There are wonderful walks from the doorstep. Dairy House Farm is close to the river and adjacent to the Wye Valley Walk. Children, dogs and horses are welcome. The Three Rivers Ride crosses Herefordshire for sixty miles. The route passes nearby through beautiful countryside, and riders get the opportunity to cross the River Wye.

clare@dairyhousefarm.org   www.dairyhousefarm.org

ROSS-ON-WYE *(B&B)*   THE HILL HOUSE   232

Howle Hill
Coughton HR9 5ST
Tel: 01989 562033

Bed and Breakfast
From £25 pppn

Mostly organic, local (named sources) and seasonal

The Hill House is family-run, laid back and relaxed. We adhere to the principles of permaculture. The food we offer guests is mostly organic, local (named sources) and seasonal. The bedrooms are wonderful. The sauna and cinema are popular. The outdoor spa is favourite. We have achieved Gold status with Wildlife Action, and have a Green Business award from Herefordshire Nature Trust. Set in 4 acres of woodland at 500 feet, the views are spectacular – south over the beautiful Wye Valley to Wales, and west towards the ancient Forest of Dean. Wildlife abounds and we have our own happy hens (ducks and pigs are planned). Phase one of the willow maze is established to be completed this year.

thehillhouse2000@hotmail.com   www.thehowlinghillhouse.com

CHALE *(B&B)*

BUTTERFLY PARAGLIDING 233

Sunacre, The Terrace
Chale PO38 2HL
Tel: 01983 731611

Bed and Breakfast, from £25 pppn
Camping, from £5 pppn

95% of the food and drink provided is organic

For a thrilling organic experience, Butterfly Paragliding run tandem flights, fun days and courses (from £65) all year round. Set up in 1994 as a centre of excellence on the Isle of Wight to provide paragliding tuition for all levels of pilot, from beginner to competition level. As a registered BHPA school we offer a relaxed and comprehensive service, and with our contacts overseas we are the original paragliding holiday company. Stay in our beautiful Edwardian house with its unrivalled sea views, set in an acre of grounds in an Area of Outstanding Natural Beauty. 95% of the food and drink provided is organic. Any other food that you require can be bought from our organic shop. Green Island Tourism Gold Award.

butterfly@paraglide.uk.com   www.paraglide.uk.com

VENTNOR *(S-C)*

GODSHILL PARK COTTAGE 234

Shanklin Road
Godshill PO38 3JF
Tel: 01983 840781

Cottage: sleeps 4
£220-£875 pw

Produce from our own farm is available to buy

Soil Association

This detached two bedroom cottage will appeal to those wanting peace and tranquillity in a luxurious environment. French windows open into the garden, where there is seating for al fresco dining. The cottage is situated on an organic working farm a quarter of a mile from the public road. Absence of light pollution ensures clear starlit skies. We have a lake stocked with roach and carp for the exclusive use of our guests. The farm is situated within an Area of Outstanding Natural Beauty. The gently undulating farmland is crossed by footpaths which lead down to the village and up to the downs. The village of Godshill is renowned for its pretty thatched cottages, 14th-century church and tea gardens.

info@godshillparkfarm.uk.com   www.godshillparkfarm.uk.com

VENTNOR *(B&B)*   GODSHILL PARK FARM   235

Shanklin Road
Godshill PO38 3JF
Tel: 01983 840781

Bed and Breakfast
Double, £90-£99 pn

Breakfast includes local and organic produce

Soil Association

Two hundred year old farm nestling in the heart of the island's countryside near the picturesque village of Godshill in an Area of Outstanding Natural Beauty. Breakfast includes local and organic produce. Free-range Isle of Wight bacon, sausages, free-range eggs, organic milk and butter, and homemade preserves using our own fruit. Our 200-acre organic farm (no pesticides, herbicides or artificial fertilizers) grows cereals, and is home to our herd of Aberdeen Angus cattle and Castlemilk Moorit sheep. Our woodlands host a least six ancient woodland plants. There are red squirrels, badgers, foxes, little owls and buzzards. The ponds are home to swans, kingfishers, various geese, ducks, moorhens and herons.

info@godshillparkfarm.uk.com   www.godshillparkfarm.uk.com

VENTNOR *(B&B)*   GOTTEN MANOR   236

Gotten Lane
Chale PO38 2HQ
Tel: 01983 551368

Bed and Breakfast, £35-£45 pppn
(based on two people sharing a room)

Homemade, organic and local produce

The Old House offers unique accommodation. Dating back to the early 14th century, it is one of the few, and probably oldest, first floor houses on the Isle of Wight. The two huge guest rooms are both traditionally decorated, with limewashed walls and wooden floors. The cast iron baths within the rooms and Persian rugs create an old-fashioned opulence. A hearty breakfast, including homemade jams and marmalades, is made from organic and local produce and served in the old creamery. A private walled garden is reserved for guests. The cottages are traditionally decorated with limewashed walls, and every effort has been made to make all three as ecologically acceptable as possible.

organic@gottenmanor.co.uk   www.gottenmanor.co.uk

VENTNOR *(S-C)*

LAKE VIEW 237

Godshill Park Farm
Godshill PO38 3JF
Tel: 01983 840781

Cottage: sleeps 6
£220-£875 pw

Breakfast can be taken in the farmhouse by arrangement

Soil Association

Lake View is a newly furbished wing of the farmhouse providing spacious accommodation all on one level. Breakfast can be taken in the Great Hall of Godshill Park farmhouse by arrangement. Lake View is situated on our 200-acre organic farm bordering Appuldurcombe estate in the heart of an Area of Outstanding Natural Beauty. French windows look onto the south-facing patio, which looks out over the garden to the millpond and the woods and farmland beyond, stretching up to the downs. Footpaths and bridleways cross the farm to the downs. The village of Godshill is renowned for its pretty thatched cottages, 14th-century church and tea gardens. Sandy beaches only a seven minute drive away.

info@godshillparkfarm.uk.com www.godshillparkfarm.uk.com

VENTNOR *(S-C)*

PHEASANT COTTAGE 238

Godshill Park Farm
Godshill PO38 3JF
Tel: 01983 840781

Cottage: sleeps 4-5
£180-£750 pw

Breakfast can be taken in the farmhouse by arrangement

Soil Association

Delightful detached cottage on an organic farm bordering Appuldurcombe estate in the heart of an Area of Outstanding Natural Beauty. Breakfast can be taken in the Great Hall of Godshill Park farmhouse by arrangement. The cottage looks out across the orchard to the nearby millpond, which has an abundance of waterfowl, and beyond to the downs. Godshill church can also be seen in the opposite direction. The 200-acre organic farm has an Aberdeen Angus herd, rare breed sheep, arable fields, pasture, wooded hills, and valleys. Footpaths and bridleways cross the farm. The picturesque village of Godshill is renowned for its pretty thatched cottages, 14th-century church and tea gardens.

info@godshillparkfarm.uk.com www.godshillparkfarm.uk.com

CANTERBURY *(S-C)*

RIPPLE FARM 239

Crundale
Canterbury CT4 7EB
Tel: 01227 730748

Farmhouse Accommodation: sleeps 5
£220-£450 pw

Organic vegetable box (order in advance)

Soil Association

An established horticultural farm specialising in organic produce, situated between the villages of Godmersham and Crundale. Spacious fully self-contained accommodation is provided in one half of the owner's Grade II listed 16th-century timber framed farmhouse. Three rooms downstairs and two large timbered bedrooms, each with a gallery, overlook fields and across the valley to the North Downs. Guests are welcome to use the garden and may also use the owner's outdoor swimming pool by arrangement. A farmers' market is held in the nearby attractive village of Wye every alternate Saturday. Excellent walking and riding country. Several beaches are less than half an hour away.

ripplefarmhols@aol.com

CANTERBURY *(S-C)*

THE RETREAT 240

Witherdens Hall
Wingham CT3 1AT
Tel: 01227 720543

Cottage: sleeps 4
£35-£100 pppn

Delicious home cooked food sourced locally (around 90% organic)

The Retreat is situated in the grounds of 16th-century Witherdens Hall. Offering a relaxing break in tranquil surroundings, the cottage has two double bedrooms, bathroom, kitchen and sitting room for guests' exclusive use. It is beautifully furnished and fitted out, with Egyptian cotton sheets, jacuzzi bath, fluffy towelling robes and a magnet and crystal healing bed with Tempur mattress for a fabulous night's sleep. Organic food and beverages can be served to order using produce from the garden and the local organic farm shop, or guests can prepare food themselves. Treatments available in the privacy and comfort of The Retreat, from acupuncture and reiki to facials (Organic Pharmacy) and hairdressing.

louisecox@fusemail.com www.witherdenshall.co.uk

MAIDSTONE *(S-C)*

ORCHARD COTTAGE 241

Parkhouse Farm
Chart Sutton ME17 3RD
Tel: 01622 843229

Cottage: sleeps 4
£281-£430 pw

Organic fruit available to buy from July-September

Soil Association

Approached down a farm track, this delightful detached cottage (circa 1850) is surrounded by orchards on a small organic fruit farm. Comfortably modernised, the south-facing rooms retain many original features and have lots of pretty extras. Outside, a patio runs round the front and sides of the house, with steps leading down to a small well and a shallow lily pond (no pets or toddlers). Sorry, no smokers. The farmland is totally organic, with 10 acres for guests to walk in and orchards to explore. The farm produces traditional top fruit only from 100 year old trees – Laxton apples, Bramley apples, cooking apples, plums and Conference pears. The apple, plum and pear orchards are registered with the Soil Association.

jeanchartsutton@aol.com

CLITHEROE *(S-C)*

COACH HOUSE 242

Clough Bottom Farm
Bashall Eaves BB7 3NA
Tel: 01254 826285

Cottage: sleeps 4
Contact for prices

Organic produce in the market town of Clitheroe (5 miles)

Organic Farmers & Growers

A Grade II listed coach house, restored to retain the original features and character. The property has its own private drive and adjoins the farmhouse orchard by the stream. The accommodation, comfortably furnished with full gas central heating, is open plan living downstairs and is complete with its own private outdoor seating area, which is ideal for barbecues. A large dining room within a converted barn is available for hire should a large party book all three cottages. The Coach House is set on an organic and conservation-minded hill farm in the idyllic and relaxing environment of the Forest of Bowland. A ten minute walk will take you to the village post office, which is open on Thursdays.

akerrison@focus-training.net www.cloughbottom.co.uk/cottages

CLITHEROE *(S-C)*

SADDLE BARN 243

Clough Bottom Farm
Bashall Eaves BB7 3NA
Tel: 01254 826285

Cottage: sleeps 6
Contact for prices

Organic produce in the market town of
Clitheroe (5 miles)

Organic Farmers & Growers

Saddle Barn is a three bedroom property in an Area of Outstanding Natural Beauty in the heart of the beautiful Ribble Valley. Lovingly converted, it retains its natural country style charm. French doors lead to a private patio area, which overlooks fields and a stream. A large dining room within a converted barn is available for hire should a party book all three cottages. Situated on the owners organic farm in the idyllic and relaxing Forest of Bowland, it is ideal for walking locally or for touring the Lakes and the Dales. Clough Bottom Farm is very close to a number of well used public footpaths – they often lead to local pubs or the farm shop. For 'foodies', the Inn at Whitewell is worth a call.

akerrison@focus-training.net www.cloughbottom.co.uk/cottages

CLITHEROE *(S-C)*

WOODCUTTER'S COTTAGE 244

Clough Bottom Farm
Bashall Eaves BB7 3NA
Tel: 01254 826285

Cottage: sleeps 4
Contact for prices

Organic produce in the market town of
Clitheroe

Organic Farmers & Growers

Woodcutter's Cottage is a lovingly converted property in an Area of Outstanding Natural Beauty in the heart of the beautiful Ribble Valley. Dating back to the 16th century, the cottage has been thoughtfully decorated to maintain its cosy and quaint feel. Private patio area overlooking fields and a stream. A large dining room within a converted barn is available for hire should a party book all three cottages. Situated on the owners' organic farm in the idyllic and relaxing Forest of Bowland. Ideal for walking locally, or for touring the Lakes and Dales. Clough Bottom is close to a number of well used public footpaths – often leading to local pubs or the farm shop. For 'foodies', the Inn at Whitewell is worth a call.

akerrison@focus-training.net www.cloughbottom.co.uk/cottages

LUTTERWORTH *(B&B)*

HIGH HOUSE 245

Lutterworth Road
Walcote LE17 4JW
Tel: 01455 552413

Bed and Breakfast
Double, £70 pn

At least 60% organic food

Welcome to our Georgian home. We have two spacious double rooms available with private bath and shower room (robes provided). There is a lounge for guests' use and rooms have wireless internet access. For breakfast, we use organic produce wherever possible and all the bread is homemade. Special diets catered for: just ring us beforehand to discuss your requirements. The area is good for both cycling and walking and we can recommend several short circuits (including pub stops). Lovely organic shop (2 miles) in an old converted barn in the village of Cotesbach. Ryton Organic Gardens (23 miles). Please mention 'Organic Places to Stay' when booking for a 5% discount on the bed and breakfast price.

info@highhousebnb.co.uk www.highhousebnb.co.uk

BOSTON *(S-C)*

ECO-LODGE 246

Rose Cottage
Station Road PE22 9RF
Tel: 01205 870062, 01205 871396

Eco Lodge: sleeps 4, £340 pw + £5 per person
Mon-Fri or Fri-Mon £170 + £5 per person

Local organic fruit and vegetables, organic dairy produce

The eco-lodge is built from wood grown and harvested in Lincolnshire. The energy sources are wind and solar power and a large woodburning range. Developed over twenty years, it is set in 8 acres of organically managed wood and meadowland. Organic produce is available to order. A large pond provides a home for mirror carp and other fish. Native tree species as well as conifers make up the wood and park. Situated in fenland six miles from the sea marshes, it is also close to the Wolds. Beautiful walking and cycling country, interspersed with occasional country pubs. Visitors' comments: a wonderful break from the real world, freedom for children, magic moments, great hospitality, somewhere precious.

gclarke@ibs-ltd.freeserve.co.uk www.internationalbusinessschool.net/ecolodge.htm

LINCOLN *(B&B)*

CHAPLIN HOUSE 247

92 High Street
Martin LN4 3QT
Tel: 01526 378795

Bed and Breakfast
£60 per room pn

Most of our produce is locally sourced, free-range and organic

Winner of Lincolnshire Tourism's Accommodation of the Year 2006 Star Award. Finalist in the Tastes of Lincolnshire Bed and Breakfast Award. You'll find a warm friendly welcome at Chaplin House, in the heart of the Lincolnshire countryside. In our barn conversion we have three ensuite rooms together with a guests' lounge and a decked area for guests to enjoy, and we have one guest room in the house. Enjoy tea with our homemade cake on arrival, relax in our peaceful garden, unwind with a book. For breakfast, we offer a range of options. Most of our produce is locally sourced, free-range and organic. In 2008 we'll be offering our own honey as we now have two bee hives. Packed lunches on request.

info@chaplin-house.co.uk www.chaplin-house.co.uk

LOUTH *(B&B)*

CLODDYGATE FARM 248

Owes Lane
Skidbrooke LN11 7DE
Tel: 01507 358679

Bed and Breakfast
£25 pppn

Almost all organic, local where possible plus fairtrade or home-grown

Cloddygate Farm is a welcoming 19th-century farmhouse in Lincolnshire Poacher Country near the historic market town of Louth. We are passionate about good, seasonal, local food and prepare full English or vegetarian breakfast using almost all organic ingredients. Farmhouse tea, dinner or light supper available by arrangement. Enjoy a comfortable room with far-reaching rural views. Close by are coastal nature reserves with marsh orchids and samphire, full of wild birds and visited by Atlantic grey seals in winter. We have lots of room for storing bikes and safe off-road parking. The quiet lanes and footpaths and miles of wild coastline are ideal for photography, walking, cycling, or just relaxing.

cloddygatefarm@tiscali.co.uk myweb.tiscali.co.uk/cloddygatefarm

LOUTH *(B&B)*

TITHE FARM 249

Church End
North Somercotes LN11 7PZ
Tel: 01507 358413

Farmhouse Bed and Breakfast, £27.50 pppn
Evening Meal (by arrangement)

Good quality food, mostly organic (around 80%) and local where possible

18th-century farmhouse set in 6 acres of organically cultivated gardens and meadowland in a peaceful rural location near Louth and the Lincolnshire coast. We provide good quality food, mostly organic and local where possible, with homemade jam and freshly picked fruit in season. As well as accommodation in the house we also have a yurt, complete with a double futon and a woodstove (see separate listing). There's plenty of wildlife in the garden – rabbits, hedgehogs, water voles, shrews, voles, mice, frogs, toads and newts are resident, and badgers, foxes, hares and squirrels visit. Tithe Farm is a great place to go bird-watching from. For several miles north and south of us the coast is a nature reserve.

biff@biffvernon.freeserve.co.uk   www.biffvernon.freeserve.co.uk

LOUTH *(Camping)*

TITHE FARM YURT 250

Church End
North Somercotes LN11 7PZ
Tel: 01507 358413

Yurt, £27.50 per person pn
Breakfast included in the price

Good quality food, mostly organic (around 80%) and local where possible

Our yurt is 16 feet in diameter and 9 feet high in the middle, made of about 150 willow rods and a lot of canvas. There's a transparent piece at the top to let the sunshine, or moonlight, in. The floor is rather solid timber. This part is a local Lincolnshire adaptation, not suited to easy transport by camel across the steppe, but then we have neither camel nor steppe. There is a woodstove, which gets the place warm in no time. Electricity is supplied but the candle lanterns are more fun. Surrounded by trees, flowers and vegetables, the yurt is set in our six-acre garden. Outside is the yurt's own lawn with picnic table. Round the back is an open air bathroom. Breakfast in the house is included in the price of your stay.

biff@biffvernon.freeserve.co.uk   www.biffvernon.freeserve.co.uk/the_yurt.htm

PRIMROSE HILL *(B&B)*

REGENT'S PARK ROAD   251

Primrose Hill
London NW1 8XP
Tel: 020 7722 7139

Double Room £75 pn, Flat: sleeps 4 £150 pn
Luxury Apartment: sleeps 2 £130-£150 pn

Organic breakfast (self-service) by
arrangement, £5 per person

Rent a room in a charming split-level two bedroom apartment in the heart of lovely Primrose Hill, or rent both rooms as a self-contained flat. Both bedrooms ensuite. Serviced daily. Use of fully equipped kitchen / living room. Premier organic mattresses in one room and top hotel quality in the other. Can be made up as a double or a twin. On arrival guests receive a generous bowl of organic fresh fruit, organic snacks and fresh flowers. A large selection of organic teas, coffee, etc freely available from the kitchen at all times. Prior booking essential, early booking recommended. Close to transport, and within walking distance to the West End. Luxury one bedroom apartment also available, £130-£150 per night.

london-availability@onetel.com

DISS *(B&B)*

STARYARD B&B   252

Millway Lane
Palgrave IP22 1AD
Tel: 01379 643787

Bed and Breakfast, £27.50-£35 pppn
Evening Meal (prior booking)

Meals prepared using at least 85% organic
ingredients

Our eco-friendly bed and breakfast was built ten years ago of locally grown larch by a 'green' architect. Set in its own grounds of approximately one acre, it is tucked behind a lovely complex of 16th-century barns in a quiet and tranquil location. Staryard has two ponds, a stream and beautiful views of the Waveney Valley. All food at Staryard is made using at least 85% organic ingredients, much of it home-grown or sourced as much as possible from local greengrocers and butchers. All meat is free-range. Packed lunches can be prepared to order at a cost of £7.50 per head. Evening meals may also be ordered when booking at a cost of £15 per head. The bustling market town of Diss is within walking distance.

staryard@btinternet.com   www.staryardbedbreakfast.co.uk

KING'S LYNN *(B&B)*

BAGTHORPE HALL 253

Bagthorpe
Nr Bircham PE31 6QY
Tel: 01485 578528

Bed and Breakfast
£35 pppn (minimum 2 nights)

Includes organic produce from the family farm

Soil Association

Bagthorpe Hall is situated in the countryside of North Norfolk, close to Sandringham and Burnham Market. The coast is only a fifteen minute drive away. The owners, Tid and Gina Morton, are devoted to organic farming and gardening. The excellent food includes organic produce from the family farm for both breakfast and dinner. Bagthorpe Hall is a large, elegant house offering a luxurious stay. Wonderful colours, good beds, and a fascinating and beautiful mural in the hall chronicling the family history. The house is surrounded by 50 acres of parkland, woodland and gardens, which are peaceful, quiet and full of birdlife. Many of the trees are over 150 years old. There is a lovely snowdrop walk in February.

enquiries@bagthorpehall.co.uk www.bagthorpehall.co.uk

NORWICH *(B&B)*

THE FOXBURGH 254

PO Box 19
Barnham Broom NR9 4BZ
Tel: 01603 759791

Bed and Breakfast, from £70 pn
Natural Health and Wellness Centre

Breakfast is organic

Demeter

Country home within a secluded estate only eight miles south-west of Norwich. We offer an informal atmosphere for only a small number of guests, who are welcomed in comfortable ensuite rooms in modern, country house style. In line with the holistic and biodynamic principles we practice and believe in, the water supply is fully energised with Grander Water Technology – one of the few properties in the country with this facility. In addition to offering bed and breakfast accommodation we are also an Holistic Therapies Centre, providing a wide range of holistic therapies. The four acres of our biodynamically managed garden provide many plants that are used in herbalism and flower remedies.

isabelle@foxburgh.co.uk www.foxburgh.co.uk

NORWICH *(B&B)*

WEST LODGE 255

24 Fakenham Road
Drayton NR8 6PR
Tel: 01603 861191

Guest House, Small Conference Centre
B&B, double £65-£125 pn

Exclusively vegetarian, all food organic and
fairtrade where possible

West Lodge is a unique venue, an intimate and friendly large Victorian house with a light, airy contemporary feel. Complimentary Wi-Fi throughout. We are an exclusively vegetarian guest house and small conference centre, ideal for retreats, workshops and day / week courses. We use as much organic / local / fairtrade produce as possible, and are happy to cater for most dietary requirements (providing they don't involve meat). Visit us as a guest for a single night's stay, or have exclusive occupancy of the house for reunions or get-togethers, where you create the atmosphere of your choice, or perhaps hire one of our rooms for workshops. Our gardens offer places to find solitude and peace.

info@vegetarian-bedandbreakfast-norwich.co.uk www.vegetarian-bedandbreakfast-norwich.co.uk

SWAFFHAM *(Hotel)*

STRATTONS HOTEL 256

4 Ash Close
Swaffham PE37 7NH
Tel: 01760 723845

Boutique Hotel, double B&B £150-£225 pn
Restaurant

Award winning restaurant serves organic
and locally sourced produce

An art boutique hotel, hidden away in its own peaceful courtyard a minute's walk from the marketplace in Swaffham. Ten individual rooms. Environmentally sensitive restoration using environmental solutions such as lambswool insulation and environmental paint systems. Award-winning restaurant, recently scooping the Considerate Hoteliers Food Award for sourcing locally, ethically and reducing air miles. Menus change daily, sourcing organic local produce to create contemporary dishes. Strattons was the first hotel in the UK to win the prestigious Queen's Award for 'Outstanding Environmental Performance', and has since picked up a handful of awards for its environmental ethos, interiors and food.

enquiries@strattonshotel.com www.strattonshotel.com

ALNWICK (S-C)

GARDEN COTTAGE 257

Lumbylaw Farm
Edlingham NE66 2BW
Tel: 01665 574277

Cottage: sleeps 2
£202-£444 pw

Booklet with information on where to buy local produce

Organic Farmers & Growers

Surround yourself with the peaceful, beautiful countryside of Lumbylaw. Our working organic farm specialises in pedigree Lleyn sheep and our prize-winning herd of South Devon cattle. Garden Cottage is centrally heated, with one double bedroom and no steps. Set amidst the picturesque Cheviot and Simonside Hills, it has its own garden and breathtaking views. You can walk in the grounds, which feature medieval Edlingham Castle and a five-arch Victorian viaduct over the valley. The cottage is adjacent to the hamlet of Edlingham and is the perfect location to explore the delights of Northumberland, both coastal and inland. Booklet for guests in the cottage, with information on where to buy local produce.

holidays@lumbylaw.co.uk www.lumbylaw.co.uk

ALNWICK (S-C)

FARM COTTAGE 258

Farmhouse
Shipley Hill NE66 2LX
Tel: 01665 579266

Cottage: sleeps 5
£280-£450 pw

Soil Association

Shipley Hill is a mixed organic farm of 450 acres situated in the heart of the beautiful Northumberland countryside. The cottage is set in an elevated position on a quiet lane leading to the farm. Visitors are very welcome to stroll around the farm. There are many fantastic walking destinations in the surrounding area, as well as miles of unspoiled sandy coastline to explore. It provides an excellent base for exploring Northumbria, with the coast, castles (Lindisfarne, Dunstanburgh, Bamburgh), miles of sandy beaches, the Cheviot hills and the Northumberland National Park, all well within a half hour drive. The town of Alnwick, with its magnificent castle and garden, is only five miles from the farm.

ALNWICK *(S-C)*

LUMBYLAW COTTAGE 259

Lumbylaw Farm
Edlingham NE66 2BW
Tel: 01665 574277

Cottage: sleeps 6
£302-£725 pw

Booklet with information on where to buy local produce

Organic Farmers & Growers

Surround yourself with the peaceful, beautiful countryside of Lumbylaw. Our working organic farm specialises in pedigree Lleyn sheep and our prize-winning herd of South Devon cattle. Lumbylaw Cottage is centrally heated with three bedrooms, two bathrooms and no steps. Set amidst the picturesque Cheviot and Simonside Hills it has its own garden and breathtaking views. You can walk in the grounds, which feature medieval Edlingham Castle and a five-arch Victorian viaduct over the valley. The cottage is adjacent to the hamlet of Edlingham and is the perfect location to explore the delights of Northumberland, both coastal and inland. Booklet for guests with information on where to buy local produce.

holidays@lumbylaw.co.uk www.lumbylaw.co.uk

BERWICK-UPON-TWEED *(B&B)*

NOAH'S PLACE 260

31 Main Street
Spittal TD15 1QY
Tel: 01289 332141

Bed and Breakfast
£20-£25 pppn

Your breakfast comes from certified organic sources

The house, built in 1792, stands on a lovely broad Georgian high street in the one-time spa town of Spittal. It is just a few minutes walk away from the sandy beach and its promenade with far-reaching views to Holy Island and over the river to Berwick itself. Noah's Place offers cosy rooms surrounded by books, pictures and antiques. Relax in the pretty walled garden, or next to a woodburning stove in the breakfast room. Most importantly you will have the security of knowing that your breakfast comes from certified organic sources. We believe food should be free of artificial additives, and produced in an environmentally friendly way using humane and conscientious farming practices. Opening season varies.

info@noahsplace.co.uk www.noahsplace.co.uk

GREENHEAD (B&B)

HOLMHEAD GUEST HOUSE 261

Hadrian's Wall
Greenhead CA8 7HY
Tel: 016977 47402

Bed and Breakfast, from £35 pppn
Evening Meal, £25

40%-80% organic over the year

Holmhead Guest House (4 stars) stands on the World Heritage Site of Hadrian's Wall and was built with stones taken from it. Set at the top of a valley beneath the ruins of a castle and beside a river, it is surrounded by fields and woodland. Guests dine at the large oak table in the lovely stone arched beamed dining room. Food is always freshly prepared, and organically grown vegetables and organically reared local meat are served wherever possible. We specialise in organically grown and produced wine, with an award winners' list from around the world. Our other speciality is Hadrian's Wall. You can read about it from our extensive library, watch videos, take a guided or a self-guided tour.

holidays@holmhead.com   www.bandbhadrianswall.com

HEXHAM (S-C)

BURNLAW BUNKHOUSE 262

Whitfield
Hexham NE47 8HF
Tel: 01434 345359

Bunkhouse: sleeps 6
£10 pn (own linen), £13 pn (linen provided)

Organic produce available in season

Soil Association

Burnlaw is on a 50-acre organic smallholding on the edge of the West Allen Valley, one of the most unspoiled and beautiful corners of Britain. Part of a complex of stone farm buildings, the bunkhouse is a converted stone-roofed cart shed. It consists of three double bunk beds. In an adjacent room there are two loos, two showers and a wash basin. Kitchen facilities are available in the Tall Barn, which is a short walk away. The Bunkhouse can be used as a place to rest up at night in conjunction with the amenities of the Tall Barn, or as an adjunct to camping in an adjacent field. Guests are welcome to wander round the farm, use the games field, and also use the nationally recognised disc golf course.

gvs38@hotmail.com   www.burnlaw.org.uk

HEXHAM *(S-C)*

BURNLAW COTTAGE 263

Whitfield
Hexham NE47 8HF
Tel: 01434 345359

Cottage: sleeps 8
£300-£500 pw

Organic produce available in season

Soil Association

Burnlaw Cottage is on a 50-acre organic smallholding in an Area of Outstanding Natural Beauty. The converted 18th-century barn is part of a complex of stone farm buildings, which is home to five households – most of whom are members of the Bahá'í Faith. On the edge of the West Allen Valley, it is one of the most unspoiled and beautiful corners of Britain. Part of the North Pennines, it has hilly uplands, steep wooded valleys, and fast flowing limestone streams. The farm has a small herd of suckler cows, horses, poultry, orchard, organic vegetable garden, and woodland. Guests are welcome to wander round the farm, use the games field, and also use the nationally recognised disc golf course.

gvs38@hotmail.com   www.burnlaw.org.uk

HEXHAM *(S-C)*

FELBRIDGE COTTAGE 264

Gibbs Hill Farm
Bardon Mill NE47 7AP
Tel: 01434 344030

Cottage: sleeps 2-4
£200-£350 pw

Organic free-range eggs, organic tomatoes, honey

Organic Farmers & Growers

Felbridge Cottage is a most attractive, surprisingly spacious two storey building on a traditional working hill farm dating back to before the 17th century. The ground floor has a large living area incorporating the kitchen, dining area and a sitting area with a welcoming log burning stove set into the large stone-built fireplace. A stairway leads up to the bedroom and bathroom. The porchway faces west towards Felbrook. Natural spring water. Organic produce is available locally. There is access, via Gibbs Hill land, to a specially created boardwalk and bird-watching hide on the nearby Greenlee Lough nature reserve. Walk the best bits of the new Hadrians Wall path from your own doorstep.

val@gibbshillfarm.co.uk   www.gibbshillfarm.co.uk/felbridge.htm

HEXHAM *(S-C)*

FELBROOK COTTAGE 265

Gibbs Hill Farm
Bardon Mill NE47 7AP
Tel: 01434 344030

Cottage: sleeps 6
£250-£600 pw

Organic free-range eggs, organic tomatoes, honey

Organic Farmers & Growers

Converted from a stable on a traditional working hill farm. Felbrook has a spacious living room in which the original wooden beams have been left exposed, complementing the huge stone fireplace and its woodburning stove. Off this room is the large kitchen / dining area with original beams and stone fireplace. Organic produce is available locally. Natural spring water. A door to the rear from the sitting room leads to a patio with barbecue area and access to the farmland behind. Towards the northern boundary of Gibbs Hill Farm there is an ancient stone circle, thought to be an early Bronze Age burial site. This site is worth the walk, not only for its historical interest, but also for the views it offers.

val@gibbshillfarm.co.uk www.gibbshillfarm.co.uk/felbrook.htm

HEXHAM *(S-C)*

FELSTREAM 266

Gibbs Hill Farm
Bardon Mill NE47 7AP
Tel: 01434 344030

Cottage: sleeps 4
£330-£520 pw

Organic free-range eggs, organic tomatoes, honey

Organic Farmers & Growers

Newly refurbished to an extremely high standard, the cottage is furnished with locally made pine furniture. There's a spacious cosy living / dining area with a welcoming log burning stove set into the large stone-built fireplace. French windows open onto a large patio with panoramic views southwards towards a lake, the Roman Wall and distant hills. At one end of this patio is a barbecue for relaxed summer evenings. Towards the northern boundary of the farm is an ancient stone circle. This site is worth the walk, not only for it's historical interest, but also for the views it offers. There is access from our land to a specially created boardwalk and bird watching hide on nearby Greenlee Lough nature reserve.

val@gibbshillfarm.co.uk www.gibbshillfarm.co.uk/felstream.htm

HEXHAM *(S-C)*

GIBBS HILL BUNKHOUSE 267

Gibbs Hill Farm
Bardon Mill NE47 7AP
Tel: 01434 344030

Bunkhouse: sleeps up to 18
£12 pppn

Organic free-range eggs, organic tomatoes, honey

Organic Farmers & Growers

Converted from an old hay barn at Gibbs Hill Farm, the bunkhouse accommodates up to eighteen people in three rooms, each of which has six bunks. The bunkhouse is centrally heated throughout, and to reduce energy consumption the barn is insulated with special panels. Low energy light bulbs are used throughout. To the rear of the bunkhouse is a large decking area where guests may enjoy the evening sun, and also access the stables by the wooden staircase. Basic items of food may be purchased. Guests may order (in the evening for the next day) a continental breakfast (£4 per person) and packed lunches (£5 per person) from the farmhouse. Organic produce is available locally.

val@gibbshillfarm.co.uk www.gibbshillfarm.co.uk/bunkhouses.htm

HEXHAM *(B&B)*

GIBBS HILL FARM B&B   268

Bardon Mill
Hexham NE47 7AP
Tel: 01434 344030

Farmhouse Bed and Breakfast, £28-£30 pppn
Packed lunches can be provided

Home or local produce, much of it organically produced

Organic Farmers & Growers

A traditional working hill farm dating back to before the 17th century. The present owners are the fourth generation to farm here. The farm carries fifty suckler cows and calves and over five hundred Swaledale cross ewes and lambs. There is also a small fold of Highland cattle. Integration into the Countryside Commission's Farm Stewardship Scheme and conversion under their DEFRA Organic Farming Scheme is indicative of the deep commitment that the family have to the countryside and environmental care. Within the farm's land there are two 50-acre areas of ancient peat bog, which have been designated SSSI and handed to the Northumberland National Park for their management.

val@gibbshillfarm.co.uk www.gibbshillfarm.co.uk/bed-breakfast.htm

HEXHAM (S-C)

THE TALL BARN 269

Burnlaw
Whitfield NE47 8HF
Tel: 01434 345359

Room: sleeps 6
£10 pn (own linen), £13 pn (linen provided)

Organic produce available in season

Soil Association

Burnlaw is on a 50-acre organic smallholding on the edge of the West Allen Valley, one of the most unspoiled and beautiful corners of Britain. Part of the North Pennines, it has hilly uplands, steep wooded valleys, fast-flowing limestone streams. The Tall Barn is part of a complex of stone farm buildings. It consists of a large room with sleeping arrangements for six people, a reception room, a kitchen, a very large studio room, two shower rooms, a bath and two loos. It is centrally heated. The farm has a small herd of suckler cows, horses, poultry, orchard, organic vegetable garden, woodland. Guests are welcome to wander round the farm, use the games field, and the nationally recognised disc golf course.

gvs38@hotmail.com www.burnlaw.org.uk

MORPETH (B&B)

THISTLEYHAUGH 270

Longhorsley
Morpeth NE65 8RG
Tel: 01665 570629

Bed and Breakfast, double £65 pn
Evening Meal, 4 course with wine £17

Organically reared meat and seasonal local produce

Organic Farmers & Growers

Thistleyhaugh is a picturesque farmhouse on the banks of the River Coquet in the heart of rural Northumberland. We offer five ensuite rooms, and guests have exclusive use of the farmhouse dining room and lounge. As well as a hearty Northumbrian breakfast, we also cook traditional roast dinners, homemade soups and puddings. The food is locally produced and seasonal. The meats we serve are organically reared, and the fish are fresh wild North Sea salmon. Set in 720 acres of organic farmland, Thistleyhaugh retains much of the charm and many of the historic features found in a traditional Georgian farmhouse. The working farm, with cattle and sheep, has been run by the same family for over 100 years.

info@thistleyhaugh.co.uk www.thistleyhaugh.co.uk

NEWCASTLE UPON TYNE *(B&B)*   DUNNS HOUSES FARM   271

Otterburn
Newcastle upon Tyne NE19 1LB
Tel: 01830 520677

Farmhouse Bed and Breakfast
£27.50-£35 pppn

Organic breakfast option (£5 supplement)

A peaceful period residence on a privately owned estate with fantastic views of Troughend Common, the Rede valley, Otterburn, the foothills of the Cheviots. Situated on a working farm in 960 hectares of the Northumberland National Park. Full Northumberland breakfast. You have the choice of a farm-reared breakfast or an organic breakfast (please note the organic breakfast needs ordering when you book). Both varieties are supplied by local suppliers where possible. Brown trout / salmon / sea trout fishing on our private mile stretch of the River Rede. Bring your own horse and explore this beautiful countryside on horseback. For walkers we are ideally placed for accessing the Pennine Way.

dunnshouses@hotmail.com   www.northumberlandfarmholidays.co.uk

EAST BRIDGFORD *(B&B)*   BARN FARM COTTAGE   272

Kneeton Road
East Bridgford NG13 8PH
Tel: 01949 20196 (early morning or evening)

Bed and Breakfast
£32 pppn

The delicious breakfast is almost always all organic

You'll receive a warm welcome at this wonderful hideaway. It's a small organic and biodynamic holding in East Bridgford, overlooking fields and the Trent Valley. Ideal for walkers and fishermen (look out for the clapper gates along the river bank path, found only on the Trent), and well set up for children. The cottage has log fires, exposed beams, gardens, a peaceful atmosphere, and good food. The delicious breakfast is almost always all organic, and includes homemade marmalade and jams. Many organic items are also available from the village shop. East Bridgford is an attractive village on the Trent Valley Way, the long distance trail (84 miles) through Nottinghamshire along the Trent Valley.

WALLINGFORD *(B&B)* FYFIELD MANOR 273

Brook Street
Benson OX10 6HA
Tel: 01491 835184

Bed and Breakfast
From £32.50 pppn (2 people sharing)

A range of organic produce is offered

Recently restored and refurbished, Fyfield Manor offers very comfortable accommodation in an interesting manor house with features which span seven centuries, many of which have been hidden for over 250 years. We pride ourselves on running an environmentally friendly bed and breakfast, using local produce, saving energy and the world's resources. A full English breakfast is served in the medieval dining room. A range of organic produce is offered, including organically grown tomatoes and fruit in season from the garden. Guests have full use of the gardens and picnic areas. The gardens, with 6 acres of natural water gardens, are a haven for wildlife and totally organic. Surcharge for single occupancy.

chris_fyfield@hotmail.co.uk www.fyfieldmanor.co.uk

WANTAGE *(B&B)* DOWN BARN FARM 274

Sparsholt Down
Wantage OX12 9XD
Tel: 01367 820272

Farmhouse Bed and Breakfast, £30-£35 pppn
Evening Meal, from £15 (by arrangement)

Most of the food is from the organic farm and garden

Organic Farmers & Growers

Down Barn is a 100-acre grassland farm set in a hollow of the Ridgeway Downs. This organic cattle and pig enterprise is quietly situated and gives the impression of being completely isolated even though it is in fact close to Oxford and the Cotswolds. A full English cooked breakfast is included in the price of the rooms, and evening meals can be served if needed (with a little advance notice). Most of the food is from the farm and garden, and is therefore all organic. Some of the special dining features that we have to offer are home cooking, home produce, and vegetarian food. The countryside is ideal for walking, off-road cycling, and riding. The whole area is renowned for its racehorse training stables.

pendomeffect@aol.com

BUCKNELL *(S-C)*

ECOCABIN 275

Obley
Bucknell SY7 0BZ
Tel: 01547 530183

Ecocabin: sleeps 4+cot, £420-£605 pw
£90-£105 pn (minimum 2 nights)

Organic foods can be delivered ready for your arrival (£5 collection charge)

Ecocabin is constructed of home-grown timber, sheep's wool, reeds, lime and clay, and heated by a wood pellet stove. It nestles peacefully in a secluded valley in the South Shropshire Hills and has stunning views. Fairtrade tea, coffee and cocoa are provided and there is a small 'honesty' shop stocking many organic products. The Marches and Mid-Wales have a delicious variety of small scale food producers that sell at local outlets and farmers' markets. We provide a 'buy local' shopping service and a selection of foods of your choice can be delivered ready for your arrival (£5 collection charge). Organic cotton bed linen, towels and chemical-free toiletries provided for your stay. No short breaks in school holidays.

kate@ecocabin.co.uk www.ecocabin.co.uk

CRAVEN ARMS *(S-C)*

BRYNMAWR FARM 276

Newcastle on Clun
Craven Arms SY7 8QU
Tel: 01588 640298

Caravan: sleeps 4-6, £200-£250 pw
Price pn on application

Organic vegetables subject to availability

Soil Association

The caravan is set on the Shropshire / Mid Wales border in the beautiful Clun Valley, an Area of Outstanding Natural Beauty. Brynmawr is a working organic farm situated within an Environmentally Sensitive Area. The farm produces organic potatoes (including seed), carrots, swedes, organic beef and lamb. Enjoy the peace and quiet and the spectacular views, whether sitting in the caravan, walking on the hill top, or sitting in the self-contained garden having tea. The farm includes the Shropshire Wildlife Trust's Rhos Fiddle Nature Reserve, a beautiful expanse of upland moorland designated as a Site of Special Scientific Interest, where you will be able see Highland cattle and Hebridean sheep.

brynmawr@farmersweekly.net www.clunvalleyorganics.co.uk

CRAVEN ARMS *(S-C)*

BUCKSHEAD COTTAGE   277

Brynmawr Farm
Newcastle-on-Clun SY7 8QU
Tel: 01588 640298

Cottage: sleeps 4, from £420 per week
Price pn on application

Pick your own organic vegetables from the
garden (subject to availability)

Soil Association

An eco-friendly traditional stone cottage with its own wind turbine and solar hot water panels. Set on the Shropshire / Mid Wales border in the beautiful Clun Valley, an Area of Outstanding Natural Beauty. Brynmawr is a working organic farm situated within an Environmentally Sensitive Area. The farm produces organic potatoes (including seed), carrots, swedes, organic beef and lamb. Enjoy the peace and quiet and the spectacular views from the hill top. The farm includes the Shropshire Wildlife Trust's Rhos Fiddle Reserve, a beautiful expanse of upland moorland designated as a Site of Special Scientific Interest, where you will be able see Highland cattle and Hebridean sheep.

brynmawr@farmersweekly.net www.clunvalleyorganics.co.uk

CRAVEN ARMS *(B&B)*

WARD FARM   278

Westhope
Craven Arms SY7 9JL
Tel: 01584 861601

Farmhouse Bed and Breakfast
Double £25-£30 pppn, Single £30-£35 pn

A variety of free-range poultry provide fresh
eggs for your breakfast

Organic Farmers & Growers

Ward Farm is a certified organic working farm with a traditional herd of Hereford cattle, sheep and three Gloucester Old Spot pigs. We also keep completely free-range poultry providing fresh eggs for your farmhouse breakfast. Spacious rooms, including a ground floor twin room suitable for wheelchair access, with lovely views across fields and all the facilities to make your stay a comfortable one. The village of Westhope is in South Shropshire's Area of Outstanding Natural Beauty and is particularly picturesque. The area is ideal for walking or cycling. Ludlow and Church Stretton are fifteen minutes by car and Shrewsbury, Much Wenlock, Ironbridge and Bridgnorth are about thirty minutes.

contact@wardfarm.co.uk   www.wardfarm.co.uk

CRAVEN ARMS *(Camping)*

WARD FARM CAMPING   279

Westhope
Craven Arms SY7 9JL
Tel: 01584 861601

Certified Location Site, £10 pn
CL club members only

Organic Farmers & Growers

Ward Farm is a certified organic working farm with a traditional herd of Hereford cattle, sheep and three Gloucester Old Spot pigs. We also keep completely free-range poultry. Our camping and caravanning Certified Location site has electric hook-ups, drinking water supply and chemical disposal point. We also have a shower room with WC and wash basin with hot and cold water. The site, which is for camping and caravanning club members only, is situated next to the farmhouse with views across the surrounding countryside. Westhope is in South Shropshire's Area of Outstanding Natural Beauty and is particularly picturesque. The area is ideal for walking and cycling, and is very peaceful.

contact@wardfarm.co.uk   www.wardfarm.co.uk/Camping.htm

LUDLOW *(B&B)*

LOWER BUCKTON   280

Buckton
Leintwardine SY7 0JU
Tel: 01547 540 532

Private Restaurant with Rooms
Dinner Bed and Breakfast, £75 pppn

All food either home produced or locally sought, bought and caught

Country house accommodation with award-winning breakfasts and delicious dinners. Situated off the beaten track in Mortimer Country on the north Herefordshire / south Shropshire borders, where England meets Wales. The productive vegetable garden, managed on organic principles, supplies the kitchen with year-round fresh seasonal produce. Carolyn and Henry are members of Slow Food, believe in the importance of low food miles, and buy all other ingredients from small local growers and producers, thus supporting the rural community and economy. Their cooking is much praised for its ingredients and flair. Open all year for short breaks, weekends, private house parties and bring your own horse holidays.

carolyn@lowerbuckton.co.uk   www.lowerbuckton.co.uk

OSWESTRY *(Hotel)*

PEN-Y-DYFFRYN HOTEL   281

Rhydycroesau
Oswestry SY10 7JD
Tel: 01691 653700

Country House Hotel, B&B from £57 pppn
Restaurant (AA two rosette good food award)

Food is healthy, locally sourced, and tends to the use of organic produce

Perched almost a thousand feet up, this silver stone former Georgian rectory is situated in the Shropshire / Welsh hills, an area of unspoilt natural beauty. The restaurant, with its huge south-facing sash windows, is central to the Pen-y-Dyffryn experience. The relaxed and almost 'retreat-like' feel of the hotel is complemented by the increasing use of local and organic produce in the kitchen, so that guests depart feeling thoroughly revitalised. Set in five acres of grounds, the hotel offers superb accommodation including some bedrooms with private patios, others with spa baths. The gardens run down to the river marking the border, the banks of which are being managed as a nature reserve.

stay@peny.co.uk www.peny.co.uk

BATH *(B&B)*

BECKFORD HOUSE   282

59 Upper Oldfield Park
Bath BA2 3LB
Tel: 01225 334959

Bed and Breakfast
Double £70-£95 pn, Single £55-£65 pn

As far as possible fresh local organic produce is used

Beckford's is a Victorian residence with open views in a quiet leafy location, a short walk from the town centre (off-street parking, Wi-Fi). The house has spacious rooms with a wide hall and landing, and high ornate ceilings. The French windows of the breakfast room overlook a small walled garden frequented by squirrels. For breakfast you'll be offered cinnamon muesli, cereals, yogurt, fruit in season, fairtrade coffees and teas, and a traditional English breakfast using fresh mushrooms and tomatoes, organic eggs and farm bacon. As far as possible fresh local organic produce is used (from Bath Farmers' Market) and breakfast is cooked to order. There's a choice of jams and spreads, some homemade.

post@beckford-house.com www.beckford-house.com

BATH *(B&B)*

MARLBOROUGH HOUSE 283

1 Marlborough Lane
Bath BA1 2NQ
Tel: 01225 318175

Vegetarian Bed and Breakfast
Double, £85-£125 pn

Organic food is a speciality of the house
(95%-100%)

Exquisitely furnished with antiques, Marlborough House is an enchanting small establishment in the heart of Georgian Bath. Served in either the elegant parlour or lovely dining room, breakfasts are cooked to order, using only the highest quality organic ingredients. Marlborough House specializes in organic foods which include a wide range of organic cereals, juices, yogurts, fresh fruits and jams, organic English cheeses, eggs and milk and a selection of excellent breads, and croissants, as well as fresh roasted continental coffees and various fair trade organic teas. Your friendly hosts will happily give you advice on your explorations of Bath, as well as the many fine walks in the gorgeous surroundings.

mars@manque.dircon.co.uk www.marlborough-house.net

BATH *(B&B)*

NUMBER FOURTEEN 284

14 Raby Place
Bathwick Hill BA2 4EH
Tel: 01225 465120

Regency Town House Bed and Breakfast
Double £65 pn, Single £35 pn

About 80% organic produce

A delightful Georgian house situated on the lower slopes of Bathwick Hill with superb views of the World Heritage City of Bath. The house is in a typical Georgian terrace, single fronted with a richly decorated interior. Bedrooms are tastefully done in an interesting mix of colours and styles. Healthy breakfasts, using organic products whenever possible, include eggs, bacon, yogurts, fruit salads and homemade jams, and are taken around a large mahogany table in the dining-room. Visit Bath's hot springs and the Roman Baths, one of the best examples of a Roman bath complex in Europe. Number Fourteen is very close to the Bath Skyline Walk (created by the National Trust), and the Kennet and Avon Canal.

BRIDGWATER (S-C)

HUNTSTILE FARM 285

Goathurst
Bridgwater TA5 2DQ
Tel: 01278 662358

Self-Catering: sleeps 2+2/3, £250-£895 pw

We can provide all meals; organic farm produce is for sale

Soil Association

Huntstile offers three self-catering options – Apple Loft, Cider House and Seed Granary. On our farm we grow a wide variety of organic vegetables, soft fruit and herbs. With a little notice we can provide breakfasts, packed lunches and evenings meals too. We cater for both meat-eaters and vegetarians. Delicious breakfasts £3.50 per person. Packed lunches £5-£7 (depending on your appetite). Evening meals around £10-£15 per person. Food is my favourite subject and I use as much of our own fresh organic produce as possible. All is available to buy from our farm gate sales area. For £6.50 you can order a mixed box of organic vegetables for your arrival, and we can also provide you with a varied organic hamper for your stay.

lizziemyers@hotmail.com www.huntstileorganicfarm.co.uk

BRIDGWATER (B&B)

HUNTSTILE FARM B&B 286

Goathurst
Bridgwater TA5 2DQ
Tel: 01278 662358

Bed and Breakfast, double from £50 pn
Evening Meal, from £10

Breakfast includes home-grown organic produce plus local organic sausages and bacon

Soil Association

A fascinating farmhouse, dating back to Henry VIII, with many original and beautiful features. Huntstile Organic Farm is set in the foothills of the Quantocks, with panoramic views across the county. We have six rooms for B&B guests (four double / family rooms and two twins). Evening meals are available from £10 per person. We are passionate about locally grown, well produced, quality food – our lives revolve around it. We grow our own organic fruit, vegetables and herbs in our two and a half acre kitchen garden. Our flock of organic chickens provides delicious eggs for breakfast. We also have a small herd of British White beef cattle. There are some lovely farm walks, and wonderful surrounding countryside.

lizziemyers@hotmail.com www.huntstileorganicfarm.co.uk

BRIDGWATER *(Camping)*

HUNTSTILE ECOTENTS 287

Goathurst
Bridgwater TA5 2DQ
Tel: 01278 662358

EcoTents: sleep 5-12, £150-£550 pw
Camping £7.50 pn, Caravans £12 pn

Organic farm produce for sale in the farm shop

Soil Association

We have recently added the Sidelands into our wildlife project. This is a beautiful part of the valley, with far-reaching views and a natural spring that feeds the wildlife lake. There are no vehicles, no electricity and no mains water. We have a water purification system for the spring water, composting loos, solar-powered showers fed from the spring (eco-friendly shampoo and soap only please). There is a recycling and composting area and a purpose-built woodburning community barbecue. The ecotents have a solid wooden base and are equipped with cooking facilities, table, benches, camp beds. All you have to do is bring your own sleeping bag and food. Very peaceful, very natural, very eco-friendly.

lizziemyers@hotmail.com   www.huntstileorganicfarm.co.uk

BRIDGWATER *(B&B)*

PARSONAGE FARM 288

Over Stowey
Bridgwater TA5 1HA
Tel: 01278 733237

Farmhouse B&B, double £55-£65 pn
Light Supper £10, Evening Meal £20-£25

We specialise in organic, home-grown food

A traditional 17th-century farmhouse and organically run smallholding in a peaceful village in the Quantock Hills, an Area of Outstanding Natural Beauty. The farmhouse has three double bedrooms (two ensuite), a cosy sitting room, log fires and quarry tiled floors. There is a walled kitchen garden with honeybees, hens, and an apple orchard with a flock of black Welsh sheep. A traditional or vegetarian English breakfast is served in front of an open fire in the dining room. Eggs from our hens, homemade breads and jams, and pancakes with maple syrup. We specialise in organic, home-grown food. Evening meals are served by candlelight. 5% discount if you arrive by bicycle, foot or public transport.

suki@parsonfarm.co.uk   www.parsonfarm.co.uk

CHARD *(B&B)*

WAMBROOK FARM 289

Wambrook
Chard TA20 3DF
Tel: 01460 62371

Farmhouse Bed and Breakfast
£28-£30 pppn, single supplement £5

Generous farmhouse breakfast or
continental options

Soil Association

Wambrook Farm is in the beautiful countryside of the Blackdown Hills, two miles from Chard. We are a working mixed organic farm. We keep sheep that lamb in the spring, suckler beef cattle, rear heifers for dairy farms, and grow corn. The farmhouse and buildings are listed (built mid 1800), with a unique granary as a focal point in the yard. We offer a generous farmhouse breakfast or continental options, and use locally grown produce. We have a lovely garden to sit in or to play badminton. Guests are welcome to walk on the farm. Wambrook is a quiet rural village in an Area of Outstanding Natural Beauty. There is a pub in the village, which is a lovely mile walk in the summer, offering excellent food.

wambrookfarm@aol.com www.wambrookfarm.co.uk

CHEDDAR *(B&B)*

BAY ROSE HOUSE 290

The Bays
Cheddar BS27 3QN
Tel: 01934 741377

Room, double £50-£70 pn
Breakfast £7.50, Evening Meal £18

100% organic diet available with advance notice

Relax at our 19th-century English country cottage. Spend a sunny summer afternoon watching the butterflies, birds and dragonflies in the garden, or explore the Mendip countryside on our doorstep. A choice of breakfasts is offered, and evening meals are available with 24 hours notice. About 30%-50% of our products and ingredients are organic, but if you specify organic as a dietary preference on the booking form you can have a 100% organic diet while staying with us. There's always organic cereal, muesli etc, organic milk, and homemade bread made entirely (or almost entirely) with organic ingredients. Some produce comes from local smallholders and allotment holders selling from their gates.

enquiries@bayrose.co.uk www.bayrose.co.uk

GLASTONBURY *(S-C)*

PADDINGTON FM TRUST 291

Maidencroft Farm
Wick BA6 8JN
Tel: 01458 832752

Farmhouse: sleeps 20, Mon-Fri £650 / Fri-Sun £325. Longhouse: sleeps 10, £15 pppn

Organic vegetables and eggs available to buy direct from farm

Soil Association

Low cost self-catering accommodation on a beautiful 43-acre organic educational farm. The farm is only a mile from the historic town of Glastonbury. Private bookings and groups of all kinds are welcome. The large farmhouse has its own private garden, picnic tables and barbecue. The longhouse, with three separate self-catering units (two units with 2 beds, one with 4-6 beds), is suitable for individuals, families or small groups. Panoramic views across the Somerset Levels to the Mendips. Glastonbury Tor is a twenty minute walk. Wildlife, walks, local attractions, tailored group activities on the farm as you wish (see our website for details of activities). Groups need to book activities on the farm in advance.

pft@onetel.net www.paddingtonfarm.co.uk

GLASTONBURY *(B&B)*

SHAMBHALA RETREAT 292

Coursing Batch
Glastonbury BA6 8BH
Tel: 01458 831797

Vegetarian Retreat
See website or contact for details

Fresh organic ingredients (100% organic)

Everything you ever wanted: Shambhala Healing Retreat on the Tor in Glastonbury with magnificent views of the Vale of Avalon. This is a sacred site from ancient times, steeped in legend. The focus is a beautiful star of hundreds of clear crystal points that energy pulses through from deep in the earth. Enjoy our flock of peace doves, water gardens and meditation spaces, beautiful rooms and lots of love. Organic vegetarian food is lovingly prepared with fresh high quality ingredients. Our treatments for mind, body and spirit are renowned. We have been voted one of the top ten retreats in the UK by the Daily Mail, and we have a 'Gold Star' award from the Good Retreat Guide. Highly recommended.

elisis@shambhalaheartcentre.com www.shambhala.co.uk

GLASTONBURY *(B&B)*   THE WHITE HOUSE   293

21 Manor House Road
Glastonbury BA6 9DF
Tel: 01458 830886

Room, double £55-£65 pn
Breakfast, £5-£7.50

Our food is organic and vegetarian

The White House is an exclusive, unconventional bed and breakfast, five minutes walk from Glastonbury High Street. Built in 1890, the house has been restored and redecorated with natural paints. Everything is arranged according to the ancient principles of Feng Shui, resulting in a happy, peaceful and relaxed atmosphere. Always conscious of the impact we have on the environment, our light bulbs are energy-saving and all household waste is recycled. Our food is organic and vegetarian. An organic cereal, fresh fruit and yogurt breakfast can be provided in your room for £5 per person per day. A full English organic vegetarian option is also available for £7.50 per person per day.

carey@theglastonburywhitehouse.com   www.theglastonburywhitehouse.com

LANGPORT *(B&B)*   3 GREAT BOW YARD   294

Bow Street
Langport TA10 9PN
Tel: 01458 253559

One double, one twin, one single
£30-£60 pppn

Organic breakfasts

Opening in Spring 2008. Tranquil comfort B&B with stunning view across the Levels. One twin / family room, one double room, and one single room, which are allergy-free using only eco decoration materials. Freeview digital TV, free Wi-Fi. Organic breakfasts, with specialist breads for toast, and spreads, cereals, fresh fruit, range of drinks, teas or coffee. All organic produce fresh from Somerset Organic Link. Front and back garden and sun space with large additional community garden. Walks and cycle rides from the house. Award-winning smokery restaurant locally. Within easy walking and cycling distance or close by car to Bath, Glastonbury, Bristol or Taunton. Qualified professional therapist.

lynn.craniosacral@hotmail.co.uk

LANGPORT *(S-C)*

MERRICKS FARM 295

Park Lane
Langport TA10 0NF
Tel: 01458 252901

Converted Barn: sleeps 2, £225 per week
£40 cottage pn S-C, £50 cottage pn B&B

Eggs, vegetables, fruit and meat are available
from the farm

Soil Association

A small converted barn on the farm lane, looking out over fields and woodland. The cottage is spacious but basic, having an entrance area by the front door that opens out onto the kitchen, living room and dining area. To the right of the entrance area is a double bedroom with ensuite shower room. Eggs, vegetables, fruit and meat are available from the farm. Should you wish it, an evening meal can be provided in the cottage. Our organic farm covers 28 acres, of which 9 acres is devoted to fruit and vegetables. We have created a large pond and planted traditional hedgerows, cider apple orchards and woodland. On the edge of the Somerset Levels, the farm is a mile and a half from the market town of Langport.

merricksorganicfarm@tiscali.co.uk www.merricksorganicfarm.co.uk

LANGPORT *(B&B)*

TIBBS HOUSE 296

Henley
Langport TA10 9BG
Tel: 01458 253022

Dining House with Rooms, double £80 pn
Dinner, around £35 per person

The emphasis is very much on food, using
local organic produce where possible

Nestling at the foot of a hill on the edge of the Somerset Levels, Tibbs House is an 1825 blue lias stone farmhouse surrounded by orchards and lush countryside. Recently refurbished as a stylish contemporary home, with three gorgeous double guest rooms. The emphasis at Tibbs House is very much on food, making use of the wonderful produce that this part of the country has in abundance. Wherever possible we like to use local organic produce. We have a large garden with lawn, terrace and pergola, and beyond the garden an orchard and vegetable garden, where we grow as much of our own produce as we can – organically of course. We also do a wide range of organic preserves, chutneys and cordials.

brendan@tibbshouse.co.uk www.tibbshouse.co.uk

MINEHEAD *(B&B)*

HINDON ORGANIC FARM 297

Nr Selworthy
Minehead TA24 8SH
Tel: 01643 705244

Farmhouse Bed and Breakfast
£35-£45 pppn

Own organic meats, other organic goods,
local produce

Soil Association

Real Farm. Real Food. Relax. Enjoy Exmoor National Park, where red deer roam, on an award-winning 500-acre organic hill farm. 18th-century accommodation with 21st-century comforts and some style. Aga-cooked breakfasts with our own homemade sausages and bacon, free-range eggs from our hens, fresh baked bread, fruit, honey on the comb, etc. Hindon is a working stock farm and country home set in an idyllic secluded location three miles from Minehead. Ducks dabble in the garden stream. Wonderful walks from the door to the moor, the South West Coast Path, the sea, Selworthy (1mile) for scrummy cream teas. We have a farm shop. Outdoor hot tub and aromatherapy treatments by arrangement.

info@hindonfarm.co.uk www.hindonfarm.co.uk

MINEHEAD *(S-C)*

HINDON COTTAGE 298

Nr Selworthy
Minehead TA24 8SH
Tel: 01643 705244

Cottage: sleeps 1-6, £299-£899 pw

Our own organic meat produce, free-range
eggs, fruit and vegetables in season

Soil Association

Real Farm. Real Food. Relax. Stay in farm style. Charming 18th-century traditional farm cottage with 21st-century comforts in the Exmoor National Park. Lovingly cared for to a high standard. Set alone on an idyllic wooded hillside in its own enclosed garden with lovely views over the fields. Peacocks wander. Red deer roam. Perfect for a country escape. Complimentary welcome basket of organic / local produce. Log fire. Central heating. Crisp cotton linen. The cottage is hidden 100 yards from the farmhouse within our 500-acre award-winning organic stock farm. Wonderful walks from the door to coast, moorland and sea. On site farm shop for our produce. Farmhouse meals. Outdoor hot tub.

info@hindonfarm.co.uk www.hindonfarm.co.uk

NETHER STOWEY *(B&B)*

THE OLD CIDER HOUSE 299

25 Castle Street
Nether Stowey TA5 1LN
Tel: 01278 732228

Guest House, from £30-£55 pppn
Evening Meal, £13.50-£19.50

Somerset sourced produce, organic where available, home-grown in season

The Old Cider House was built in 1910 and produced local cider until the 1960s. Now a 4-star guest house with five ensuite rooms, the proprietors, Ian and Lynne, are enthusiastic about producing good home cooking using seasonal and local ingredients. They grow as many of their own vegetables as possible in the summer, and keep organically fed hens for fresh eggs. Meat comes from the local butcher, and they subscribe to a local organic box scheme. Ian has also recently set up the Stowey Brewery, producing a small range of real ales for in-house consumption. The thriving village of Nether Stowey, designated a Rural Centre, is situated at the foot of the largely unexplored Quantock Hills.

info@theoldciderhouse.co.uk www.theoldciderhouse.co.uk

WELLS *(B&B)*

THE MILLER'S HOUSE 300

Burcott Mill
Burcott BA5 1NJ
Tel: 01749 673118

Guest House
Bed and Breakfast, £25-£35 pppn

Our wholemeal bread is made by a local baker using our own organic flour

Soil Association

The Miller's House (circa 1750) is a charming Grade II listed building adjoining Burcott Mill. There has been a mill on this site for over a thousand years, and few such watermills still operate commercially today. We specialise in the production of 100% organic wholemeal stoneground flour made from organic English wheat grain. Our breakfasts are highly praised by our guests. We offer a selection of locally made organic yogurts, marmalades and honey, West Country honey roast sausages and bacon to go with your free-range eggs, and of course our wholemeal bread is made by a local baker using our own organic flour. A private tour of the working mill with our miller is a feature of your stay here.

theburts@burcottmill.com www.burcottmill.com

WHEDDON CROSS *(B&B)*

CUTTHORNE 301

Luckwell Bridge
Wheddon Cross TA24 7EW
Tel: 01643 831255

Country House, B&B £35-£44 pppn
Dinner, £18-£21

Approximately 50% organic produce over
the year

Hidden in a private valley, deep in the heart of the glorious Exmoor countryside, Cutthorne is a delightful country house with a rare tranquillity that is truly off the beaten track. At the centre of this 25-acre estate is the impressive Georgian farmhouse, which retains much of its original character and charm. We offer superb bed and breakfast accommodation in a choice of three ensuite guest rooms or two adjoining cottages. We grow our own organic fruit, vegetables and salads, and provide eggs from our own hens. All our meals are traditionally prepared and cooked in an Aga. Delicious home-baked puddings. Local organic produce used whenever possible. Fully licensed with some organic wines.

durbin@cutthorne.co.uk www.cutthorne.com

WINCANTON *(B&B)*

LOWER FARM 302

Shepton Montague
Wincanton BA9 8JG
Tel: 01749 812253

Bed and Breakfast in the Barn, sleeps 6
£45 pppn (weekends minimum 2 nights)

Home produced, organic, local (at least 80%
organic)

A stylish self-contained barn attached to an 18th-century farmstead surrounded by organic farmland in deepest Somerset dairy country. Comfortable beds, crisp cotton sheets, downy duvets, toile de Jouy curtains, limewashed walls, polished wood floors. The big window in the barn overlooks hens scratching in the orchard, an inspiring acre of compost-grown vegetables (we have been growing organic vegetables since 1983), abundant flower borders, and orchards. Breakfast consists of home-produced, local and organic ingredients. The bread is baked from organic wheat grown in the village. We can usually supply organic vegetables if you wish to cook for yourselves in the barn kitchen.

enquiries@lowerfarm.org.uk www.lowerfarm.org.uk

STOKE-ON-TRENT *(S-C)*

ROWAN HOUSE 303

Tythe Barn
Alton ST10 4AZ
Tel: 01889 591844

Self-Catering: sleeps 7+, £460-£650 pw
Short Breaks, from £315

Complimentary organic breakfast basket, in-house catering

4-star self-catering accommodation on the edge of the historical and picturesque village of Alton, within the Staffordshire Moorlands in the Peak District. The pretty south-facing enclosed garden is organically managed. Rowan House is run as sustainably as possible and we support the local environment and economy. You will find a selection of fairtrade teas and coffees, and a homemade cake to welcome you. There are miles of walks right from the front door – beautiful woods, deep valleys, open moorland and old country tracks. We have a selection of maps and books to help you decide where to go. We also help guests plan bespoke weekends to include catering, guided walks and climbing.

emily@simplystaffordshire.co.uk www.simplystaffordshire.co.uk

STOKE-ON-TRENT *(B&B)*

THE CHURCH FARM 304

Holt Lane
Kingsley ST10 2BA
Tel: 01538 754759

Farmhouse Bed and Breakfast
£25-£28 pppn

100% organic breakfast can be provided on request

Surrounded by beautiful countryside the farmhouse is situated in the quaint village of Kingsley, above the lovely Churnet Valley. The Grade II listed house provides luxury accommodation with oak beamed rooms and beautiful period furnishings. It has a cottage garden with a large lawn. A full English breakfast is served using organic and local produce. 100% organic breakfast provided on request. The 50-hectare farm (dairy, poultry, beef) is a working farm with a tree ringed farmyard and friendly farm animals. Not far from the Churnet Valley steam railway station, close to the Staffordshire Way footpath, five and a half miles from Alton Towers. An ideal base for exploring both the Potteries and the Peak District.

thechurchfarm@yahoo.co.uk

BECCLES *(B&B)*

2 THE OLD HALL 305

Barsham
Beccles NR34 8HB
Tel: 01502 714661

Bed and Breakfast, £18 pppn +£5 per car pn
Evening Meal, £5 per person

Around 98% organic – and 99%
supermarket-free

We offer cycle-friendly accommodation in a 16th-century old hall on a 3-acre organic smallholding in the peaceful Waveney Valley. We grow much of our own food, and welcome informal visitors to share our lifestyle and the idyllic surroundings. We are a non-smoking, vegetarian, child friendly household. As our guests you share our home (no TV or private tea making facilities). We have a variety of rooms and can accommodate up to fifteen people. We also have a self-catering option sleeping up to eight in bunk beds. We are interested in food preservation (bottling, drying, juice, wine), spinning, dyeing, knitting, cycling, yoga, massage, green living. We can arrange cycle tours to suit your particular requirements.

graham@bikeways.org.uk www.bikeways.org.uk

HALESWORTH *(B&B)*

BRIGHTS FARM 306

Bramfield
Halesworth IP19 9AG
Tel: 01986 784212

Bed and Breakfast
£35 pppn

Breakfast includes organic produce from our farm

Soil Association

A classic three storey Grade II listed 15th-century farmhouse set at the heart of a working organic mixed farm. Breakfast is served in the garden room overlooking the farm pond. Organic and fresh locally produced ingredients are cooked for breakfast, including organic produce from the farm (eggs, bread, damson jam, raspberries, strawberries). This is a traditional Suffolk farm with three generations living on and involved with the farm. It has a Site of Special Scientific Interest, which is one of only 236 sites in England. From the farm you can access twelve miles of grass walks passing old meadows, ancient woods and ponds. One mile to The Queen's Head, where many ingredients are sourced from local organic farms.

mail@brightsfarm.co.uk www.brightsfarm.co.uk

LOWESTOFT *(B&B)*

PINETREES 307

Park Drive
Beccles NR34 7DQ
Tel: 01502 470796

B&B, double from £50 pn, single from £40 pn
Packed Lunch, £3.50 (on request)

We use organic, fair trade and local produce
throughout

Enjoy the contemporary design and many eco-friendly features at Pinetrees, set in six and a quarter acres of the peaceful Waveney Valley at Beccles. Pinetrees is a small family business. We offer a wide range of breakfasts, including free-range eggs from our own hens. Although we don't have the Soil Association stamp of approval, all our foods are sourced organically, locally, and are free of harmful fertilizers and pesticides and anything which may damage the environment and wildlife. We can provide a wholesome packed lunch for £3.50 if requested the night before. Beccles is on Route 1 of the National Cycle Network and the North Sea Cycle Route. £5 discount per room for cyclists and walkers.

info@pinetrees.net www.pinetrees.net

POLSTEAD *(B&B)*

MARIA MARTINS COTTAGE 308

Martins Lane
Polstead CO6 5AG
Tel: 01206 262380

Bed and Breakfast, £20 pppn
Evening Meal, £8-£10 (including wine)

Our own organically grown produce is used
in the meals

This historical building is the homestead for a smallholding run on ecological principles. The smallholding consists of 18 acres, mostly pasture, developing woods, an orchard and a vegetable garden. Our income comes mainly from the sheep stud, specialised catering, and furniture made from local hardwoods. The half acre vegetable garden and twenty-five fruit and nut trees provide for four families, as well as providing household meals for countless visitors. We grow anything from three quarters of a ton of potatoes to exotic vegetables annually. Home-grown potatoes, sheep meat, leeks, brassicas, green salads, eggs, apples, hazelnuts, summer preserves and honey all figure large in our diet.

GUILDFORD *(Hotel)*

ASPERION 309

73 Farnham Road
Guildford GU2 7PF
Tel: 01483 579299

Small Hotel
Double £85-£120 pn, Single £50 pn

Our aim is to use organic, free-range and
fairtrade products wherever possible

Asperion offers contemporary accommodation within walking distance of historic Guildford town centre and the main line train station. We aim to create a high quality guest experience that is ethical, sustainable and rewarding. Our fifteen stylish and comfortable ensuite rooms and suites are luxuriously decorated, and feature cutting-edge technology. We are passionate about food and are committed to providing our guests with high quality, freshly cooked food. Our aim is to use organic, free-range, fairtrade and local produce wherever possible. Relax and unwind with delicious food and drink in our organic bar (tapas menu). All Asperion's wines and spirits are organic. We also offer an organic beer.

enquiries@asperion.co.uk www.asperion.co.uk

GUILDFORD *(Hotel)*

HILLSIDE HOTEL 310

Perry Hill
Worplesdon GU3 3RF
Tel: 01483 232051

Small Hotel
Double £75-£105 pn, Single £65 pn

Our aim is to use organic, free-range,
fairtrade and local produce wherever possible

Soil Association

Situated on the beautiful rolling landscape of Surrey, the Hillside Hotel is adjacent to Whitmore Common. Set in award-winning gardens, the privately owned and run hotel has fifteen ensuite bedrooms. From the moment you are greeted at the door of the converted Georgian Post Office we aim to make you feel instantly at home and relaxed. Our large and comfortable sitting room overlooks the beautiful gardens and Koi-filled pond. All food is prepared on-site within our own kitchens. We take great pride in our personal attention to detail and have organic certification with the Soil Association for food served in the hotel. The village of Worplesdon is four miles from both Guildford and Woking.

info@thehillsidehotel.com www.thehillsidehotel.com

BATTLE *(B&B)*

BLACKLANDS   311

Crowhurst
Battle TN33 9AB
Tel: 01424 830360

Farmhouse Bed and Breakfast, £40 pppn
Camping, £7 pppn

At least 95% organic

This old farmhouse, part of which is timber framed and dates from 1679, lies in rolling Sussex hills and dense woods. Blacklands is on a smallholding which has been farmed along organic lines for over twenty years. As well as rearing Angora Cross goats, the smallholding is involved in dairy and horticulture. The owners are practising architects, working from home, and offer environment conscious designs. We offer bed and breakfast and camping. The breakfast is almost completely organic and includes home-grown fruit and homemade bread. The campsite is near the goats, under majestic oaks and beech trees, with a view of the sea on the horizon. The nearest beach is about seven miles away.

info@oliverarchitects.co.uk

BRIGHTON *(Hotel)*

FIVEHOTEL   312

5 New Steine
Brighton BN2 1PB
Tel: 01273 686547

Small Hotel, B&B £35-£70 pppn
Minimum stay 2 nights at weekends

Freshly prepared organic breakfasts

This period townhouse offers beautiful panoramic sea views and overlooks a classic regency square in Brighton. FiveHotel has ten rooms. The majority of our rooms are ensuite with views over the square and sea. Crisp white linen and luxurious duvets. Complimentary Wi-Fi throughout. We serve a selection of fresh breakfasts to order. Our organic breakfast is made from fresh produce sourced from local farms on the Sussex South Downs. We also serve a vegetarian breakfast. FiveHotel is a stone's throw from the beach and the famous Brighton Palace Pier, and a short stroll from the city. With a backdrop of the Sussex Downs and traditional English countryside, it is a great base for exploring.

info@fivehotel.com www.fivehotel.com

BRIGHTON *(Hotel)*

PASKINS TOWN HOUSE   313

18/19 Charlotte Street
Brighton BN2 1AG
Tel: 01273 601203

Town House Hotel
Bed and Breakfast, £30-£65 pppn

Local organic, local farm, homemade

A 'green' hotel, environmentally friendly, and serving organic food. Paskins Town House, in the heart of one of Victorian England's most perfectly preserved conservation areas, is in a tranquil street lined with fine four-storey buildings (built around 1810), with intricate cast iron balconies and gracious bow fronts. Healthy cuisine. We pride ourselves that most of our fresh ingredients are organic, and many are grown on local Sussex farms, including the eggs, tomatoes and mushrooms. The beach is at the end of the road. Paskins is not far from the South Downs Way, imposing chalk cliffs, Beachy Head (with views across the sea), picturesque medieval villages, forests and bird sanctuaries.

welcome@paskins.co.uk www.paskins.co.uk

BRIGHTON *(B&B)*

THE BRIGHTON HOUSE   314

52 Regency Square
Brighton BN1 2FF
Tel: 01273 323282

Guest House
Bed and Breakfast, £40-£65 pppn

Big organic buffet-style breakfast (at least 80% organic)

The Brighton House is a recently refurbished historic Regency townhouse, centrally located by the West Pier. Christine and Lucho are proud of their environmental and health concerns, and wish this to reflect in their 14-room guesthouse. The large buffet-style breakfast, suitable for both vegetarians and non, is almost entirely organic, with the exceptions being made known (if it's not organic, we say so). The environmental ethos goes to behind the front of house, with careful recycling, energy-efficient heating systems, and electricity exclusively from renewable sources. Come and experience the clean ensuite rooms and relax in our down duvet decked beds. Parking available.

info@brighton-house.co.uk www.brighton-house.co.uk

HEATHFIELD *(S-C)*

THE COACH HOUSE 315

Beech Hill Farm
Rushlake Green TN21 9QB
Tel: 01435 830203

Cottage: sleeps 2-3
£295-£370 pw

In season fruit, vegetables, naturally reared
rare breed lamb / mutton

Organically run 20-acre smallholding with two small lakes, formal gardens, traditional pasture. WWOOF host, committed to sustainable ways of living wherever possible. SEEDA Sustainable Business Award for resource efficiency. BETRE Green Action Award for rain harvesting scheme for vegetable, fruit and flower production. Green Tourism Gold Award. The artistically converted 18th-century coach house (separate entrance) is set within its own private garden with views over the unspoilt ancient High Weald, making it a wonderful place to relax and unwind. Public transport and food on your doorstep leaflets. Fine textiles, locally spun yarn and fleece, all from our rare breed Black Wensleydale Longwools.

julia@desch.go-plus.net   www.sussexcountryretreat.co.uk/coach.htm

HEATHFIELD *(Camping)*

HIDDEN SPRING 316

Vines Cross Road
Horam TN21 0HG
Tel: 01435 812640

Caravan and Camping Site
£8.50 per unit pn (hook-up inclusive)

Organic apples and pears, organic ciders,
vineyard honey

Soil Association

Close to the village of Horam, providing a good range of day-to-day needs, this rural caravan club site offers the chance to stay on a working vineyard and organic apple and pear orchards. Sited at the top of the farm it affords views over the vines to the south-west, perfect to catch the best of the sun. The farm shop stocks estate wines, organic ciders and organic apple juice as well as some of the lowest food mile organic fruit in season. Under new ownership and with plans to extend the organic management and planting in the coming years, we look forward to meeting you. The picturesque Cuckoo Trail, the route of a disused railway line which passes through Horam, is well worth walking or cycling along.

hiddenspring@btconnect.com   www.hiddenspring.co.uk

HEATHFIELD *(S-C)*

THE STUDIO SANCTUARY 317

Beech Hill Farm
Rushlake Green TN21 9QB
Tel: 01435 830203

Studio: sleeps 2
£285-£300 pw

In season fruit, vegetables, naturally reared
rare breed lamb / mutton

Organically run 20-acre smallholding with two small lakes, formal gardens, traditional pasture. WWOOF host, committed to sustainable ways of living wherever possible. SEEDA Sustainable Business Award for resource efficiency. BETRE Green Action Award for rain harvesting scheme for vegetable, fruit and flower production. Green Tourism Gold Award. The studio offers dedicated space and seclusion for single / small groups, master classes / workshops, or as a personal retreat for rest and artistic inspiration. We welcome walkers and cyclists as part of the East Sussex Paths to Prosperity Programme. Fine textiles, locally spun yarn, fleece — all from our rare breed Black Wensleydale Longwools.

julia@desch.go-plus.net www.sussexcountryretreat.co.uk/studio.htm

HEATHFIELD *(B&B)*

WIMBLES FARM 318

Vines Cross
Horam TN21 9HA
Tel: 01435 812342

Farmhouse Bed and Breakfast
From £32.50 pppn

Home-grown organic fruit jams, jellies,
compôte, tomatoes, courgettes, eggs

A wonderful place for wildlife and nature lovers to experience the utter peace and tranquility of this delightful 18th-century farm / oasthouse. Comfortable beamed rooms beside the lily lake, with fresh flowers and hospitality tray. The delicious breakfast, served in the farmhouse kitchen, is prepared using home-grown or local produce (50%-80% organic) and organic home baked bread. Organic home produce includes fruit, vegetables, preserves, and our own organic free-range eggs. Guests' TV lounge and garden. Farm walks, coarse fishing, pottery studio. Local pub serving good food within a mile. We are close to the Eastbourne coast and the South Downs for walking, cycling, horse riding, etc.

susan_ramsay@tiscali.co.uk www.wimblesfarm.com

HOVE *(B&B)*

AT WILBURY 319

39 Wilbury Crescent
Hove BN3 6FJ
Tel: 01273 720019

Bed and Breakfast
Double from £50 pn, Single from £27.50 pn

All cooked food is organic, as is most other food and drink

At Wilbury is in a quiet residential street seven minutes walk from Hove train station and twenty minutes from Brighton station. We have two guest bedrooms which both overlook the large garden. We offer a substantial cooked breakfast that can include whatever you want but usually is a combination of eggs, vegetarian sausages, potato cakes, tomatoes, mushrooms etc, cereals, homemade bread, freshly made scones, croissants, honey, jams, fresh fruit and fruit juices. Fish such as smoked salmon, kippers, smoked haddock available on request. All cooked food is organic, as is most other food and drinks. Breakfast can be taken in the garden, or in the dining room overlooking the conservatory.

peters@atwilbury.co.uk   www.atwilbury.co.uk

ROBERTSBRIDGE *(B&B)*

SLIDES FARM B&B 320

Silverhill
Robertsbridge TN32 5PA
Tel: 01580 880106

Bed and Breakfast, £40 pppn
Dinner (by arrangement)

Local farm produce, with the emphasis on organic and free-range

Slides Farm B&B is set in 20 acres of fields and pasture, on high ground in a secluded position above the historic village of Robertsbridge. It has magnificent views over the Sussex Weald, an area noted to be of outstanding natural beauty. Each of our ensuite rooms are stylish and contemporary, with their own garden and terrace area. We pride ourselves in serving a delicious breakfast using the best of local farm produce, with the emphasis on organic (around 70%) and free-range wherever possible. Breakfast options include full English with local Salehurst bacon and sausages, local Wealden smoked haddock with organic poached egg, or Parmesan scrambled eggs with locally smoked salmon.

info@slidesfarm.com   www.slidesfarm.com

RYE *(B&B)*

HAYDEN'S 321

108 High Street
Rye TN31 7JE
Tel: 01797 224501

Bed and Breakfast, £40-£50 pppn
Lunch (daily), Evening Meal (Fri, Sat)

Almost all our food is organic and / or local

Located in a beautiful 18th-century town house, Hayden's is a family-run eco-friendly B&B in the centre of the ancient market town of Rye. Visitors have access to the rear terraces, which have panoramic views across Romney Marsh and out to the sea. Enjoy our home cooking, prepared using organic local produce, as you gaze at the views. We serve breakfast and lunch every day, and also open for evening dining on Fridays and Saturdays. As well as paying attention to natural wholesome food, we use green cleaning products in the kitchen, home laundry and rooms. We also think recycling is very important and participate in community trade waste recycling schemes for both glass and cardboard.

haydens_in_rye@mac.com   www.haydensinrye.co.uk

UCKFIELD *(Camping)*

WAPSBOURNE FARM 322

Sheffield Park
Nr Uckfield TN22 3QT
Tel: 01825 723414

Yurt: sleeps 4, £84.60 pn
Tent pitches, £8 pppn

Organic food hamper (milk, eggs, cheese, vegetables, bread) to order

Soil Association

Have a yurt experience by a trickling stream, with comfy beds and a cosy woodstove. Our 150-acre organic farm is situated at Sheffield Park. Wildlife includes deer, badgers, foxes, rabbits, hedgehogs, a nesting pair of herons, moorhens, wild duck, geese, hawks, larks and robins – with owls and nightjars (and bats) to look out for at night. Bluebells, wild honeysuckle, blackberries. Come camping on our organic farm. The tent sites nestle by the stream. Organic food hamper to order with local organic produce, including award-winning cheeses, green top milk, fresh baked bread, local organic eggs. Pick your own organic vegetables on site. There are signposted short walks to enjoy. Midpoint on the Ouse Valley Way walk.

management@wowo.co.uk   www.wowo.co.uk

WINCHELSEA *(B&B)*

WICKHAM MANOR FARM 323

Wickham Rock Lane
Winchelsea TN36 4AG
Tel: 01797 226216

Farmhouse Bed and Breakfast
£27.50-£40 pppn

Organic lamb, beef, pork

Soil Association

Wickham Manor is an historic property built in the 16th century and now owned by the National Trust. It is the family home of Sally and Mason Palmer, and the centre of their 750-acre organic farm which surrounds the historic town of Winchelsea (the smallest town in England). The farm is home to many species of wildlife such as badgers, rabbits, foxes, swans and herons. Situated in the heart of the Sussex countryside, the manor offers comfortable oak-beamed bedrooms with wonderful views, a beautiful breakfast / dining room where Sally will serve you a traditional full English breakfast, and lovely gardens where you can sit and relax after a long day exploring the many local historic places of interest.

info@wickhammanor.co.uk   www.wickhammanor.co.uk

KEYMER *(B&B)*

HEALING ARTS B&B 324

8 Ockley Way
Keymer BN6 8NE
Tel: 01273 846188

Double room (for a single person)
From £35 pppn

Mostly organic food (around 90%)

Healing Arts Bed and Breakfast is in a quiet residential area close to the South Downs. Relax in the peaceful, light environment. The food is mostly organic (around 90%). Breakfast is vegetarian, and includes a variety of cereals, breads, honey, jams, fresh fruit, yogurt and fruit juices. A range of treatments and courses in healing, art and creativity are available. The area is ideal for walking and cycling. There are some beautiful walks (a number from the door), with wonderful views and many wild flowers up on the Downs. The small village of Keymer is mentioned in the Domesday Book. There are two pubs in the village serving good food. Fifteen minutes walk to Hassocks station, ten minutes by train into Brighton.

patricia@keymer.force9.co.uk   www.homeopathyplus.net

STEYNING *(B&B)*

NASH MANOR   325

Horsham Road
Steyning BN44 3AA
Tel: 01903 814988

Bed and Breakfast, double £70 pn
Workshops, from £80 pp for 2 days

75% of the food is organic over the year

Family-run bed and breakfast situated in the beautiful Sussex countryside. Totally refurbished, Nash Manor has six guest rooms (ensuite or with private bathrooms). Set in 8 acres, we use as much organic produce as possible when available. We grow our own vegetables and herbs, and have our own chickens. We have recently been awarded Gold by the Green Tourism Business Scheme. In the grounds we have a stone circle and a labyrinth. At Nash Manor we hold weekend workshops on health related or creative subjects. Close to the South Downs, this is a tranquil setting for walking and cycling. We have an online shop, Nash Naturals, where we sell organic clothing, towels, plant wax candles, etc.

info@nashmanor.co.uk www.nashmanor.co.uk

CHIPPENHAM *(B&B)*

GOULTERS MILL   326

Goulters Mill Farm
Nettleton SN14 7LL
Tel: 01249 782555

Bed and Breakfast, £31-£40 pppn
Summer House: sleeps 2, £200-£350 pw

Average around 50% organic

Soil Association

Goulters is a 16th-century secluded mill house situated one and a half miles upstream from picturesque Castle Combe. Under its stone tile roof the house is filled with pictures and books, and has big carved stone fireplaces. Nestling in its own 26 acres of wooded valley and wildflower meadows, there has been a mill on this site since Saxon times. The organic smallholding produces lamb. On the steep sides of the south face of the valley the grazing is specially managed to preserve a colony of the blue butterfly (both the Common Blue and the Adonis Blue). Bounded by the Bybrook, our three-quarter acre typical English cottage garden is open to the public for charity with the National Gardens Scheme.

alison@harvey3512.freeserve.co.uk www.freespace.virgin.net/lf.mackelden/Castle_Combe

SWINDON *(B&B)*

LOWER SHAW FARM   327

Old Shaw Lane
Shaw SN5 5PJ
Tel: 01793 771080

Courses and Learning Holidays
Contact us for a programme

90% of the food we give our guests is
organic

Once a dairy farm deep in rural North Wiltshire, Lower Shaw Farm now has another life. It is a 3-acre organic oasis in an area of new development, with large organic vegetable, herb and flower gardens, poultry and black mountain sheep. There are wildlife areas with native shrubs and trees, ponds and play spaces. The outbuildings have been converted into dormitories, meeting rooms and workshops, and it is now a flourishing meeting place and residential centre, running courses, conferences and learning holidays. These include rural crafts, family activities, yoga and singing. The food is mostly home-grown or local and organic, and is all freshly prepared. Not far away are the Ridgeway Path and Avebury stone circle.

enquiries@lowershawfarm.co.uk   www.lowershawfarm.co.uk

SWINDON *(B&B)*

PREBENDAL FARM   328

Icknield Way
Bishopstone SN6 8PT
Tel: 01793 790485

Farmhouse Bed and Breakfast
£30-£40 pppn

Organic breakfasts are provided

Prebendal Farm, built in 1863, is only a mile from the Ridgeway – the most ancient road in Europe. The classic Victorian redbrick farmhouse is enclosed within its own extensive walled gardens, which sweep away from the house in a succession of ancient terraces to the medieval fish pond. This working arable farm is situated in Bishopstone, a beautiful chalk downland village with an exquisite Norman church and a multitude of thatched cottages clustered around an old mill pond. Organic breakfasts are provided, using produce from the famous Eastbrook Farm next door. The Royal Oak pub, which is just five minutes walk from Prebendal farmhouse, offers an extensive organic menu.

prebendal@aol.com   www.prebendal.com

SWINDON *(B&B)*

THE ROYAL OAK   329

Cues Lane
Bishopstone SN6 8PP
Tel: 01793 790481

Bed and Breakfast, double £60 pn
Bar snacks, full lunches, evening meals

The finest organic meat and good quality,
often home-grown, ingredients

The Royal Oak has been the heart of the village of Bishopstone since around 1650 and is now part of Helen Browning's organic food and farming business centred on Eastbrook Farm. B&B is in two rooms set away from the hubbub of the bar. Wake up to a glorious breakfast mostly provided by our own pigs and hens. Lunch and supper menus use the best meat and eggs from our own organic livestock, our own garden fruit, berries from our hedgerows, game from the farm, as seasons dictate. Open 11am-3pm and 6pm-11pm Monday to Friday. Saturdays and Sundays we open at noon and serve lunch till after 4pm. Simple supper menus Sunday and Monday evenings. Organic wines and champagnes.

royaloak@helenbrowningorganics.co.uk www.helenbrowningorganics.co.uk

BROMSGROVE *(B&B)*

WOODCOTE FARM   330

Dodford
Bromsgrove B61 9EA
Tel: 01562 777795

Farmhouse Bed and Breakfast
Double, £65 pn

We use mostly organic produce for
breakfasts

Soil Association

Beautiful 18th-century listed farmhouse set in a mature moated Victorian garden. We have been offering guests accommodation for many years. We provide bed and breakfast, the use of a separate kitchen for self-catering, and self-contained apartments in a barn conversion. We use mostly organic produce for breakfasts. Woodcote Farm has 50 acres of grassland rearing organic sheep and cattle. Attractive farm and woodland walks are on the doorstep. Situated between Bromsgrove and Kidderminster the farm is near the pretty village of Chaddesley Corbett. We are within two miles of historic houses, gardens and villages. The farm is ideally placed to explore Worcestershire and the West Midlands.

woodcotefarm@btinternet.com www.woodcotefarm.com

MALVERN (Camping)

CAVES FOLLY CAMPSITE 331

Caves Folly Nurseries
Evendine Lane WR13 6DU
Tel: 01684 540631

Campsite
£5 pppn

Shop on site selling organic fruit and vegetables, free-range eggs, etc

Soil Association

Have a quiet night camping in our wild flower meadow at just £5 per person per night. The nursery shop on site sells organic fruit and vegetables and other local produce. Our wildflower meadow has secluded little areas to allow you to spend a tranquil night with nature. Old codgers camping (tent and breakfast provided), £15 per person. We provide a two-man tent, sleeping mat and pillows, and a cooked breakfast. You provide a sleeping bag. Please note that our eco-campsite is only available to anyone who turns up either on foot or by bicycle. We are lucky to have an excellent public transport network in Colwall, with regular buses and trains. The eco-campsite is ten minutes walk from the train station.

pleck@cavesfolly.com www.cavesfolly.co.uk

MALVERN (B&B)

OLD COUNTRY HOUSE 332

Old Country Farm
Mathon WR13 5PS
Tel: 01886 880867

Farmhouse Bed and Breakfast
Double £60-£90 pn, Single £35-£55 pn

80% certified organic food on average

600 year old family home with a large and beautiful garden. Relax in the big farmhouse kitchen. The extensive farmhouse buffet breakfast encompasses organic and local food wherever possible. Enjoy the freedom of walking in the grassland, traditional orchards and ancient woodland of this 220-acre farm. The whole farm is managed for the benefit of wildlife and landscape, and to encourage the understanding of our relationship – physical, spiritual and creative – with the natural world. We have a Herefordshire Nature Trust Green Business award and a Gold Wildlife Award. Visitors staying at the bed and breakfast can view the fascinating cider house and hop kilns building at their discretion.

ella@oldcountryhouse.co.uk www.oldcountryhouse.co.uk

MALVERN *(S-C)*

THE LIGHTHOUSE   333

Old Country Farm
Mathon WR13 5PS
Tel: 01886 880867

Green Oak House: sleeps 8-12
Please contact for prices and details

Welcome pack of organic and local food
provided

The Lighthouse is in a wonderful position in the orchards, overlooking the Malvern Hills. This is a newly built green oak building, with a large music / sitting room suitable for group use, smaller study / bedroom, three double bedrooms with baths / showers, and further sleeping space for up to four people. Organic mattresses and bedlinen on the double beds. In the nearby studio / garage are facilities for washing clothes, cleaning palettes, etc. Two to four more beds available in the studio. Hang your work and host a final party at the 'Gallery in the Granary'. All the facilities of Old Country Farm are open to our guests. The Lighthouse is self-contained accommodation but meals for groups can be provided by arrangement.

ella@oldcountryhouse.co.uk www.oldcountryhouse.co.uk

MALVERN *(S-C)*

THE PLECK   334

Caves Folly Nurseries
Evendine Lane WR13 6DU
Tel: 01684 540631

Bungalow: sleeps 2/4/6, £35/£60/£90 pn
£350-£400 pw

On-site shop sells organic fruit and
vegetables, free-range eggs, etc

Soil Association

The Pleck is a newly built two bedroom bungalow with shower room, spacious kitchen / diner, open plan lounge with double sofa bed. It is set in our organic nursery, with lovely views to the Malvern Hills across the wild flower meadow. Facilities include seating and a barbecue area (we sell locally produced charcoal in our organic shop). Wonderful walks and bike rides in the area. We are one of only a handful of commercial producers of organically grown plants in the UK. We have been growing plants organically for over ten years. None of our plants or grounds are sprayed with chemicals. Everything is maintained or dealt with naturally, either by the fauna or us, resulting in a nursery heaving with wildlife.

pleck@cavesfolly.com www.cavesfolly.co.uk

WORCESTER *(S-C)*

THE STEADING 335

Upper Wick Farm
Rushwick WR2 5SU
Tel: 01905 422243

Cottage: sleeps 2+2
£200-£275 pw (pppn by arrangement)

Home cooked meals can be provided made with our own seasonal organic produce

Soil Association

Upper Wick Farm is to the south-west of Worcester city, two miles from the magnificent Cathedral and Royal Worcester Porcelain works. We are a working organic farm of 300 acres rearing our own organic beef, lamb, chicken and eggs plus a large variety of vegetables, herbs and fruit that we sell at our own shop in the village. The Steading is all on the ground floor. It has a large double bedroom with room for a further bed / cot for children, family bathroom, fully equipped kitchen, large lounge (with sofa bed) / dining room with a beautiful aspect across the farm towards the Malvern Hills. The farm is bordered by the River Teme, a Site of Special Scientific Interest due to the wealth of wildlife it supports.

roots@rushwick.com

WORCESTER *(B&B)*

THE TALBOT 336

Knightwick
Worcester WR6 5PH
Tel: 01886 821235

Coaching Inn, B&B £37-£42 pppn
Restaurant

Strong emphasis on organic (40%-60%) and locally produced ingredients

In a peaceful setting on the River Teme, this traditional coaching inn has been welcoming enthusiasts of good food since the late 14th century. There is a strong emphasis on organic and locally produced ingredients (with the exception of fish delivered from Cornwall and Wales), and traditional, seasonal and sometimes ancient recipes, all reworked with an imaginative flair and real emphasis on wholesome flavour. Homemade preserves, breads, black pudding and raised pies. Many of the vegetables, salads and herbs come from our own organic kitchen garden, and wild food is gathered from the fields and hedgerows. Home brewed ales are produced in our own brewery behind the inn.

info@the-talbot.co.uk www.the-talbot.co.uk

DONCASTER *(B&B)*

THE FIELDGATE CENTRE 337

Mill Field Road
Fishlake DN7 5GH
Tel: 01302 842210

Vegan Bed and Breakfast, £27.50-£35 pppn
Evening Meal (by arrangement)

All food is organic vegan using much home-grown produce

A four-acre organic smallholding with a café, shop, conference room, three ensuite B&B rooms in the farmhouse and a caravan site. B&B includes either a continental breakfast (organic cereal, our own organic bread and preserves) or our famous full cooked vegan breakfast. Evening meals by arrangement. We have an organic vegan café with fresh teas, coffees, cakes, ice-creams and other constantly changing goodies. In the shop there are organic fruit and vegetables as well as a range of wholefoods, almost all of which are organic. We make our own jams, chutneys, relishes and pickles, available here and at local farmers' markets. We are members of the caravan and camping club, but open to non-members.

info@fieldgatecentre.org www.fieldgatecentre.org

DRIFFIELD *(S-C)*

WOLD VIEW 338

Foston on the Wolds
Driffield YO25 8BJ
Tel: 01262 488382

Apartment: sleeps 2
£226-£340 pw

Complimentary fruit basket, milk and eggs

Soil Association

A traditional first floor property, adjacent to the owner's house and small organic nursery business. Very comfortably furnished to provide excellent and cosy holiday accommodation, it overlooks the rear courtyard and vegetable garden. Small sun terrace with chairs (french window access from the lounge) and use of the owner's garden. The very pleasant outlook extends out over the surrounding countryside. The cottage is in a quiet and secluded position in the small village of Foston, deep in the Yorkshire Wolds. There are many lovely country walks in the immediate area, and plenty of local sights to visit. Visit the East Coast of Yorkshire, the North Yorkshire Moors, and even York itself.

www.theinternetfarmshop.com/foston-nurseries.htm

GUISBOROUGH *(Hotel)*

PINCHINTHORPE HALL   339

Pinchinthorpe
Guisborough TS14 8HG
Tel: 01287 630200

Country House Hotel, B&B from £65 pppn
Restaurant and Bistro

Menus include fresh seasonal produce from
our Georgian kitchen garden

Organic Food Federation

17th-century country house hotel situated in natural woodland within the North Yorkshire Moors National Park. Menus change daily, according to the choice of fresh seasonal produce available from our kitchen garden. Whenever possible all other produce is bought from local producers within a fifty mile radius, using organic as first choice and free trade if obtained from abroad. Our pedigree herd of Dexter cattle provides the chefs with beef that is second to none. The Manor Restaurant is grand but intimate, whereas the Brewhouse Bistro is less formal. The on-site brewery is certified by the Organic Food Federation, and the brewery tour includes a set meal. NB the kitchen garden is not certified organic.

nybrewery@pinchinthorpe.wanadoo.co.uk www.pinchinthorpehall.co.uk

HEBDEN BRIDGE *(B&B)*

MYRTLE GROVE   340

14 Old Lees Road
Hebden Bridge HX7 8HL
Tel: 01422 846078

Vegetarian Bed and Breakfast
Double £55-£65 pn, Single £35-£55 pn

Organic when possible; home-grown fruit,
homemade jams, home baked bread

Beautifully furnished stone cottage overlooking the small town of Hebden Bridge. The self-contained ensuite guest room has scenic views of the Calder Valley and across to Heptonstall. I cook vegetarian, and use organic produce wherever I can. I grow a wide selection of fruit (rhubarb, raspberries, gooseberries, damsons, blackcurrants, redcurrants), which is served with yogurt at breakfast time. What doesn't get eaten is bottled or made into jam and served throughout the year. I bake my own bread using organic products and buy local eggs and vegetables whenever possible. Plenty of footpath walks begin from the house. It's a pleasant walk down to the town with its thriving organic cafés and delicatessens.

myrtlegrove@btinternet.com www.myrtlegrove.btinternet.co.uk

HOWDEN *(S-C)*

THE STRAW BALE CABIN 341

Barmby Grange
Eastrington DN14 7QN
Tel: 01430 410662

Straw Bale Cabin: sleeps 2 £245-£280 pw
Weekend and mid week available

Complimentary larder basics, honesty shop, vegetable box to order

Unique cottage built with locally grown straw bales and other natural materials. Powered with renewable energy. The cosy, well equipped cabin stands in the corner of a wildflower meadow, overlooking a delightful pond. Curvy, clay-plastered walls, oak beams and deep oak windowsills give the cabin the feel of an old country cottage. Organic towels, bedding and cleaning materials are provided. Herbs growing on the doorstep. Miles of bramble-laden hedgerows in season. Local, organic and fairtrade food available. Peaceful rural location. Explore this unspoilt corner of East Yorkshire. Free use of bicycles. Excellent train links for the complete environmentally friendly holiday. Station collection service.

carol@homegrownhome.co.uk www.homegrownhome.co.uk

HUDDERSFIELD *(B&B)*

THE WEAVERS SHED   342

88 Knowl Road
Golcar HD7 4AN
Tel: 01484 654284

Bed and Breakfast, £50-£75 pppn
Restaurant

Dishes include organically grown produce from the kitchen garden

The Weavers Shed Restaurant with Rooms is a former cloth finishing mill in the centre of the village of Golcar. Set in the heart of the Colne Valley it was converted to a restaurant over twenty-five years ago and adjoins the former mill owner's residence, which now comprises five spacious luxury guest rooms. The restaurant offers a menu of suitably rustic dishes, in a setting of rough stone walls and flagstone floors. It is one of the few restaurants in the North to have its own kitchen garden. The restaurant grows fruit, vegetables and herbs as organically as possible on over an acre of land, which is picked on an almost daily basis. Eggs are provided by the restaurant's own chickens and ducks.

info@weaversshed.co.uk www.weaversshed.co.uk

PICKERING *(S-C)*

BEDFORD CORNER   343

Little Edstone Farm
Little Edstone YO62 6NY
Tel: 01751 431369

Self-Catering: sleeps 4+2
£400-£930 pw

Organic eggs and organic seasonal
vegetables always available to purchase

Soil Association

Little Edstone House and Farm is set amidst wonderful countryside on the edge of the North York Moors National Park. The beautiful cottages were created from a 300 year old stone barn, with many of the original features remaining, and are all heated by renewable energy. Facilities include a heated indoor pool, tennis court, gym, sauna, table tennis, outdoor children's play area and a pets corner. You are also welcome to explore the woodland which, although small, is home to a variety of wildlife. Organic eggs and organic seasonal vegetables are always available to purchase direct from the owners. There is also an organic farm shop, which is Soil Association certified, in nearby Pickering.

pj.littleedstone@btinternet.com www.littleedstone.co.uk

PICKERING *(S-C)*

FOXCOVER   344

Little Edstone Farm
Little Edstone YO62 6NY
Tel: 01751 431369

Self-Catering: sleeps 4+1
£380-£840 pw

Organic eggs and organic seasonal
vegetables always available to purchase

Soil Association

Little Edstone House and Farm is set amidst wonderful countryside on the edge of the North York Moors National Park. The beautiful cottages were created from a 300 year old stone barn, with many of the original features remaining, and are all heated by renewable energy. Facilities include a heated indoor pool, tennis court, gym, sauna, table tennis, outdoor children's play area and a pets corner. You are also welcome to explore the woodland which, although small, is home to a variety of wildlife. Organic eggs and organic seasonal vegetables are always available to purchase direct from the owners. There is also an organic farm shop, which is Soil Association certified, in nearby Pickering.

pj.littleedstone@btinternet.com www.littleedstone.co.uk

PICKERING *(S-C)*

SEPTEMBER LOFT 345

Little Edstone Farm
Little Edstone YO62 6NY
Tel: 01751 431369

Self-Catering: sleeps 2+1
£290-£610 pw

Organic eggs and organic seasonal
vegetables always available to purchase

Soil Association

Little Edstone House and Farm is set amidst wonderful countryside on the edge of the North York Moors National Park. The beautiful cottages were created from a 300 year old stone barn, with many of the original features remaining, and are all heated by renewable energy. Facilities include a heated indoor pool, tennis court, gym, sauna, table tennis, outdoor children's play area and a pets corner. You are also welcome to explore the woodland which, although small, is home to a variety of wildlife. Organic eggs and organic seasonal vegetables are always available to purchase direct from the owners. There is also an organic farm shop, which is Soil Association certified, in nearby Pickering.

pj.littleedstone@btinternet.com www.littleedstone.co.uk

PICKERING *(S-C)*

STANDFIELD HALL COTT 346

Standfield Hall Farm
Westgate Carr Road YO18 8LX
Tel: 01751 472249

Cottage: sleeps 4, £280-£766 per week
Free organic breakfast hamper

Our certified organic farm shop has a wide
selection of organic produce

Soil Association

The cottage is situated on our 67-acre working organic farm, where delicious organic vegetables, eggs and beef are produced. All the produce, plus much more, can be bought from our certified organic farm shop. A complimentary organic breakfast hamper (worth £20) and fresh flowers will be in the cottage at the beginning of your holiday. The 4-star accommodation has a fully fitted farmhouse kitchen and a lounge with a woodburning stove on the ground floor, and king-size double and twin bedded rooms and a bathroom on the first floor. Outside there's a private patio and a large garden with barbecue and picnic table. The farm is down a quiet country lane, a mile from the small market town of Pickering.

mike@theorganicfarmshop.com www.theorganicfarmshop.com

PICKERING *(S-C)*

THE WHEELHOUSE 347

Little Edstone Farm
Little Edstone YO62 6NY
Tel: 01751 431369

Self-Catering: sleeps 8+2
£740-£1,550 pw

Organic eggs and organic seasonal
vegetables always available to purchase

Soil Association

Little Edstone House and Farm is set amidst wonderful countryside on the edge of the North York Moors National Park. The beautiful cottages were created from a 300 year old stone barn, with many of the original features remaining, and are all heated by renewable energy. Facilities include a heated indoor pool, tennis court, gym, sauna, table tennis, outdoor children's play area and a pets corner. You are also welcome to explore the woodland which, although small, is home to a variety of wildlife. Organic eggs and organic seasonal vegetables are always available to purchase direct from the owners. There is also an organic farm shop, which is Soil Association certified, in nearby Pickering.

pj.littleedstone@btinternet.com www.littleedstone.co.uk

PICKERING *(S-C)*

WESTEND 348

Little Edstone Farm
Little Edstone YO62 6NY
Tel: 01751 431369

Self-Catering: sleeps 4+1
£380-£840 pw

Organic eggs and organic seasonal
vegetables always available to purchase

Soil Association

Little Edstone House and Farm is set amidst wonderful countryside on the edge of the North York Moors National Park. The beautiful cottages were created from a 300 year old stone barn, with many of the original features remaining, and are all heated by renewable energy. Facilities include a heated indoor pool, tennis court, gym, sauna, table tennis, outdoor children's play area and a pets corner. You are also welcome to explore the woodland which, although small, is home to a variety of wildlife. Organic eggs and organic seasonal vegetables are always available to purchase direct from the owners. There is also an organic farm shop, which is Soil Association certified, in nearby Pickering.

pj.littleedstone@btinternet.com www.littleedstone.co.uk

SALTBURN BY THE SEA (B&B)   THE ROSE GARDEN   349

20 Hilda Place
Saltburn by the Sea TS12 1BP
Tel: 01287 622947

Bed and Breakfast
Double £30 pppn, Single £40 pn

Carefully sourced high quality produce,
mainly organic / local / fairtrade

The Rose Garden is a gracious, totally non-smoking Victorian terraced house. It is close to the shops and the train station, and within five minutes walk to the sea. 4-star accommodation. We have two excellently furnished ensuite double / twin bedrooms appointed to a high standard. Well stocked tea tray with mineral water and a selection of teas, coffee, hot chocolate, herbal drinks and biscuits and organic chocolates. We believe that food should be produced in an environmentally friendly way using humane methods. We therefore use mainly organic / fairtrade / locally produced products, and are more than happy to cater for those with various dietary requirements, such as vegetarians and vegans.

enquiries@therosegarden.co.uk www.therosegarden.co.uk

SCARBOROUGH (S-C)   SPIKERS HILL FARM   350

West Ayton
Scarborough YO13 9LB
Tel: 01723 862537

Cottages: sleep 4-6
£195-£495 pw

Local organic produce can be bought at the farmers' market (two miles)

Soil Association

Spikers Hill Farm Holiday Cottages are situated on a 500-acre working organic farm (cows, sheep, crops) in a quiet, peaceful location. Converted from farm workers' cottages. they have fantastic views overlooking the beautiful Forge Valley to the North Sea at one side, and rolling farmland to Wykeham forestry at the other (where beautiful sunsets may be seen). Fishing can be arranged locally; please ask for details. Local organic produce can be bought at the farmers' market in Wykeham (two miles away) on Fridays, and there's a farm shop in Pickering selling lots of organic foodstuffs (some local). Set within the North Yorkshire National Park, the farm cottages are six miles from the coast at Scarborough.

janet@spikershill.ndo.co.uk www.spikershill.ndo.co.uk

SETTLE *(Hotel)*

AUSTWICK TRADDOCK 351

Austwick
Settle LA2 8BY
Tel: 015242 51224

Small Hotel, B&B from £70 pppn
Fully certified organic restaurant

The award-winning restaurant uses organic, local and seasonal ingredients

Soil Association

Nestling in the unspoilt village of Austwick and flanked by the three peaks of Ingleborough, Penn-y-Ghent and Whernside with glorious views of the Forest of Bowland, this stylish, cosy and friendly hotel offers an authentic country house experience. There are stunning walks from the front door through Crummackdale, the Norber Erratics and the famous Limestone Pavements (as featured in Wainwright's Limestone Country), enabling you to enjoy the wonders of the surrounding countryside and work up a hearty appetite for the delicious organic food on offer at The Traddock's fully certified organic restaurant. The restaurant won 'Organic Restaurant of The Year' Award in 2006. AA Rosette.

info@austwicktraddock.co.uk www.austwicktraddock.co.uk

SKIPTON *(B&B)*

WHARFE VIEW 352

Main Street
Burnsall BD23 6BP
Tel: 01756 720643

Bed and Breakfast
From £24 pppn

As many organic products as possible are sourced locally for your breakfast

Soil Association

Wharfe View Farm House B&B is a family-run bed and breakfast accommodation situated in the beautiful village of Burnsall in the Yorkshire Dales. We offer two large spacious double and twin rooms and a private sitting / dining room with colour TV and open log fire. As many organic products as possible are sourced locally for our full English breakfast, and we offer organic cereals, fruit juice and fruit. The farm is a working organic farm with sheep and some cattle. Guided farm walk. Wharfe View Farm is an excellent base for many walks, including the first few days of the Dales Way walk (Ilkley to Windermere). Free off road parking is available to those staying with us who are doing the local three dale walk.

richard.hirst@ukgateway.net www.burnsall.net

STAITHES *(S-C)*

RIDGE HALL COTTAGES 353

Ridge Lane
Staithes TS13 5DX
Tel: 01943 466988

Cottages: sleep 2-6, £290-£650 pw
Short Breaks (smaller cottages only)

Welcome basket of seasonal local produce
and home produced preserves

These imaginatively designed cottages have panoramic views of Borrowby Edge, Roxby, and eastward to the sea and Staithes Valley. We will be happy to share our enjoyment of our organic kitchen garden with guests. The kitchen garden is backed up by a 60-foot polytunnel providing exotic fruit and vegetables to complement the traditional orchard and plots. Ridge Hall gets its water from a spring at Twizzy Ghyll, which is just filtered and purified. Rainwater is collected to water the gardens. A wind vane is soon to be situated in the kitchen garden. Future projects include planting a small vineyard, building a new greenhouse, a hen house for fresh eggs and a natural swimming lake.

relax@ridgehallcottages.co.uk www.ridgehallcottages.co.uk

YORK *(B&B)*

CORNMILL LODGE B&B 354

120 Haxby Road
York YO31 8JP
Tel: 01904 620566

Vegetarian Guest House
Bed and Breakfast, £25-£40 pppn

Vegetarian and vegan options, using organic
produce (around 90%) where possible

A deceptively large Edwardian terraced house, built on the site of an 18th-century mill in a popular residential area of this historic city. Comfortable accommodation in a friendly atmosphere. Start the day with a choice of vegetarian or vegan breakfasts. The delicious menu is prepared using organic produce wherever possible, with enough to satisfy the heartiest appetite. Cornmill Lodge is within fifteen minutes walk of York Minster and the city walls – in fact most of this beautiful city is accessible on foot. To the west lie the Yorkshire Dales, to the north the Yorkshire Moors. The rugged cliffs, bird sanctuaries and sandy beaches of Yorkshire's Heritage Coast are less than an hour's drive away.

cornmillyork@aol.com www.cornmillyork.co.uk

YORK *(B&B)*

YORK ALTERNATIVE B&B 355

82 Scarcroft Road
York YO24 1DD
Tel: 01904 625931

Bed and Breakfast
£26 pppn

Serving locally produced and organic foods
(choice of traditional or vegetarian menu)

A comfortable Bed and Breakfast with lots of character, only ten minutes walk from the railway station and into the city centre. Everyone comments on the delicious breakfasts. Whenever possible produce will be organic, local, homemade and fairtrade. I buy organic products from local shops – Alligator, Tullivers, and Out of This World, an organic supermarket in the city centre. All breads and preserves are homemade. I also cater for special diets such as vegan, gluten-free, diabetics, etc. The secluded back garden attracts many varieties of birds and insects. York is very cycle-friendly, with cycle lanes in many parts of the city. I welcome cyclists, and can house your bike in a lock-up garage overnight.

direddeer@nahurac.freeserve.co.uk   www.yorkalternativebandb.co.uk

CASTLEWELLAN (S-C)

BURRENWOOD FARM 356

38 Burrenbridge Road
Castlewellan BT31 9HT
Tel: 028 4377 0241

Apartments: both sleep 4
£350 pw

Complimentary organic farm produce

Soil Association

Burrenwood Farm is located at the northern foot of the Mourne Mountains, midway between Tollymore and Castlewellan forest parks. Enjoy the freshest of food on your doorstep. Burrenwood is an organic vegetable farm growing all sorts of food on 12 acres for weekly delivery to a hundred households, and for free to our guests. Situated between the Irish Sea and two scenic lakes, the Burren River flows by these five fields next to a 60-acre woodland. There is plenty of space to roam, and all manner of outdoor pursuits in the area. In keeping with the theme of room to breathe, both apartments boast huge conservatories with spiral staircases, offering ever-changing wonderful views of mountain and sea.

burrenwood@btinternet.com www.burrenwood.com

NEWTOWNARDS (B&B)

ANNA'S HOUSE 357

35 Lisbarnet Road
Comber BT23 6AW
Tel: 028 9754 1566

Bed and Breakfast
£37.50-£45 per person sharing

We offer delicious organic food (around 75%-80% organic)

A serene and secret place ten miles from Belfast City Airport. Our splendid house, set on its own 20 acres, has panoramic views over our wildfowl lake and 2-acre organic garden. Enjoy the rich natural flavour of our organic food. Freshly baked bread and scones every morning. The full Irish breakfast is a favourite, but often business people and the health conscious prefer a lighter alternative. We are the only signatories in Northern Ireland to the Soil Association's Catering Code of Practice. The field in front of our house supplies central heating for our extension (a geothermal system). Solar panels supply our hot water. We're in the process of converting to organic pastures, copses and shrubberies.

anna@annashouse.com www.annashouse.com

NEWRY *(S-C)*

PLUMTREE COTTAGE 358

25 Lurganconary Road
Kilkeel BT34 4LL
Tel: 028 3025 4595

Cottage: sleeps 4+2
£600-£650 pw

Fresh organic fruit and vegetables available for guests to buy in season

Soil Association

Plumtree Cottage is set in idyllic landscaped gardens on a 100-acre organic farm at the foot of the majestic Mourne Mountains and within walking distance to the Blue Flag Cranfield beach. This charming cottage has the perfect blend of luxury and comfort, with underfloor heating powered by geothermal heating systems. During your stay on the farm fishing is available on the White Water River; there is complimentary use of bicycles and outdoor wear, a children's playground on site, and guests can explore one of the many nature trails. Hiking, horse riding, sailing and golf in the area. Fresh organic fruit and vegetables available to buy from the farm depending on season. Organic produce can be bought locally.

info@lurganconaryfarms.com www.lurganconaryfarms.com

NEWRY *(S-C)*

SAND COTTAGE 359

27 Lurganconary Road
Kilkeel BT34 4LL
Tel: 028 3025 4595

Cottage: sleeps 4+2
£600-£650 pw

Fresh organic fruit and vegetables available for guests to buy in season

Soil Association

Set in idyllic landscaped gardens on a 100-acre organic farm at the foot of the majestic Mourne Mountains and within walking distance to the Blue Flag Cranfield beach. This charming cottage has the perfect blend of luxury and comfort, with underfloor heating powered by geothermal heating systems. During your stay fishing is available on the White Water River, there is complimentary use of bicycles and outdoor wear, a children's playground on site, and guests can explore one of the many nature trails. Hiking, horse riding, sailing and golf in the area. Fresh organic fruit and vegetables available for guests to purchase from the farm, depending on the season. Organic produce can also be bought locally.

info@lurganconaryfarms.com www.lurganconaryfarms.com

OMAGH *(S-C)*

GLENHORDIAL FARM   360

9a Waterworks Road
Omagh BT79 7JS
Tel: 028 8224 1973

Dorm / Private Rooms, £12-£15 pppn
Closed 1 November to 1 March

Fruit and vegetables grown to organic
standards available in season

Imagine driving down a long country lane, with flowery banks and ancient hedges, to a place that feels like home. This remote, peaceful, small family farm nestles at the edge of the Sperrin mountains and offers simple self-catering accommodation with both private and dorm rooms. Here you can breathe fresh air, wander green valleys, participate in community activities, plant a tree and offset your carbon. Our green ethos is a threaded through the farm. We grow our own vegetables and fruit according to organic / permaculture principles. Feel free to explore the gardens and learn from them. Produce is available to buy in season. Introduction to organic gardening workshops. We are WWOOF hosts.

marella@omaghhostel.co.uk www.omaghhostel.co.uk

KILCHRENAN *(B&B)*

ROINEABHAL 361

Roineabhal Country House,
Kilchrenan, Taynuilt PA35 1HD
Tel: 01866 833207

Bed and Breakfast, £45-£55 pppn
Dinner, £35 including wine

100% organic meals for a small surcharge

Roineabhal is situated in the very picturesque village of Kilchrenan. Friendly family atmosphere. You can relax in front of the log fire, meander round the grounds or walk in open country, or just sit outside in the sun-traps and listen to the tumbling burn. Fine cuisine – local Scottish game and seafood are on the menu daily. Fresh bread, muffins and shortbread are just a few baked items available on a regular basis. Vegetarian food can be prepared, and 100% organic meals are available at slight extra cost. Nearby, lonely Glen Nant is a hidden treasure teeming with wildlife, and a great place for gentle or strenuous walks. Loch Awe provides rambles, fishing, and some of the finest scenery in Scotland.

maria@roineabhal.com www.roineabhal.com

KINTYRE *(Hotel)*

BALINAKILL HOTEL 362

Balinakill Country House Hotel,
Clachan, Tarbert PA29 6XL
Tel: 01880 740206

Small Hotel, B&B from £45 pppn
Dinner, 3 course £28.95

About 70% of all the food we offer is organic

Balinakill Hotel is set in 6 acres of parkland grounds and looks out between hills to the Sound of Jura and Islay beyond. Most of the food in our AA Rosetted restaurant is sourced locally – venison from the hills behind the hotel, totally free-range eggs from next door, superb seafood from the waters around Kintyre and organic beef and lamb from the Borders. Our dry goods come from Greencity workers co-op and are all fairtrade, GM-free and organic. We do not use chemicals for cleaning and our 6-acre grounds are pesticide-free. Hot stone massage, reflexology and other therapies are available. Green Tourism Silver Leaf. Hotel Reservation Service Hotels of the Year 2006 (Green Award). AA Rosette.

info@balinakill.com www.balinakill.com

KINTYRE *(S-C)*

BALLIMENEACH COTTAGE 363

Kildalloig Estate, by Campbeltown
Mull of Kintyre PA28 6RE
Tel: 07784 896907

Cottage: sleeps 8
£470-£995 pw

Organic beef and lamb to order

Soil Association

The cottage is set within its own large garden, very close to the sea on the beautiful Mull of Kintyre on the west coast of Scotland. In a secluded position with outstanding sea views, this lovely house is ideal for families. Situated on the Kildalloig Estate, providing acres of unspoilt and remote rolling countryside with stretches of secluded beaches and stunning sea views, including the fascinating Island of Davaar with its cave painting and wild goats. Kildalloig is an organic farm producing organic beef and lamb. Organic breeding stock includes Aberdeen Angus heifers, pedigree registered Blueface Leicester, Blackface and North Ronaldsay rams or ewe lambs. Natural spring water supply.

BrenNeish@aol.com www.kintyrecottages.com/ballimeneach-cottage.html

KINTYRE *(S-C)*

FISHERMAN'S COTTAGE 364

Kildalloig Estate
Campbeltown PA28 6RE
Tel: 07784 896907

Cottage: sleeps 2
£350-£650 pw

Organic beef and lamb to order

Soil Association

Fisherman's Cottage is set on a secluded beach. This cosy single storey accommodation enjoys a very romantic and peaceful setting with spectacular views over the Kilbrannan Sound to Arran and the Island of Davaar. Situated on the Kildalloig Estate, providing acres of unspoilt and remote rolling countryside with stretches of secluded beaches and stunning sea views, including the fascinating Island of Davaar with its cave painting and wild goats. Kildalloig is an organic farm producing beef and lamb. Organic breeding stock includes Aberdeen Angus heifers, pedigree registered Blueface Leicester, Blackface and North Ronaldsay rams or ewe lambs. Natural spring water supply.

BrenNeish@aol.com www.kintyrecottages.com/fishermans-cottage.html

KINTYRE *(S-C)*　　　ISLAND COTTAGES　　　365

Kildalloig Estate
Campbeltown PA28 6RE
Tel: 07784 896907

Cottages: sleep 2-4
£220-£430 pw

Organic beef and lamb to order

Soil Association

In a superb, secluded location by the sea on the 160-acre private island of Davaar, these two unique cottages enjoy stunning views. Otter (sleeps 2) and Island (sleeps 4) are an adjoining pair of cosy and spacious lighthouse keepers' cottages. Natural spring water supply. The cottages share a walled enclosure with the neighbouring caretaker. Set at the northern tip of Davaar Island, they are connected to the mainland by a causeway, revealed by the sea for six hours at low tide. On arrival and departure, and for arranged shopping trips, visitors will be ferried by Landrover across the causeway (leaving their cars at the quayside). Kildalloig is an organic farm producing beef and lamb.

BrenNeish@aol.com　www.kintyrecottages.com/island-cottages.html

KINTYRE *(S-C)*　　　THE LOOKOUT　　　366

Kildalloig Estate
Campbeltown PA28 6RE
Tel: 07784 896907

Cottage: sleeps 2
£300-£550 pw

Organic beef and lamb to order

Soil Association

The Lookout is a former wartime lookout post situated 100 yards away from the lighthouse enclosure. This cottage has an extra sitting room and sun terrace, formed from the original lookout, with superb long distance views from windows all around. The Lookout has its own area of lawn. Set at the northern tip of Davaar Island, the cottage is connected to the mainland by a causeway revealed by the sea for six hours at low tide (a 15 minute walk). On arrival and departure, and for arranged shopping trips, visitors will be ferried by Landrover across the causeway (leaving their cars at the quayside). Kildalloig is an organic farm producing beef and lamb. Natural spring water supply.

BrenNeish@aol.com　www.kintyrecottages.com/the-lookout.html

KINTYRE *(S-C)*

STABLE COTTAGE 367

Kidalloig Estate, Campbeltown
Mull of Kintyre PA28 6RE
Tel: 07784 896907

Cottage: sleeps 4
£360-£700 pw

Organic beef and lamb to order

Soil Association

Stable Cottage lies within a quarter mile of a secluded beach (reached via a steep track) near the southern tip of the romantic Mull of Kintyre. There are marvellous walks through woodland on the estate, on the coast (where seals, otters, and a variety of birds can be seen), and in the hills, where golden eagles soar. This spacious ground floor cottage, near to a working farm, stands in its own secure garden with fine sea views towards Ailsa Craig. Kildalloig is an organic farm producing beef and lamb. Organic breeding stock includes Aberdeen Angus heifers, pedigree registered Blueface Leicester, Blackface and North Ronaldsay rams or ewe lambs. Natural spring water supply.

BrenNeish@aol.com www.kintyrecottages.com/stable-cottage.html

STRONTIAN *(S-C)*

HONEYSUCKLE HOUSE 368

Bluebell Croft, 15 Anaheilt
Strontian PH36 4JA
Tel: 01967 402226

House: sleeps 8+, £1,100-£1,650 pw
Supper, 1-5 course £6-£40

As far as possible all our produce is grown on the croft following organic principles

A single house with six ensuite bedrooms sleeping 12-16 (£1,500-£2,200 pw), or two houses separated by the conservatory sleeping 8+ (Honeysuckle) and 2-4+ (Rose). 5-star, with simple luxury throughout. A generous hamper can be ordered for your arrival, with more available during the week. The hamper could contain homemade bread, eggs, preserves, home smoked goodies such as bacon, cheese, fish, and seasonal vegetables, fruit, salads from the polytunnel / garden. We also offer a range of cooked meals, such as a casserole in the Aga waiting for you on arrival, supper during the week, or a full 2-5 course dinner from the 'Rural Chef of the Year'. We will pick guests up from the station at no extra cost.

billandsukie@bluebellcroft.co.uk www.bluebellcroft.co.uk

STRONTIAN *(S-C)*

ROSE COTTAGE 369

Bluebell Croft, 15 Anaheilt
Strontian PH36 4JA
Tel: 01967 402226

Cottage: sleeps 2-4+, £450-£750 pw
Supper, 1-5 course £6-£40

As far as possible all our produce is grown
on the croft following organic principles

Rose Cottage has two ensuite rooms. The house is rated 5-star, with simple luxury throughout. A generous hamper can be ordered for your arrival, with more available during the week. The hamper could include homemade bread, eggs, preserves and home-smoked goodies such as bacon (from our own pigs), cheese and fish, and depending on the season we hope to include fresh vegetables, fruit and salads from the polytunnel / garden. We will also be offering a range of cooked meals, such as a casserole in the oven waiting for you on arrival, supper during the week, or a full 2-5 course dinner from the 'Rural Chef of the Year'. We will pick guests up from the station at no cost to encourage use of the train.

billandsukie@bluebellcroft.co.uk www.bluebellcroft.co.uk

GIRVAN *(B&B)*

DRUMSKEOCH FARM B&B 370

Drumskeoch Farm
Pinwherry KA26 0QB
Tel: 01465 841172

Vegetarian Bed and Breakfast, £25-£35 pppn
Evening Meal (by prior arrangement)

All food is organic and where possible
locally produced

A warm welcome and a comfortable relaxing stay awaits you in this unique organic vegetarian / vegan bed and breakfast. The traditionally and naturally renovated rural farmhouse has beautiful views of the surrounding hills, sunrises, sunsets, and the unspoilt night sky. The food is all organic, vegetarian / vegan and home cooked. The farmhouse also has its own water source. Packed lunches and evening meals are available, and special dietary requirements are catered for. The bedding, towels, toiletries, and the paint on the walls are all organic. Our light bulbs are low energy. The loo is low flush. We run courses in rural sustainable crafts – willow structures, treebogs, drystone dyking, herbal medicine.

drumskeoch@wildmail.com www.drumskeoch.co.uk

DOLLAR *(B&B)*

KENNELS COTTAGE 371

Dollarbeg
Dollar FK14 7PA
Tel: 01259 742476

Bed and Breakfast
£30-£35 pppn

All the food we use is either local or organic

Set in one acre of garden, Kennels Cottage 4-star bed and breakfast is a fresh, stylish former gamekeeper's cottage. White walls, soft white sofas, the odd splash of gold, and light airy ensuite bedrooms all go to create a calm, peaceful atmosphere. Guests have use of their own sitting room and reading area. Breakfast is sourced locally using organic and free-range products wherever possible. We have our own hens so our eggs are very fresh, and we also grow some of our own produce. We use environmentally friendly cleaning products as much as we can, and recycle as much as possible. We also offer classic car hire and classic car hire packages. The cottage is an ideal base to tour Scotland.

tanya.worsfold@btinternet.com www.guesthousescotland.co.uk

DUMFRIES *(B&B)*

CLEARVIEWS B&B 372

Carsethorn
Dumfries DG2 8DS
Tel: 01387 880537

Bed and Breakfast
From £30 pppn

The extensive breakfast menu includes many organic items

Relax in the tranquillity of Clearviews Bed and Breakfast in the tiny village of Carsethorn. We have one ensuite guest room of superior quality with a king-size bed and stunning sea views. The room has all modern facilities. Breakfast is served from an extensive breakfast menu which has many organic items, including organic bread and porridge with real coffee and local organic free-range eggs. Goats milk available. See otter and porpoise along with a stunning variety of birdlife from the comfort of your bedroom. Enjoy the sea air from our private beach garden. Stroll for miles on the deserted seashore collecting fossils. Take a short walk to the friendly local pub. Explore this hidden south-west corner of Scotland.

alan.cairns2@btinternet.com

BUNCHREW *(Hotel)*

BUNCHREW HOTEL   373

Bunchrew
Inverness IV3 8TA
Tel: 01463 234917

Country House, B&B £75-£130 pppn
Restaurant

Organic produce (35%-45%), natural and
wild produce, local produce

17th-century Scottish mansion only yards from the sea. Set amidst 20 acres of beautiful landscaped gardens and woodland where no pesticides are used, and where areas are left deliberately wild to provide a natural habitat for wildlife. Award-winning food, fresh, local or organic, served in the wood panelled dining room overlooking the sea. The chef uses naturally reared meat and fish, which wherever possible is locally and organically produced. Try the smoked duck or organic smoked salmon from the Summer Isles and organic muesli from Brin Herbs near Farr. Bunchrew House grows its own organic potatoes, herbs and cooking apples, and uses locally produced organic vegetables.

enquiries@bunchrew-inverness.co.uk   www.bunchrew-inverness.co.uk

DRUMNADROCHIT *(B&B)*

SHENVAL B&B   374

Glenurquhart
Drumnadrochit IV63 6TW
Tel: 01456 476363

Bed and Breakfast, £22 pppn
Dinner, £18-£23 (by prior arrangement)

Mostly organic, Scottish and international
cuisine with a French touch

On the gateway to Glen Affric National Nature Reserve and only ten minutes' drive from Loch Ness, Shenval Bed and Breakfast nestles in a secluded and peaceful hamlet. You will find a heartfelt friendly welcome in our comfortable bed and breakfast. Always freshly prepared on the premises, our fare is mostly organic and includes seasonal fruit and vegetables from our own organic garden. Packed lunches available. Optional evening meal. Vegetarians and vegans catered for. Hill and forest walks, cycling, bird-watching and fishing are readily available from our very doorstep. We are delighted to share our thirty years experience of hill walking in the Highlands and our extensive knowledge of the area.

info@shenval-welcome.co.uk   www.shenval-welcome.co.uk

FORT WILLIAM *(B&B)*   CUILDORAG HOUSE   375

Onich
Fort William PH33 6SD
Tel: 01855 821529

Vegetarian / Vegan B&B, £20-£27.50 pppn
Evening Meal, £17.50 (by arrangement)

Breakfast up to 50% organic, evening meal
80%-100% organic

Cuildorag House is a vegetarian and vegan bed and breakfast, situated ten miles south of Fort William in the village of Onich. The house has mountain and loch views to the south and west. A warm welcome and delicious home cooked meals are our speciality. Our house is set within 1.5 acres of mature garden where we grow, without chemicals, a variety of fruit and vegetables which we use in the preparation of our evening meals (3 courses with coffee). The garden is also home to our free-range hens, who provide the eggs for your large and delicious breakfast, and is visited by deer, red squirrels, badgers and pine martens. Walk the 150 metres to the shore of the loch. You may spot otters and basking sharks.

enquiries@cuildoraghouse.com   www.cuildoraghouse.com

FORT WILLIAM *(S-C)*   GREAT GLEN CHALETS   376

Torlundy Farm
Torlundy PH33 6SW
Tel: 01397 703015

Chalets: sleep 4
£330-£560 pw

Scottish Organic Producers Association

Eight Finnish chalets on an organic farm, individually sited with superb views of three of the highest mountains in the British Isles These two bedroom chalets are pine panelled throughout, and fitted with three full length double glazed windows in the living room to make you feel part of the great outdoors. A variety of birds will feed from your balcony, and roe deer are frequently seen in the early morning amongst the trees. Torlundy Farm breeds Highland ponies, Highland cattle and Cheviot sheep. You are welcome to walk along any of the attractive tracks which lead down to the River Lochy, or up on to the hill which has wonderful views down Loch Linnhe. Fort William is three miles down the road.

info@fortwilliam-chalets.co.uk   www.fortwilliam-chalets.co.uk

FORT WILLIAM *(S-C)*

LONE PINE LODGE · 377

Torlundy Farm
Torlundy PH33 6SW
Tel: 01397 703015

Lodge: sleeps 7
£550-£950 pw

Scottish Organic Producers Association

Superb log house from Carolina USA. Lone Pine Lodge is in an attractive rural location on an organic farm, with superb views of the spectacular north face of Ben Nevis and down Loch Linnhe. The one and a half storey timber house has an open plan living room with a cathedral ceiling and large windows, and doors which open onto the balcony. Experience the peace and tranquillity from this elevated site, overlooking fields and forest to the mountains. The early morning and late evening views are often amazing. Enjoy a farm walk up into the hills behind, or take a couple of hours out and discover the fun of fly fishing – there's a trout loch just twenty yards from your balcony. Fort William is four miles away.

info@fortwilliam-chalets.co.uk www.fortwilliam-chalets.co.uk/lonepine.htm

FORT WILLIAM *(Hotel)*

OLD PINES HOTEL · 378

Spean Bridge
Fort William PH34 4EG
Tel: 01397 712324

Small Hotel, B&B £40-£52.50 pppn
Dinner, B&B £77.50-£90 pppn

50%-70% organic ingredients

Old Pines is a small yet high quality hotel with a relaxed atmosphere. Set among mature Scots Pines in 30 acres of grounds north of the village of Spean Bridge, three hundred yards below the famous Commando Memorial. We consciously source organic ingredients for our homemade bread, pasta, ice cream, cakes and preserves. We have our own vegetable garden growing organic potatoes, carrots, leeks, salads, fruits and herbs. Only fresh local seafood, beef, venison and lamb are used to create the sumptuous contemporary Scottish dishes. Take a stroll down the quiet country lanes for amazing views of Ben Nevis, Loch Lochy and the Great Glen, and work up an appetite for dinner.

enquiries@oldpines.co.uk www.oldpines.co.uk

INVERNESS *(B&B)*

MARDON 379

37 Kenneth Street
Inverness IV3 5DH
Tel: 01463 231005

Bed and Breakfast
From £28 pppn

Preferential supply of organic food whenever available (around 90% organic)

A family-run guest house centrally located in Inverness, five minutes from the city centre. Six ensuite bedrooms, from singles to one family room. Private off-road parking. Our aim is to provide a healthy, friendly and comfortable stay. Landlady Val is a practising Nutritional Therapist and strongly supports the organic movement. The breakfast menu ranges from a Full Scottish Breakfast to a Continental selection, with a wide choice of fruits, yogurts and cereals. Much of our cooked ingredients are single-sourced from a local farm which specialises in free-range animals. Therapies available from Val include reflexology, Indian head massage, manual lymphatic massage. General nutritional guidance.

enquiries@mardonguesthouse.co.uk www.mardonguesthouse.co.uk

LAGGAN *(B&B)*

THE RUMBLIE 380

Gergask Avenue
Laggan PH20 1AH
Tel: 01528 544766

Bed and Breakfast, £32.50 pppn
Evening Meal, £25 (by arrangement)

Breakfast is around 70% organic, evening meals 80% to 90% organic

The Rumblie experience is about quality organic food and service in a relaxed Highland home. Our focus is on local produce, and on many occasions this would be Rumblie-grown by organic methods and organic seed stock. We use organic products extensively, and follow an ethical approach with many fairtrade goods. All this and other measures led to our Gold Green Tourism Business Scheme award. We offer a home-cooked evening meal for guests on a set menu based on seasonal produce. This will be 80% to 90% organic depending upon what is available at the time. We can provide a pick-up service in our hybrid car for those guests who are planning to travel here by train or bus.

mail@rumblie.com www.rumblie.com

NAIRN *(Hotel)*

BOATH HOUSE HOTEL   381

Boath House Hotel and Spa,
Auldearn, Nairn IV12 5TE
Tel: 01667 454896

Regency House, B&B £95-£140 pppn

Restaurant (lunch, dinner)

Home-grown, local (organic 60%-90%)

Beautiful Georgian mansion (4 rosettes, 3 red stars) set in 20 acres of lawns, woodland and streams. Eight rooms individually decorated to a very high standard. The grounds were set out around 1730, prior to the building of the present house. Lake with brown trout. A wildflower meadow and woodland walks have now been established. The kitchen gardens provide most of the vegetables and herbs for the award-winning restaurant. Organic meats, cheeses and vegetables are sourced locally through several suppliers. Supporters of the Slow Food movement. The Spa specialises in Ayurvedic treatments, using only organic petrochemical-free ingredients sourced from pure plant and flower extracts.

wendy@boath-house.com www.boath-house.com

NAIRN *(S-C)*

HIDDENGLEN HOLIDAYS 382

Laikenbuie
Grantown Road IV12 5QN
Tel: 01667 454630

Lodges, Chalet, Caravan
£144-£600 pw

Organic lamb (frozen), eggs, excess vegetables

Soil Association

Watch roe deer and osprey among the abundant wildlife on a tranquil croft with a beautiful outlook over a trout loch amid birch woods. Guests are welcome to tour the croft, collect eggs, feed pet lambs (if there are any), meet the animals. Large warm lodges (quality unbeaten) provide luxury accommodation, plus a chalet or residential caravan, all kept very clean and well equipped. For the more adventurous there is a camping area. Safe for children, with play area, bikes and a boat. An excellent holiday centre, low rainfall, plentiful sunshine, few midges. Near Loch Ness, sandy beaches, Moray Firth dolphins, Cairngorm Mountains, Speyside distilleries, golf, skiing, walking, pony trekking, fishing.

info@hiddenglen.co.uk www.hiddenglen.co.uk

IONA *(Hotel)*

ARGYLL HOTEL 383

Iona
Isle of Iona PA76 6SJ
Tel: 01681 700334

B&B £27-£65 pppn, HB £44-£102 pppn
Restaurant (breakfast, lunch, dinner)

The best of local produce and vegetables
from our certified organic kitchen garden

Soil Association

Built in 1868 as the village inn, the hotel overlooks the Sound of Iona to the pink and blue hills of Mull. We have a strong environmental ethos, and this encompasses the entire range of activities surrounding the hotel's day-to-day management. For the past forty years the hotel has had its own organic garden, producing fresh produce for the kitchen. Eggs are local and free-range. We also promote Scottish organic meat. Baking and dry goods are sourced from Greencity Wholefoods (fairtrade and organically produced goods). We have achieved a gold standard for sustainability in the Green Tourism Business Scheme. The natural features of the Isle of Iona offer lots of walking and exploring opportunities.

reception@argyllhoteliona.co.uk www.argyllhoteliona.co.uk

IONA *(S-C)*

IONA HOSTEL 384

Lagandorain
Isle of Iona PA76 6SW
Tel: 01681 700781

Hostel
Adult £17.50 pn, Child £12 pn

We sell our own traditionally reared
Hebridean mutton and duck eggs

Iona Hostel is situated on my working croft at the north end of the Isle of Iona. It is simply and beautifully furnished, has five bedrooms (sleeping two to six in bunkbeds), and has a wonderful kitchen / sitting room with woodburning stove. The views are spectacular. Iona Hostel holds a Green Tourism Gold Award and is graded as 4-star by the Tourist Board. Lagandorain croft has been worked for countless generations. The fields are now grazed by our flock of black Hebridean sheep from which we produce beautiful blankets and mutton, in season. The only fertiliser used on the hay parks is seaweed from the beach. We are members of Linking Environment and Farming and the Slow Food Movement.

info@ionahostel.co.uk www.ionahostel.co.uk

IONA *(S-C)*

LAGANDORAIN COTTAGE 385

Lagandorain
Isle of Iona PA76 6SW
Tel: 01681 700642

Cottage: sleeps 4-5
£450 pw

We sell our own traditionally reared
Hebridean mutton and duck eggs

The well equipped and homely cottage is situated on my working croft at the north end of the Isle of Iona. It is the only house on Iona where at night you can see no other house lights – only the stars. The views (in the daytime) out past Staffa to Skye are fabulous. The croftlands of Lagandorain have been worked traditionally for countless generations and are a botanical gem. A very special and beautiful place, reaching from the beach below the cottage to the highest point on the island. The fields are now grazed by our flock of black Hebridean sheep from which we produce beautiful blankets and mutton, in season. Such richness needs only time and space and care – the way it's been done for generations.

john@lagandorain.f9.co.uk www.lagandorain.com

IONA *(Hotel)*

ST COLUMBA HOTEL 386

Iona
Isle of Iona PA76 6SL
Tel: 01681 700304

Small Hotel, Dinner B&B £61-£91 pppn
Restaurant (breakfast, lunch, dinner)

All meals and baking are home-cooked using organic ingredients where possible

Situated next to Iona Abbey the hotel is owned by a partnership of ten individuals, nine of whom live and work on Iona. We aim to continue the tradition of hospitality that this hotel has offered for more than 100 years. Our sun lounges, dining room and many of our rooms enjoy spectacular views over the sound of Iona towards the mountains of Mull. All our food and baking is prepared from scratch on the premises. Our garden is run on organic principles and supplies much of the vegetables and most of the salads used in the kitchen. We should have full organic certification by spring 2008. All other food is sourced as locally as possible and we use fair trade products where available. Free broadband internet.

info@stcolumba-hotel.co.uk www.stcolumba-hotel.co.uk

BALMACLELLAN *(S-C)*

WEST HOLMHEAD 387

Craig Farm
Balmaclellan DG7 3QS
Tel: 01644 420636

Cottage: sleeps 5, £300-£500 pw
Short Breaks (out of season)

Surplus organic beef, lamb, apples, plums, courgettes

Biodynamic Agricultural Association

West Holmhead is an old stone cottage on the edge of our organic (biodynamic) farm in deepest Galloway. The cottage has beamed ceilings and a big birchwood garden, and looks out through trees onto green fields and hills. Sometimes we can provide fresh organic eggs, apples, meat – please ask. You'll find an excellent organic farm shop within thirty minutes drive (Beeswing). We have a mixture of sheep and cattle (White Galloways), orchid meadows, bluebell woods, splashy burns, heather moor, and abundant wildlife. From the front door you can walk or cycle (there's a pair of traditional bikes for your use) along the quiet 'Hidden Road' to Balmaclellan, through dark forests and over the green hills.

mas@craigfarm.co.uk www.craigfarm.co.uk

KIRKPATRICK DURHAM *(S-C)*

CRAIGADAM COTTAGE 388

Kirkpatrick Durham
Castle Douglas DG7 3HU
Tel: 01556 650233

Cottage: sleeps 4-6
£500-£550 pw

Organic lamb, organic vegetables, wild game

Scottish Organic Producers Association

Craigadam Estate covers 25,000 acres of farmland, lochs and moorland. It is committed to organic farming and is run with conservation and sustainability in mind. The self-catering cottage has three twin bedrooms individually decorated to a theme – African, Florentine, and Scottish. The cottage has a comfortable sitting / dining room with French windows and a lovely view of the orchard. The orchard is particularly suitable for sitting out, for barbecues and for children. Visitors can choose to come to the house for a meal or to make use of other facilities, or cater for themselves (the luxury fitted kitchen has all modern appliances) in one of the most pleasant homes from home in Dumfries and Galloway.

inquiry@craigadam.com www.craigadam.com/accommodation/index.htm

KIRKPATRICK DURHAM *(B&B)* CRAIGADAM 389

Kirkpatrick Durham
Castle Douglas DG7 3HU
Tel: 01556 650233

Country House, B&B £42 pppn
Dinner £22

Organic lamb, organic vegetables, wild game

Scottish Organic Producers Association

A tastefully converted 18th-century farm steading within a working farm. Craigadam has been a past winner of the Taste of Scotland awards for its quality home cooking. Meals, including a hearty Galloway breakfast, are sumptuous and are enjoyed in our oak-panelled dining room around our magnificent oak table. We use organic lamb and organic vegetables. Sample our game cooking. The venison is wild, as are the pheasants and partridges. Honesty bar and wine list. Craigadam Estate is committed to organic farming and is run with conservation and sustainability in mind. The 25,000 acres of farmland, lochs, moorland and woodland are rich in wildlife. An ideal location for hiking, rambling, bird-watching.

inquiry@craigadam.com www.craigadam.com

EDINBURGH *(B&B)* GLENORA GUEST HOUSE 390

14 Rosebery Crescent
Edinburgh EH12 5JY
Tel: 01313 371186

Bed and Breakfast
Double, from £80 pn

100% of the food that we serve is organic

The Glenora Guest House is a beautiful Victorian townhouse in the centre of Edinburgh. After a full refurbishment we have been awarded 4 stars by the Scottish Tourist Board. We serve a continental buffet and full cooked breakfast, all of which is entirely organic, in our large bright dining room on the ground floor. We also offer complimentary tea and coffee making facilities in the bedrooms, again all of which is both organic and fairtrade. The guest house is located in Edinburgh's West End, where quiet streets with terraces of fine Victorian townhouses and private gardens exist close to the city centre. The nearby railway station at Haymarket makes excursions to other parts of Scotland very convenient.

enquiries@glenorahotel.co.uk www.glenorahotel.co.uk

EDINBURGH *(B&B)*

TANTALLON B&B 391

17 Tantallon Place
Edinburgh EH9 1NZ
Tel: 0131 667 1708

Bed and Breakfast
£26-£30 pppn

Breakfast is between 70%-90% organic

Tantallon Place is situated in the Grange, a quiet conservation area with tree-lined streets and Victorian houses, close to the centre of Edinburgh. Breakfast is between 70%-90% organic. We offer a cooked breakfast with organic free-range eggs from East Lothian, organic wholemeal bread, grilled organic sausages and bacon, grilled tomatoes, mushrooms, freshly squeezed orange juice, homemade jams and marmalade, plus a wide range of teas and coffee. If you prefer, there's a lighter option with freshly made fruit salads, fresh grapefruit and melon, natural yogurt, local honey, organic porridge oats or muesli, scrambled or poached eggs, vegetarian sausages, and poached undyed smoked haddock.

mcw@ecosse.net www.tantallonbandb.co.uk

WEST CALDER *(S-C)*

SWALLOW COTTAGE 392

South Cobbinshaw
West Calder EH55 8LQ
Tel: 01501 785436

Cottage: sleeps 6
£250-£600 pw

Farm grown organic vegetables, eggs and milk

Scottish Organic Producers Association

Beautiful, traditional, rural cottage overlooking picturesque Cobbinshaw Loch and the Pentland Hills. Tasteful decoration throughout, with spectacular views from all the rooms, makes for a relaxing holiday retreat. The stone cottage boasts a secure enclosed garden with barbecue, outdoor tables and chairs. The cottage is situated on our organic farm, where we grow vegetables and run an organic box scheme. Farm grown organic vegetables, eggs and milk available. You are welcome to meet our animals. Superb walking from the doorstep. Local attractions include fishing, golfing, hillwalking, bird-watching. West Calder train station, with frequent railway connections, is five minutes drive from the cottage.

cobbinshawloch@aol.com www.cobbinshawloch.co.uk

GRANTOWN-ON-SPEY *(B&B)*   EDEN HOUSE   393

Cromdale
Grantown-on-Spey PH26 3LW
Tel: 01479 872112

Bed and Breakfast, from £42 pppn
Evening Meals (by arrangement)

Mainly organic food, supplemented with fine local produce and fairtrade

Be assured of luxury combined with ethics at this elegant Victorian house, overlooking the River Spey and Cromdale Hills, on the fringes of the Cairngorm National Park. The Eden House has three individually styled and sumptuous guest rooms. Everything from oxygen bleached bedlinen and fluffy towels to tea bags and complimentary toiletries is either organic or fairtrade – or both. Evening meals (winter months only) are available by arrangement. Guests can enjoy a wee dram (of the organic variety of course) by a crackling fire in the elegant drawing room, and reflect on the day's events before retiring for the evening. The house is set in half an acre of restful gardens, complete with ponds and summerhouse.

enquiries@theedenhouse.co.uk   www.theedenhouse.co.uk

MORAY *(S-C)*   MARCASSIE FARM   394

Rafford
Forres IV36 2RH
Tel: 01309 671700

Self-Catering
£185-£385 per unit pw

Own eggs, wheatgrass, surplus vegetables, herbs available in season

Soil Association

We run an organically certified smallholding growing small quantities of grains, vegetables, herbs and fruit. We are currently stock-free, apart from a small flock of laying hens and some geese. Eggs, wheatgrass, surplus vegetables and herbs are available to buy in season. A locally sourced organic fruit and vegetable box, meat and cheese are also available on request. We run a sawmill and a bespoke joinery manufacturing facility on site, specialising in Scottish timber and timber products. Accommodation is in the self-contained west wing of our farmhouse or in one of our chalets. Marcassie Farm is close to Forres, Findhorn, Cairngorm, Speyside and the attractive coastline of the Moray Firth.

info@marcassie.co.uk   www.marcassie.co.uk

ISLE OF MULL *(S-C)*   HAUNN COTTAGES   395

Calgary
Isle of Mull PA75 6QX
Tel: 01688 400249

Cottages: sleep 2-5
£160-£510 pw

Organic produce sometimes for sale

Scottish Organic Producers Association

The Haunn cottages are remote, situated on our organic farm at the end of a two mile farm track. The sense of peace and quiet is strong. Surrounded by herb-rich grassy fields and with the dramatic Treshnish coastline five minutes walk away, the three crofters cottages (with thick rounded corner stone walls) provide a unique, simple yet comfortable place to stay. The fourth cottage, extensively renovated using sheep's wool insulation, solar-heated water, reclaimed maple floors and environmentally friendly paints, sits on its own with wonderful views from an open plan kitchen / living room. Sheep tracks lead to hidden settlements in secluded glens and along wide open grassy raised beaches.

enquiries@treshnish.co.uk   www.treshnish.co.uk/haunn.html

ISLE OF MULL *(S-C)*   ISLE OF ERRAID   396

Fionnphort
Isle of Mull PA66 6BN
Tel: 01681 700384

Shared Cottages
Contributions between £120 and £260 pw

The fruit and vegetable garden is managed organically

The beautiful and tiny island of Erraid stands at the southernmost tip of Mull, only a short way from the island of Iona. Comprising sandy beaches, lush peat bogs and stark craggy granite outcrops, the island, which has been in the care of the Findhorn Foundation for over twenty years, offers sanctuary to a small community as they enjoy a simple but richly rewarding life. Being here allows them to connect with nature and the elements in a very immediate way, be it growing fruit and vegetables, caring for the animals, confronting the tides and weather or simply enjoying the rugged landscape of the island itself. The heart of the community is the organic garden, and much of the work here is outdoors.

paul@erraid.fslife.co.uk   www.erraid.com

ISLE OF MULL (B&B)

Fionnphort
Isle of Mull PA66 6BL
Tel: 01681 700677

Bed and Breakfast, £32-£38 pppn
Evening Meal (by arrangement)

Organic / locally sourced ingredients used
for meals where possible

Staffa House is situated in the village of Fionnphort on the Hebridean island of Mull. Inside the house, away from the hustle and bustle at the jetty, you will find a peaceful atmosphere. Meals are served in the lovely conservatory with views west to the Sound of Iona (great for sunsets) and east to Ben More. We believe that food plays a central role in offering genuine welcome and hospitality. Ali is a qualified chef with twenty years experience. Her professional skills and passion for organic / local, ethically sourced food ensures that nourishing meals are made with love and care, attractively presented and delicious to eat. A place to relax, unwind and feel close to the elemental rocks and seas on your doorstep.

enquiries@staffahouse.co.uk www.staffahouse.co.uk

ISLE OF MULL (S-C)

TRESHNISH COTTAGES 398

Calgary
Isle of Mull PA75 6QX
Tel: 0845 458 1971

Cottages: sleep 2-6
£175-£530 pw

Organic produce sometimes for sale

Scottish Organic Producers Association

Situated on a dramatic peninsula with wonderful views and abundant wildlife, Treshnish is a working organic farm with local breeds of cattle and sheep. The Treshnish cottages (with a Gold Award from the Green Tourism Business Scheme) are located around the stone farm buildings and provide a peaceful base from which to explore this magical part of the island. The cottages are all individually decorated with a mixture of modern and antique furnishings. The flora and fauna on the headland is rich and varied, and we farm in a way as to benefit and protect its biodiversity. On the farm itself there is plenty to explore, and within a few miles of here there are several secluded sandy beaches.

enquiries@treshnish.co.uk www.treshnish.co.uk/treshnish.html

ORKNEY *(S-C)*

NEW HOLLAND BOTHY   399

New Holland Organic Farm
Holm KW17 2SA
Tel: 01856 781345

Bothy: sleeps 2
£120-£250 pw

Home reared organic meat (beef, pork, lamb)

Scottish Organic Producers Association

Comfortable self-catering accommodation for two people in a converted farm bothy. It is surrounded by beautiful countryside on the main island of Orkney. New Holland is a working organic farm with cattle, sheep and hens. We can supply our own organic meat (beef, pork, lamb), sausages, and sometimes our own potatoes. We are passionate about our way of farming here, and love to discuss our methods and aims with our visitors, who are free to walk around our 900 acres of pastures and heather. There are scenic walks along breathtaking cliffs or beautiful deserted beaches. Orkney is also a well known bird-watchers' paradise, with many native and migrating species to be seen.

info@holidayorganic.co.uk   www.holidayorganic.co.uk

ORKNEY *(B&B)*

WOODWICK HOUSE   400

Evie
Orkney KW17 2PQ
Tel: 01856 751330

Country House, B&B £34-£50 pppn
Evening Meal, 3 course approx £28

Organic or organically grown wherever possible

Warm and welcoming historic country house overlooking the island of Gairsay and beyond. An extraordinary, peaceful location set in unique and beautiful surroundings on this sheltered part of Orkney. Only twenty minutes from Stromness and Kirkwall, and within easy reach of the main historic sites, bird reserves and sandy beaches. With its twelve acres of bluebell woodland, a burn cascading down to the sea and its own bay, this is an ideal location for bird-watching, seal watching or simply relaxing. A member of 'Eat Scotland' and 'Taste of Orkney' for our farmhouse-style cuisine, which makes use of the excellent prime local produce and seafoods, using organic / organically grown wherever possible.

mail@woodwickhouse.co.uk   www.woodwickhouse.co.uk

ROUSAY (S-C)

ROUSAY HOSTEL 401

Trumland Organic Farm
Rousay KW17 2PU
Tel: 01856 821252

Hostel, £10-£12 pppn
Camping, £5 pppn

Organic produce may be available to buy

Soil Association

A working organic farm within easy walking distance from the pier. Modern, purpose-built and well equipped, the hostel has two dormitories and one single room, showers, kitchen and laundry facilities. The camp site is adjacent to the hostel. Campers have use of the hostel facilities. Organic produce may be available to buy from the farm. We are also WWOOF hosts. Visitors can walk to a shop, restaurant and pub. Bike hire is available at the hostel. A walker and birdwatcher's paradise (we are close to an RSPB reserve), the island has many footpaths of outstanding scenic and environmental beauty. Rousay's small friendly community creates a unique welcome for the visitor to this beautiful Orkney island.

trumland@btopenworld.com   www.hostel-scotland.co.uk/hostel

SOUTH RONALDSAY (B&B)

ORCADIAN WILDLIFE 402

Gerraquoy Organic Farm
St Margaret's Hope KW17 2TH
Tel: 01856 831240

Orkney Island Tours, £850 pppw all inclusive
Short Breaks, £300-£450 per person

We do our best to provide organic food, utilising our own organic produce

Scottish Organic Producers Association

Orcadian Wildlife runs tailor-made birdwatching, wildlife and culture tours from April to October for up to a maximum of four guests. We specialise in a blend of wildlife tours (featuring our seabirds and birds of prey) and Orkney's 5,000 year old Neolithic monuments. The base for your holiday will be our traditional family farmhouse and organic smallholding, embellished with a small herd of the placid and beautiful Shetland cattle, one of the rarest breeds in the UK. We produce our own organic beef and eggs, and have access to locally reared pork and lamb, so the farmhouse food that we serve is fresh and tasty. The price for six nights is £850 and includes accommodation, meals, and guiding services.

enquiries@orcadianwildlife.co.uk   www.orcadianwildlife.co.uk

SOUTH RONALDSAY *(S-C)*   THE PEEDIE HOUSE   403

Gerraquoy Organic Farm
St Margaret's Hope KW17 2TH
Tel: 01856 831240

Cottage: sleeps 2
£300 pw

Our own organic beef and free-range eggs
for sale

Scottish Organic Producers Association

VisitScotland 4 Star graded. Designed and constructed to enable full disabled access, and to the highest green tourism standards with solar-powered water heating, full roof and wall insulation, underfloor heating. The cottage has a double bedroom, bathroom with shower, first class kitchen facilities and a large conservatory overlooking the island of Copinsay. Organic beef is for sale, produced on the farm from our small herd of native Shetland cattle, as well as free-range eggs produced by our own chickens. As part of our Orcadian Wildlife and Gerraquoy Farm businesses we offer to share our knowledge of Orkney's wildlife and 5,000 year old neolithic sites, with day or half-day tours at preferential rates.

enquiries@orcadianwildlife.co.uk www.orcadianwildlife.co.uk

SOUTH RONALDSAY *(S-C)*   WHEEMS BOTHY   404

Wheems
Eastside KW17 2TJ
Tel: 01856 831537

Hostel, £8 pppn
Camping from £3 pppn

Organic salads, vegetables, eggs available

Soil Association

Wheems Farm is an ecological and organic 10-hectare smallholding on the barrier island of South Ronaldsay. The 200 year old buildings have been renovated using traditional materials. Wheems Bothy is a simple, inexpensive summer hostel sleeping up to eight. The hostel is built over the barn and overlooks cliffs and quiet sandy bays, with a five minute downhill walk to the beach. It is a family-run concern, complementing the farm and Christina Sargent's textile artwork. Home produce (organic salads, vegetables, eggs) is available, along with some other basics. Two miles east of St Margaret's Hope, the hostel is fifteen miles south of Kirkwall by road across the causeways linking the islands.

christina.sargent@wheems.fsworld.co.uk

ABERFELDY *(S-C)*

CRUCK COTTAGE   405

Drumdewan
Dull PH15 2JQ
Tel: 01887 820071

Cottage: sleeps 2, from £425 per week
Short breaks are available

Buy organic produce from our farm shop, or
eat in our farm shop café

The ultimate in luxury for the discerning couple, whether on honeymoon, a romantic break, or just a 'get away from it all' experience. No expense has been spared in the decoration of the cottage, the fittings, or the wonderfully landscaped garden. This idyllic 5-star experience will leave you refreshed, invigorated and rejuvenated. Situated in the small village of Drumdewan the cottage is only two minutes walk from our farm shop. Here you can choose from an array of organic produce from Highland Perthshire and beyond (discount available for guests). You can even have a box of produce ready for your arrival, or you could choose to eat in the farm shop café where the majority of the food is organic.

info@aberfeldycountrycottages.co.uk www.aberfeldycountrycottages.co.uk

DOUNE *(S-C)*

THE GLED COTTAGE   406

Doune
Stirling FK16 6AX
Tel: 01786 850213

Cottage: sleeps 4-5, £395-£595
Visitors are welcome to book dinner

Includes fresh vegetables, fruit and herbs
from the organic garden

This charming and comfortable cottage stands in its own garden, facing south in the midst of farmland, with distant views to the Gargunnock Hills. Nearby, across the fields, is an old tower built to mark the very centre of Scotland. Visitors are welcome to book dinner at Mackeanston House (two minutes drive away and five minutes walk), where Fiona cooks delicious food based on the best local produce and fresh vegetables, fruit and herbs from her organic garden. Meals are served in the dining room or in the conservatory overlooking the garden. Menus regularly include local fish, game and beef from hill and river, delicious homemade Aga baked breads. Organic venison, and fish, used where possible.

fiona@mackeanstonhouse.co.uk www.stirling-flexible-lettings.co.uk

DOUNE *(B&B)*

MACKEANSTON HOUSE 407

Doune
Stirling FK16 6AX
Tel: 01786 850213

Country House, B&B £43-£45 pppn
Dinner, 4 course £26

Includes fresh vegetables, fruit and herbs
from the organic garden

Here at Mackeanston the Graham family offer you a warm welcome and a touch of luxury in the heart of Scotland, where you will wake to the sound of the skylark, drink in the pure air of the highlands, and enjoy the panorama of lochs and mountains which make up the beautiful Trossachs area. Fiona's imaginative cooking is a major feature, based on the best local produce and fresh vegetables, fruit and herbs from her organic garden where possible. Meals are served in the dining room or in the conservatory overlooking the garden. Menus regularly include local fish, game and beef from hill and river, delicious homemade Aga-baked breads. Organic venison and fish used where possible.

fiona@mackeanstonhouse.co.uk www.stirling-flexible-lettings.co.uk/mackeanston

GLENFARG *(S-C)*

BRACKEN LOG CABIN 408

Duncrievie Farm
Glenfarg PH2 9PD
Tel: 01502 502588

Log Cabin S4468: sleeps 2
Usually available for short breaks

Organic restaurant, organic farm shops,
organic café all within 15 minutes drive

Scottish Organic Producers Association

New luxury log cabin offering every comfort, with a king-size four-poster bed, double spa bath, and sauna. The log cabin is centrally situated on an organic farm, with stunning panoramic views over the village. We have been awarded the Green Tourism Business Scheme Gold Award for excellence in environmental practice. The cabin has a thermostatically controlled ground source heating system. We have our own fresh water supply. We provide information on the local farmers' market, organic produce providers and farm shops. Jamesfield Organic Centre (organic restaurant, shop, butchery, bakery) and Pillars of Hercules (organic café, farm shop) are within fifteen minutes drive of Duncrievie Farm.

mail@hoseasons.co.uk www.hoseasons.co.uk

GLENFARG *(S-C)*

FINGASK LOG CABIN 409

Duncrievie Farm
Glenfarg PH2 9PD
Tel: 01502 502588

Log Cabin S4394: sleeps 2
Usually available for short breaks

Organic restaurant, organic farm shops,
organic café all within 15 minutes drive

Scottish Organic Producers Association

A luxury one bedroom log cabin built from Finnish logs. The log cabin is centrally situated on an organic farm, with stunning panoramic views over the village. We have been awarded the Green Tourism Business Scheme Gold Award for excellence in environmental practice. The cabin has a thermostatically controlled ground source heating system, a wind turbine supplies electricity, and we have our own fresh water supply. Lots of local information is provided, including info on the local farmers' market, organic produce providers and farm shops. Jamesfield Organic Centre (organic restaurant, shop, butchery, bakery) and Pillars of Hercules (organic café, farm shop) are both within fifteen minutes drive.

mail@hoseasons.co.uk www.hoseasons.co.uk

GLENFARG *(S-C)*

HILTON LOG CABIN 410

Duncrievie Farm
Glenfarg PH2 9PD
Tel: 01502 502588

Log Cabin S4345: sleeps 2+1
Usually available for short breaks

Organic restaurant, organic farm shops,
organic café all within 15 minutes drive

Scottish Organic Producers Association

One bedroom log cabin with wooden floors throughout. The log cabin is centrally situated on an organic farm, with stunning panoramic views over the village. We have been awarded the Green Tourism Business Scheme Gold Award for excellence in environmental practice. The cabin has a thermostatically controlled ground source heating system, a wind turbine supplies electricity, and we have our own fresh water supply. Lots of local information is provided, including info on the local farmers' market, organic produce providers and farm shops. Jamesfield Organic Centre (organic restaurant, shop, butchery, bakery) and Pillars of Hercules (organic café, farm shop) are both within fifteen minutes drive.

mail@hoseasons.co.uk www.hoseasons.co.uk

KILLIN *(B&B)*

INVERTAY HOUSE 411

Killin
Stirling FK21 8TN
Tel: 01567 820492

Guest House
Dinner, B&B from £54 pppn

45%-65% organic over the year

Situated on the outskirts of the picturesque village of Killin, at the western end of Loch Tay. This former manse, the oldest part dating from 1744, stands in extensive walled gardens looking out across the River Lochay with spectacular views of the Tarmachan Mountains, Beinn Ghlas and Ben Lawers, and the wonderful Breadalbane countryside. All meals are prepared using only fresh produce, including an abundance of organically grown seasonal fruit, herbs and vegetables from our own garden, homemade jams and preserves, and honey from our beehives. The dinner menu changes daily. All produce used is carefully sourced and supplied directly to us from the highest quality producers in Scotland.

invertay@btinternet.com www.invertayhouse.co.uk

LOCHEARNHEAD *(Hotel)*

MONACHYLE MHOR 412

Balquhidder
Lochearnhead FK19 8PQ
Tel: 01877 384622

Lochside Hotel, B&B from £47.50 pppn
Restaurant (lunch, dinner)

Includes seasonal produce from our organic garden

A small family-run farmhouse hotel in the heart of the Trossachs. Peacefully set in 2,000 acres, it enjoys magnificent views across two crystal-clear lochs. The menu in the award-winning restaurant changes daily. Most of our produce comes from within a thirty mile radius. Fish is delivered from the west coast, selected for optimum freshness and quality. Our organic garden supplies as many herbs as we can manage, plus all the basics from strawberries and salads to high summer favourites like broad beans and carrots, then on to cabbages and kale as the season progresses. We are great believers in preserving the best of our produce, from homemade jams and pickles to cured beef and bacon.

monachyle@mhor.net www.mhor.net

LOGIEALMOND *(B&B)*

GREENACRES 413

Chapelhill
Logiealmond PH1 3TQ
Tel: 01738 880302

Bed and Breakfast, double from £50 pn
Single from £32 pn

Minimum 70% organic, at times it may be as much as 85%-90%

Set in lovely rural countryside with far-reaching views of the surrounding hills, only a few miles from Perth. Organically home-grown or locally sourced food for breakfast. The house is secluded, quiet, comfortable, and elegantly furnished. It is surrounded by a sheltered half-acre garden, which is a sanctuary for birds, and includes an organic fruit and vegetable garden, hens providing free-range eggs, decorative fantail pigeons and a wildlife pond. Greenacres is a plant collector's paradise. It has held the Gold Award from the Green Tourism Business Scheme for excellence in environmental practice for the past three years. Runner up in The Big Tree Country Awards 2007 for business development.

enquiry@bedandbreakfast-perthshire.co.uk www.bedandbreakfast-perthshire.co.uk

PITLOCHRY *(S-C)*

CONVALLOCH LODGE 414

Atholl Estates Office
Tulliemet PH18 5TH
Tel: 01796 481355

Lodge: sleeps 10-12
£1,020-£2,080 pw

Atholl Glens Organic Meat (beef and lamb)

Scottish Organic Producers Association

Situated in an attractive and secluded highland location, with elevated views over lower Strathtay, Convalloch is surrounded by organic farmland. As part of Atholl Estates, guests receive tickets to nearby Blair Castle, where tours of the organic home farm run throughout the year (at an additional cost). The estates' farms are part of the Atholl Glens Organic Meat co-operative, producing top quality organic beef and lamb, which can be pre-ordered (delivered frozen). Alternatively, Atholl Glens sell fresh meat at the Perth Farmers' Market (20 miles away) on the first Saturday of the month. Organic fruit and vegetable boxes are also available to order from a local company. River and hill loch fishing available nearby.

enquiries@atholl-estates.co.uk www.athollestateslodges.co.uk

PITLOCHRY *(S-C)*

GLEN BRUAR LODGE 415

Atholl Estates Office
Blair Atholl PH18 5TH
Tel: 01796 481355

Lodge: sleeps 18
£1,300-£1,770

Atholl Glens Organic Meat (beef and lamb)

Scottish Organic Producers Association

Set in a dramatic glen, nine miles along a private track from the public road at the village of Calvine, Glen Bruar is the ideal remote retreat for up to eighteen people. Many miles of pony and foot tracks start from the front door. Free from the trappings of everyday life (no TV or mobile signal), guests can watch wildlife such as red deer and golden eagles, pat the lodge's farm animals and enjoy organic produce. The lodge is part of Atholl Estates, most of which is under organic status. The estates' farms are part of the Atholl Glens Organic Meat co-operative, producing top quality organic beef and lamb, which can be pre-ordered (delivered frozen), as can organic fruit and vegetable boxes from a local company.

enquiries@atholl-estates.co.uk   www.athollestateslodges.co.uk

PITLOCHRY *(S-C)*

OLD BLAIR LODGE 416

Atholl Estates Office
Blair Atholl PH18 5TH
Tel: 01796 481355

Lodge: sleeps 10-12
£1,250-£2,600 pw

Atholl Glens Organic Meat (beef and lamb)

Scottish Organic Producers Association

Originally an inn, Old Blair is located minutes walk from historic Blair Castle (part of Atholl Estates) and is surrounded by the castle's organic home farm. Tours of the farm run regularly throughout the year (admission charge). The estates' farms are part of the Atholl Glens Organic Meat co-operative, producing top quality organic beef and lamb, which can be pre-ordered (delivered frozen). Organic fruit and vegetable boxes are available from a local company. Perth (35 miles away) has a large farmers' market on the first Saturday of the month. Old Blair is only a short walk from the village of Blair Atholl. The house is ideally located for hill walking and mountaineering. Pony trekking can be provided on the estate.

enquiries@atholl-estates.co.uk www.athollestateslodges.co.uk

ACHNASHEEN *(Hotel)*

POOLEWE HOTEL   417

Poolewe
Achnasheen IV22 2JX
Tel: 01445 781241

Vegetarian Retreat, £49 pppn (£540 pppw)
Complementary therapies included

Minimum 50% organic, produced locally

Many people have discovered the wonderful value and the benefits of complementary health, and we offer a holiday that combines these benefits with gentle exercise, great food, like-minded company, all in the beautiful setting of Poolewe. Your holiday is all inclusive of accommodation, delicious food, daily therapy treatments and daily Pilates. The retreat will have over 50% organic produce in its menu and will be as local as possible. We have an organic bistro, which is family friendly. The restaurant menu will be aiming for 90% organic, but presently is around 65%. All food served during your week with us is delicious vegetarian. We love food, and we are sure you will love our meals and tasty snacks.

sandra1463@tiscali.co.uk www.poolewehotel.co.uk

DINGWALL *(B&B)*

SOLUS OR   418

Findon Hill
Culbokie IV7 8JH
Tel: 01349 877828

Bed and Breakfast
£30 pppn

A healthy natural breakfast is provided; all our produce is organic

The Harmonology Centre evolved from an organic therapeutic centre to incorporate a Visit Scotland 4-star Bed and Breakfast. Set in 3 acres with panoramic views of mountains, sea, forest and pastures. Our emphasis is on 'natural'. This includes organic food, structured purified water throughout, and an EMG stress-free environment. We pick our own cherries, plums, herbs. Forest walks provide us with chanterelles, bilberries. We are beautifully located. Visit castles, gardens. View dolphins, seals, black swans, red kites and buzzards. Experience Pictish Trails, hill walks and stunning beaches. Return, relax on the patio, or treat yourself to a massage or sauna and steam shower – naturally chemical-free.

info@harmonology.eu www.harmonology.eu/holidays.htm

DUNDONNELL (S-C)

TOM'S BOTHY 419

Achmore
Scoraig IV23 2RE
Tel: 01854 633354

Bothy: sleeps 5
£10 per day per adult (prices negotiable)

Fresh vegetables, fruit, herbs, eggs, home baked bread, all organic

The bothy is furnished with a fully equipped kitchen and is very comfortable, with a large woodburning stove that also heats the water. There is a bath in the bothy and a basic outside loo. Five minutes walk away behind the trees lies Chris and Anna's house and their 3-acre organic garden, where they grow and harvest the best quality organic vegetables, fruit and herbs. Depending on the season, fresh vegetables, fruit, herbs, eggs and home baked bread (all organic) are available. Sometimes there may be the opportunity to catch fish, or lobsters and crabs in creels. Tom's Bothy is situated on the south side of Loch Broom. There are many local hill and coastal walks that offer breathtaking views.

anna@scoraig.com

TAIN (B&B)

WEMYSS HOUSE B&B 420

Bayfield
By Tain IV19 1QW
Tel: 01862 851212

B&B, double or twin ensuite £80 per room
Evening Meal, £28 (by arrangement)

Organic / local / home produce available

Set in a peaceful rural landscape near Tain in the Highlands of Scotland, Wemyss House has three comfortably furnished ensuite rooms (two doubles and a twin) and stunning views over the Cromarty Firth to the mountains beyond. Enjoy a full traditional Scottish breakfast. Organic produce is important at Wemyss House. Christine and Stuart grow most of their own vegetables in the two-acre garden, where the roaming free-range chickens provide the eggs for your breakfast. Together with homemade organic bread, homemade preserves and other locally sourced organic and traditional fare, you can be assured of a good wholesome start to your day. Four-course evening meals plus coffee by arrangement.

stay@wemysshouse.com www.wemysshouse.com

ULLAPOOL *(S-C)*

LECKMELM COTTAGES　421

Leckmelm Estate
Loch Broom IV23 2RL
Tel: 01854 612471

Cottages: sleep 2-6, £190-£600 pw
Green Weekends

Meat and vegetables according to seasonal
availability

Biodynamic Agricultural Association

Eleven cottages in a rural situation, some by the loch, with the farm at the heart of Leckmelm Estate. STB Green Tourism Business Scheme Gold standard. Leckmelm Farm produces vegetables from the walled garden using biodynamic methods and markets via a box scheme and farm gate sales. We keep Highland Cattle predominantly for conservation grazing of species rich grassland and production of store calves. The family of pigs produce many sets of piglets each year, which are either sold locally or kept for home produced meat. Meat is reared organically but not certified due to the expense. There are plenty of good walks in the stunning landscape of Wester Ross from your doorstep.

organicholidays@leckmelmholidays.co.uk　www.leckmelmholidays.co.uk

ULLAPOOL *(Camping)*

LECKMELM FARM　422

Leckmelm Farm Wild Camping
Leckmelm Estate, Loch Broom IV23 2RL
Tel: 01854 612471

Camping £5 pppn

Meat and vegetables according to seasonal
availability

Biodynamic Agricultural Association

Basic camping facilities in a walled garden with an on-site tipi. Situated on Leckmelm Farm the tipi sleeps two, or alternatively it can be used as a living room in addition to tents. The tipi has a groundsheet inside with rugs. It's in a very sheltered spot close to the loch, where you can swim in warm weather and fish. Long drop compost loo and tap nearby. We aim to manage the land in a way that benefits the environment and peripheral ecosystems as well as providing jobs and homes for local people. We are involved in the Rural Stewardship scheme and have been using traditional cropping techniques, tree planting in shelterbelts and grazing the pastures using traditional breeds of animal.

info@leckmelmholidays.co.uk　www.leckmelmholidays.co.uk

WESTER ROSS *(S-C)*

COILLE BHEAG 423

14 Midtown of Inverasdale
Poolewe IV22 2LW
Tel: 01445 781783

Crofter's Cottage: sleeps 6, £245-£470 pw
Eco-Lodge: sleeps 4, £345-£570 pw

Our own produce (mixed salads, herbs, vegetables), free-range eggs

Two properties available for rent: a fully renovated crofter's cottage furnished in traditional style with a solid fuel fire, and a modern open-plan luxury eco-lodge with energy-efficient heating. Our 6-acre family croft has its own meadowland and wood, access to the shores of Loch Ewe, and amazing views of the wild, rugged mountains. Home-grown vegetables and fruits are available in season. Ready prepared salads and herbs with fresh ingredients from the croft. Fresh, new laid free-range eggs. Wester Ross is one of the most beautiful parts of the Scottish Highlands. Near stunning coastal beaches, the Torridon Mountains, and world-famous Inverewe Garden. Pets welcome in the cottage, but not in the lodge.

alasdairwright@btinternet.com www.coillebheag.com

WESTER ROSS *(S-C)*

RHIDORROCH COTT 424

Rhidorroch Estate
Glen Achall IV26
Tel: 01463 731360

Cottage: sleeps 4
From £250 pw

Organic produce from the farm

Scottish Organic Producers Association

We farm sheep and cattle on the hills in a remote and beautiful glen with a large organic garden. You are welcome to join in the work and share the produce during your stay. We keep a supply of beef, lamb and venison in the deep freeze if you would like to try some. Rhidorroch Estate is a wonderful place for bird-watching, with many rare birds visiting during the summer. For those interested in nature photography there are many interesting plants and wildlife. Enjoy swimming in the river pools and exploring the river gorge and waterfalls. The pony tracks are challenging and varied for mountain bikes, which can be hired in the village. We keep Highland ponies for riding and to herd the cattle.

scobiecoulmore@yahoo.co.uk www.rhidorrochlodge.co.uk/cottage.htm

WESTER ROSS *(S-C)*

RHIDORROCH LODGE 425

Rhidorroch Estate
Glen Achall IV26
Tel: 01463 731360

Lodge: sleeps 10
From £900 pw

Organic produce from the farm

Scottish Organic Producers Association

We farm sheep and cattle on the hills in a remote and beautiful glen with a large organic garden. You are welcome to join in the work and share the produce during your stay. We keep a supply of beef, lamb and venison in the deep freeze if you would like to try some. The estate is a wonderful place for bird-watching, with many rare birds visiting during the summer. For those interested in nature photography there are many interesting plants and wildlife. Enjoy swimming in the river pools and exploring the river gorge and waterfalls. The pony tracks are challenging and varied for mountain bikes, which can be hired in the village. We keep Highland ponies for riding and to herd the cattle.

scobiecoulmore@yahoo.co.uk   www.rhidorrochlodge.co.uk/lodge.htm

HAWICK *(B&B)*

NETHER SWANSHIEL 426

Hobkirk, Bonchester Bridge
Scottish Borders TD9 8JU
Tel: 01450 860636

Bed and Breakfast, £35 pppn
Dinner, £20 (by arrangement)

Home produce, local organic produce (about 75% organic)

Hobkirk is a tiny hamlet in unspoilt Scottish Borders country. It is a centrally heated family house with two twin-bedded guest rooms with private bathrooms, and one single room for overspill. The house was built in the 18th century as a manse and has an acre of garden. We rent a field in which our free-range Black Rock hens, Swedish geese and Jacobs sheep cohabit happily. We use no chemicals in their upkeep or in the garden, and supplement our food supplies from local organic sources. We make our own bread, marmalade and jams, and cook in an Aga. Why not step back in time and enjoy the peace? Then walk the hills and visit abbeys and gardens. Home-cooked evening meal on request.

auld@swanshiel.wanadoo.co.uk   www.netherswanshiel.fsnet.co.uk

GALASHIELS *(S-C)*

THE HEN HOOSE 427

Over Langshaw Farm
Langshaw TD1 2PE
Tel: 01896 860244

Cottage: sleeps 4
From £300 pw

Organic milk, eggs, garden fresh vegetables, ice-cream

Scottish Organic Producers Association

Stone cottage on a 500-acre working organic farm in the beautiful border country. The south-facing sun room and traditional materials give the cottage much charm. Natural materials include cotton sheets, oak and recycled pitch pine floors, and organic paint. 'Start you off' food hampers with organic and local produce. Eggs and, in season, garden fresh vegetables available to buy, plus Over Langshaw farmhouse ice-cream. An 'all seasons' place, in spring you'll see the sweet young lambs. In summer wildflowers and butterflies fill the clover meadows. Autumn colours and hazy days will bring out the photographer in you. Winter can be as cold and wild as it likes; you'll be snug and warm in your 'hoose'.

bergius@overlangshaw.fsnet.co.uk www.overlangshaw.com

GALASHIELS *(B&B)*

OVER LANGSHAW FARM 428

Langshaw
Galashiels TD1 2PE
Tel: 01896 860244

Farmhouse Bed and Breakfast
From £30 pppn, Evening Meal from £15

Garden vegetables, eggs, homemade breads, marmalades, ice-cream

Scottish Organic Producers Association

A welcoming family farm with wonderful views in the beautiful Borders. The farmhouse is a 'log fires and wooden shutters' sort of place, with a lovely double guest room and a large family guest room (private bathrooms). Delicious meals include fresh farm eggs, homemade breads and marmalades, garden vegetables, local and organic foods. Over Langshaw delicious farmhouse ice-cream now available. Being an organic sheep and dairy farm, there's lots of wildlife and flora to see on the pleasant farm walks. Hedgehogs, owls and birds enjoy the wild garden, which also has a nature trail. Out on the farm you'll see gentle cows and sheep enjoying the clover-rich pasture, completing the idyllic scene.

bergius@overlangshaw.fsnet.co.uk www.overlangshaw.com

WALLS *(Hotel)*

BURRASTOW HOUSE 429

Walls
Shetland ZE2 9PD
Tel: 01595 809307

Country House Hotel
Dinner, B&B £70 pppn

70%-90% organic (salads and vegetables from our own garden)

18th-century house on a promontory facing the island of Vaila, on the remote and peaceful west coast of Shetland. Burrastow welcomes you with peat fires, a cosy library, and all the marvellous food you could want after a day's exploring. Delicious cuisine using fresh Shetland produce – lamb which is almost 100% organic and natural, locally raised beef and pork, a wide variety of freshly caught fish. Salads and vegetables come from the garden. Fine fresh ingredients, simply cooked with uncomplicated sauces that enhance or complement the natural favours. Organic wines. Otters and seals may be seen from the windows and wild orchids flourish in the grounds. The hotel is open from April to October.

burr.hs@zetnet.co.uk   www.users.zetnet.co.uk/burrastow-house

LYNDALE *(S-C)*

LAUNDRY COTTAGE 430

Lyndale House
Lyndale IV51 9PX
Tel: 01470 582329

Cottage: sleeps 2
£300-£650 pw

Surplus organic produce may be available

Soil Association

Laundry Cottage offers an intimate and romantic holiday retreat, having been lovingly and sympathetically restored from an original estate building. Renovated with flair and imagination, the single storey cottage provides unique accommodation, combining modern comforts with traditional ambience. Surplus fresh produce from Lyndale's one and a half acre certified organic walled garden may be available to buy. Lyndale's organic produce can also be bought from the farmers' market in Portree on Thursdays. The cottage enjoys lovely views over woodland teeming with wildlife and flowers. There is easy walking access right from the door, and the cottage is within a very short walk of the sea.

linda@lyndale.net   www.lyndale.net/the-laundry.php

LYNDALE *(S-C)*

LYNDALE GATE LODGE 431

Lyndale House
Lyndale IV51 9PX
Tel: 01470 582329

Gate Lodge: sleeps 4
£370-£850 pw

Surplus organic produce may be available

Soil Association

This delightful Grade B listed 'ink pot' style gate lodge stands in the grounds of Lyndale Estate, nestling in the woods at the top of the private drive. Renovated to a high standard, it offers cosy, comfortable, self-catering accommodation of great character. Surplus fresh produce from Lyndale's certified organic one and a half acre walled garden may be available to buy. Lyndale's organic produce can be bought from the farmers' market in Portree on Thursdays. Guests enjoy the freedom of the Lyndale estate grounds and the nearby shorefront. It's just a short stroll down the wooded driveway to the sea, with panoramic views to the Outer Hebrides. The seashore teems with birds and other wildlife.

linda@lyndale.net www.lyndale.net/gate-lodge.php

LYNDALE *(S-C)*

STABLE COTTAGE 432

Lyndale House
Lyndale IV51 9PX
Tel: 01470 582329

Cottage: sleeps 2
£300-£650 pw

Surplus organic produce may be available

Soil Association

Stable Cottage offers an intimate and romantic holiday retreat, having been lovingly and sympathetically restored from an original estate building. Renovated with flair and imagination, the single storey cottage provides unique accommodation, combining modern comforts with traditional ambience. Surplus fresh produce from Lyndale's one and a half acre certified organic walled garden may be available to buy. Lyndale's organic produce can also be bought from the farmers' market in Portree on Thursdays. Stable Cottage enjoys lovely views over woodland teeming with wildlife and flowers. There is easy walking access right from the door, and the cottage is within a short walk of the sea.

linda@lyndale.net www.lyndale.net/lyndale-cottages.php

SUTHERLAND *(B&B)*

RUDDYGLOW PARK 433

Loch Assynt
By Lairg IV27 4HB
Tel: 01571 822216

Country House, double B&B from £115 pn
Dinner, B&B from £155 pn

We aim to be as organic as possible (average at least 90% organic)

Small, exclusive boutique bed and breakfast (5-star) located in the beautiful north-west Highlands of Scotland. Luxurious accommodation combining antique furniture, original paintings and individually designed rooms. A much loved 4-acre garden, full of well established trees and shrubs, surrounds the house, giving a feel of incredible space, peace and tranquillity. As breakfast is the most important meal of the day, we pride ourselves on ours. Lots of fresh organic fruits and fruit juices, delicious smoothies, homemade venison sausages, local free-range eggs, organic breads, and delicious jams and honeys. Dinners are designed to be both relaxing and delicious – just what's required after a long day out.

info@ruddyglowpark.com www.ruddyglowpark.com

ISLE OF HARRIS *(Hotel)*

SCARISTA HOUSE 434

Sgarasta Bheag
Isle of Harris HS3 3HX
Tel: 01859 550238

Small Hotel, B&B £175-£199 room pn
Dinner, 3 course £39.50

Organic, local, home-grown, homemade

The views from Scarista House, a Georgian former manse, are stunning – heather-covered mountains, the ocean, and a three mile long shell sand beach. It is one of the most beautiful and remote places to stay in Britain. We offer traditional comfort in well furnished guest rooms and two self-catering 'cottages'. We aim for natural, skilled cooking of the ingredients most immediately available, especially the island's wild seafood, lamb, beef and game. We carefully source organic, local or home-grown vegetables and herbs wherever possible. We bake our own bread and cakes, and make our own jam, marmalade, ice cream and yogurt. Three course dinner, £39.50 per person. Wines from £10 a bottle.

timandpatricia@scaristahouse.com www.scaristahouse.com

NEWTON STEWART *(S-C)*

LOW CRAIGLEMINE 435

Whithorn
Newton Stewart DG8 8NF
Tel: 01988 500730

Cottage: sleeps 6, 200-£400 pw
Bothy: sleeps 3, £150-£270 pw

Surplus garden vegetables gratis, (organic meat, dairy, bread available locally)

Biodynamic Agricultural Association

Attractively refurbished self-catering accommodation on a 130-acre organic farm in bonnie Galloway. Near the coast on the Machars peninsula, the farm lies between the quiet villages of Glasserton and Monreith. Share the simple life tending the goats, sheep, cows and bees, or just relax and enjoy your holiday in tranquil surroundings. Beautiful gardens, sandy beaches and spectacular rocky cliffs form a unique habitat for a variety of flora. The area is host to a multitude of wild animals and birds – peregrine falcon, red kite, barn owl, eagle, otter, seal, hare. The peninsula is steeped in natural, historical and archaeological interest, with cup and ring marked stones, standing stones and stone circles.

andykirstyhurst@tiscali.co.uk www.lowcraiglemine-farm-holidays.co.uk

BRECHFA *(S-C)*

LLYSTYN FARM   436

Brechfa
Carmarthen SA32 7RB
Tel: 01267 202463

Barn Conversion: sleeps 6
£230-£440 pw

Organic produce can be delivered by arrangement

Soil Association

Situated on a 200-acre organic beef and sheep farm with beautiful views across the valley. The barn conversion provides excellent spacious family accommodation, with pine furnishings, exposed beams and stone walls. A large games room provides facilities, including table tennis and a 6ft snooker table. You are welcome to explore the farm, which is located half a mile off the road up an unmade farm track. It includes 14 acres of broadleaf woodland, ancient flower meadows and varied bird life in an area known as Brechfa Forest. Free guided walks of the farm on request. Within fifty minutes drive you'll find the National Botanic Garden of Wales, castles, gold mines, wonderful coastline, beaches.

cliffcarnell@hotmail.com

FFYNNONDDRAIN *(S-C)*

LLECHEIGON FARMHOUSE   437

Clynmelyn
Ffynnonddrain SA33 6EE
Tel: 01267 237842

Farmhouse: sleeps 12
£550-£1,000 pw

Organic produce available to order

Quality Welsh Food Certification Ltd

Llecheigon Farmhouse is a traditional detached farmhouse three miles north of Carmarthen town. Enjoying panoramic views over hills and glorious countryside, this attractive, spacious and very comfortable farmhouse is ideal for large family gatherings. Set on a working organic farm, the owners are very happy to show visitors around. It is within easy reach of many of this beautiful area's attractions, such as Oakwood theme park, Pembrey country park, Gwili steam railway, the National Botanic Garden of Wales, and many lovely sandy beaches. Organic vegetable and fruit boxes are available by pre-ordering through Organics To Go at Werndolau Farm. There is also an organic shop in Carmarthen town.

www.llecheigon.co.uk

LLANBOIDY *(B&B)*

MAESGWYN ISAF 438

Llanboidy
Whitland SA34 0ET
Tel: 01994 448758

Farmhouse Bed and Breakfast
£26 pppn

Continental buffet breakfast (about 80% organic and local)

Small, clean, quiet bed and breakfast on a farm in beautiful Carmarthenshire, on the border with Pembrokeshire. Experience an ecological stay (Green Dragon Environmental Standard Level 2), where sustainability is offered without compromising your comfort and well-being. Everything provided is homemade or locally sourced, organic or fairly traded. Enjoy the atmosphere, beauty and wildlife on a piece of land managed with love and respect. Talk with us about our organic fruit and vegetable gardens. Visit our stone circle, extended woodlands, new shelter woods and meadows. Enjoy the birds, the flowers, the stars, and the wonderful views from the hill where the wind turbine proudly stands.

carters@gn.apc.org   www.maesgwynisaf.co.uk

LLANDOVERY *(B&B)*

BEILIGLAS 439

Myddfai
Llandovery SA20 0QB
Tel: 01550 720494

Bed and Breakfast, £25 pppn
Evening Meal (by arrangement)

Organically grown garden produce in season

An old farmhouse with a friendly atmosphere on the unspoiled northern border of the Brecon Beacons National Park. Optional evening meal with traditional home cooking, using a wide range of seasonal organic produce from the garden (or locally produced) wherever possible. Packed lunches on request. If you prefer self-catering there's a comfortable two bedroom cottage with central heating and log burner (all ground floor, suitable for the less mobile). Organically grown garden produce available in season. A grocery box can be provided upon request. Beiliglas is home to Herbs at Myddfai, a small organically run nursery growing herbs and native flowers. You're welcome to enjoy the garden area.

gill@myddfai.com   www.myddfai.com

LLANDYSUL *(S-C)*

PEN PYNFARCH 440

Llandysul
Carmarthen SA44 4RU
Tel: 01559 384948

Cottage: sleeps 4-6, £220-£375 pw
Weekend, from £130

Organic / local food box (to order),
vegetarian catering for groups of 5+

A self-contained cottage, part of the range of stone farm buildings, in a peaceful woodland valley. Simple décor using traditional and reclaimed materials and antique furniture. Woodburner with a supply of logs from site. Green electricity. Recycling facilities. An organic / local food box can be ordered from a local company. Pen Pynfarch is a smallholding working towards sustainability and hosts a seasonal programme of arts and environment workshops and holidays. We offer vegetarian catering (bed, full board, use of studio, £45 pppn). Meals are cooked with wholefoods and organic vegetables and fruit, using local produce plus our own eggs, honey and garden produce. Meals will be around 75% organic.

enquiries@penpynfarch.co.uk www.penpynfarch.co.uk

LLANDYSUL *(S-C)*

PENYRALLT FACH 441

Penyrallt Home Farm
Pentre-Cwrt SA44 5DW
Tel: 01559 370341

Cottage: sleeps 4, £250-£400 pw (Sat-Sat)
Short Breaks, £30 pppn (Oct-May)

Our farm shop sells meat, milk, eggs and basic groceries

Soil Association

Converted from an old piggery, this comfortable cottage, with woodburning stove and exposed beams, is all on one floor. Fully equipped kitchen / dining / sitting room. Two bedrooms, simply and attractively furnished. All bed linen and towels supplied. All fuel and electricity included in the price. The cottage is situated on an organic dairy and sheep farm in the beautiful Teifi Valley. Penyrallt Home Farm is a Soil Association demonstration farm and visitors are welcome to walk around the farm, woods and fields. The farm shop sells meat, milk, eggs, basic groceries. Freshly home-baked cakes, scones and bread, made with organic and fairtrade ingredients, can be ordered either in advance or during your stay.

djwj@penyrallt.freeserve.co.uk www.penyrallt.co.uk

LLANELLI *(B&B)*

BRYNGWENYN FARM B&B 442

Pontyberem
Llanelli SA15 5NG
Tel: 01269 843990

Farmhouse Bed & Breakfast
From £25 pppn, Evening Meal £15
Packed Lunch (on Request)

Local produce and home-grown vegetables

Soil Association

Comfortable ensuite accommodation in a 17th-century farmhouse located in peaceful countryside with panoramic views across the Gwendraeth Valley. Enjoy superb breakfasts cooked for you on the Aga, with eggs laid by our free-range hens and homemade preserves. Evening meals can be provided by arrangement, and are prepared using local produce and home-grown vegetables. Bryngwenyn is an organic farm with a flock of eighty Suffolk / Lleyn cross ewes. Two Angora goats share the orchard with rabbits, chickens, ducks, geese, and Sandy the Golden Guernsey. Children are very welcome, and are able to join in with farm activities. Our farm shop sells a good selection of organic and local produce.

elizabeth.hedges@btinternet.com www.bryngwenynfarm.co.uk

LLANELLI *(S-C)*

BRYNGWENYN 443

Bryngwenyn Farm Cottages
Pontyberem, Llanelli SA15 5NG
Tel: 01269 843990

Cottages: sleep 5, £300-£495 per week
Short Breaks, from £150 (min 2 nights)

Our farm shop has a good selection of organic and local produce

Soil Association

The three self-catering cottages are architect-designed conversions of a former barn. They are comfortably furnished with two or three bedrooms. Situated just across the yard from Bryngwenyn Farmhouse, the cottages are located in peaceful countryside with panoramic views across the Gwendraeth Valley. Evening meals can be provided for self-catering guests by prior arrangement, and are prepared using local produce and home-grown vegetables. Meals can be taken in the farmhouse, or brought to your cottage. We also sell produce from our farm shop. Bryngwenyn is an organic farm with a flock of eighty Suffolk / Lleyn cross ewes. Children are very welcome, and are able to join in with the farm activities.

elizabeth.hedges@btinternet.com www.bryngwenynfarm.co.uk/Cottages.htm

LLANSTEFFAN *(S-C)*

HEARTSPRING CENTRE   444

Heartspring Retreat Centre
Hill House, Llansteffan SA33 5JG
Tel: 01267 241999

Apartments: sleep 2-6, from £195 for 3
nights. 5-day Retreats, all inclusive from £380

Organic vegan meals available and organic
vegetable boxes to order

Heartspring is a small retreat centre specialising in relaxing and nurturing holidays in a stunning coastal setting. We are easy to reach and have a neutral spiritual focus. We use toxic-free paints, natural furnishings, with our own spring water. We offer three self-catering vegetarian apartments, and can provide organic meals and fruit and vegetables from our gardens. Organic vegetable boxes are also available through Organics To Go at Werndolau Farm. We also offer tailor-made retreat programmes which include organic meals and a choice of many complementary therapies. Heartspring Retreat Centre offers an inspiring, tranquil environment to help those looking to find their own healing and peace.

info@heartspring.co.uk   www.heartspring.co.uk

LLANWRDA *(B&B)*

GLANMARLAIS FARM   445

Llansadwrn
Llanwrda SA19 8HU
Tel: 01550 777425

Farmhouse Bed and Breakfast, £25 pppn
Evening Meal, 4 course £15 (by arrangement)

Organic produce served (also available to
buy)

Soil Association

Glanmarlais is a 200 year old working farm beautifully situated in the Towy Valley. We produce organic lamb, bacon and pork (and will shortly produce beef), all from rare or endangered breeds. Comfortable accommodation, with ample room for indoor relaxation should the weather invite you to sit by the open log burning fire. Organic foods are available – most meat and vegetables served are home-grown or locally produced organic. The farm is surrounded by secluded woodland and hill pastures, with our own meandering stream. Farm walks connect with the local footpath network. Children are welcome, and they can help feed and handle farm animals such as chickens, geese, ducks, sheep and pigs.

john@glanmarlaisfarm.co.uk   www.glanmarlaisfarm.co.uk

PENCADER *(B&B)*

HOLLYVILLE COTTAGE B&B 446

Hollyville
Maesycrugiau SA39 9DL
Tel: 01559 395301

Bed and Breakfast
£25-£35 pppn

Own honey and free-range eggs, home baking (organic ingredients)

A traditional Welsh cottage set in the beautiful and peaceful Teifi Valley, offering comfortable and friendly accommodation. We use as much organic produce from local suppliers as possible. We are developing our own vegetable garden and do not use any chemicals on our fruit and vegetables. I am also a hobby beekeeper, and honey is served each morning on the breakfast table, together with homemade jams using fruit collected from the garden. Our rare breed hens produce our eggs, freshly collected with deliciously golden yolks for you to enjoy however you like them. We bake award-winning Welsh cakes too. We actively encourage guests to recycle, and try hard to be as eco-friendly as possible.

bizzylizzy_hollyville@btinternet.com   www.dreamwales.com

PENDINE *(B&B)*

CLYNGWYN FARM B&B 447

Marros
Pendine SA33 4PW
Tel: 01994 453214

Farmhouse Bed and Breakfast
From £22 pppn

Breakfast includes organic produce when available

Soil Association

B&B on a working organic farm at the heart of Carmarthen Bay. Breakfast includes organic produce when available. Clyngwyn Farm is set in 100 acres of farmland. Surrounded by woodland and streams, the farm is in a peaceful, idyllic location with an abundance of wildlife and fauna. An ideal setting for the family as we have many animals, such as sheep, cows, horses, ducks, geese and dogs. We have recently erected thirty nest boxes over the farm. Riding, clay shooting, beautiful beaches and coastal walks are all within walking distance. Amroth, less than a mile away, is a small coastal village set within breathtaking countryside and outstanding coastline. Colby Woodland Garden (National Trust) nearby.

clyngwyn@tiscali.co.uk

PENDINE *(S-C)*

CLYNGWYN COTTAGES 448

Clyngwyn Farm
Marros SA33 4PW
Tel: 01994 453214

Cottages: sleep 2-6, £250-£475 per week
Breakfast, 4 course £4.50

Seasonal organic farm produce may be available

Soil Association

Four cottages on a working organic farm (three adapted for wheelchair use) at the heart of Carmarthen Bay. Clyngwyn is set in 100 acres of organic farmland. Seasonal organic farm produce may be available. Surrounded by woodland and streams the farm is in a peaceful, idyllic location with an abundance of wildlife and fauna. Amroth, a small coastal village set within beautiful countryside, is less than a mile away. We are one mile from a blue flag beach. The Pembrokeshire Coast Path, which takes you along one of the most outstanding stretches of coastline in Britain, starts at Marros. A Welsh farmhouse breakfast is available in the farmhouse for people staying in the cottages (by arrangement).

clyngwyn@tiscali.co.uk

ABERAERON *(Camping)*

NATURESBASE 449

Tyngwndwn Farm
Cilcennin SA48 8RJ

Campsite
Adults £6 pppn, Children £3 pppn

Organic, local and fair trade shop on site

Our campsite is a little different from most campsites in the UK. It is set in 9 acres of organic flower-rich meadows with a meandering stream and hedgerows ablaze with wildlife, just minutes from Aberaeron and Cardigan Bay. We believe in providing quality uncrowded and sustainable camping, where adults can relax enjoying the open countryside and children can enjoy the rugged excitement nature has to offer. The facilities include beautiful showers and loos. Our on-site shop provides organic, local and fair trade produce, breakfast and packed lunches. Our rammed earth pizza oven is fired up once a week for visitors to make their own organic pizzas. Explore the tracks and trails on foot or bike.

gyles@naturesbase.co.uk www.naturesbasecamping.co.uk

ABERAERON *(S-C)*

TY-RHOS COTTAGE 450

Ty-rhos Organic Farm
Upper Aberarth SA46 0LA
Tel: 01545 571430

Cottage: sleeps 2-4
£160-£200 pw

Seasonal organic salad and vegetables gratis

Soil Association

Ty-rhos is set in 31 acres of organic farmland, two acres of which is used for protected horticulture, with the remainder being natural grassland and habitat for wildlife conservation. We produce salads and seasonal vegetables for the wholesale market and several local outlets. The cottage (double bedroom, lounge with kitchen area, shower room) is adjacent to the farmhouse. Seasonal organic salad and vegetables are available gratis. An abundance of birds, butterflies and wild flowers can be seen on the farm. The farm has all the feeling of remoteness, being set well back from a country lane, yet it is only two miles from the Georgian harbour town of Aberaeron and the Ceredigion Heritage Coastline

walsh@ty-rhos.freeserve.co.uk

CARDIGAN *(B&B)*

GWYNFRYN 451

Sarnau
Cardigan SA44 6QS
Tel: 01239 654408

Bed and Breakfast
£27-£32 pppn

Organic meats, milk, eggs, cereals

A small family-run bed and breakfast in some of the most spectacular coast and countryside in south-west Wales. Situated on the coast road, yet within easy reach of Cardigan Bay, this Edwardian farmhouse offers a friendly family welcome. Ample off-road parking. Each of our comfortable rooms has colour television, tea and coffee making facilities, hairdryer, ensuite or private bathroom, full central heating. You can feel really at home, coming and going as you wish throughout the day. Our organic food is, where possible, sourced locally, our organic meats coming from the nearby Trefere Fawr Farm. Having enjoyed your breakfast with us, you could visit their organic farm shop and take home a treat.

SEHoughton@tred.freeserve.co.uk   www.stayinwales.co.uk

LAMPETER *(S-C)*

THE FARMHOUSE 452

Treberfedd Farm
Dihewyd SA48 7NW
Tel: 01570 470672

Farmhouse: sleeps 7
Short breaks start from £89

Seasonal rare breed organic beef and lamb
from our farm

Soil Association

A country retreat with all the comforts of a modern home, with spacious accommodation for up to seven people. The house occupies an idyllic position, with panoramic views over rolling green hills to the front and organic fields at the back. The poet Dylan Thomas once described the Aeron Valley as 'the most precious place in the world'. Come and find out what makes it so special. The beautiful Cardigan Bay coast is fifteen minutes away, with great sandy beaches to discover. You can spend time exploring the Treberfedd nature trail and then enjoy a hearty meal around the farmhouse table. Organic beef and lamb from our farm is seasonally available to guests as well as organic vegetables from local growers.

jack@treberfedd.co.uk   www.treberfedd.co.uk/white_house.php

LAMPETER *(S-C)*

GRANARY COTTAGE 453

Treberfedd Farm
Dihewyd SA48 7NW
Tel: 01570 470672

Barn Conversion: sleeps 5
Short breaks start from £89

Seasonal rare breed organic beef and lamb
from our farm

Soil Association

Created from one of the farm's lovely traditional buildings, this cottage provides beautiful contemporary accommodation whilst retaining much of the character of its origins. It has a large open plan living space with limewashed walls and original stone features. An attractive summer room gives fantastic views of the woodland and surrounding valley. This cottage is an ideal holiday getaway. The beautiful Cardigan Bay coast is just fifteen minutes away and there is a nature trail to explore around our organic farm. Organic beef and lamb is available from Treberfedd, and fresh seafood is seasonally available at the nearby harbour towns of Aberaeron and New Quay. Short breaks start from just £89.

jack@treberfedd.co.uk   www.treberfedd.co.uk/granary_cottage.php

LAMPETER *(S-C)*

THE OLD CART HOUSE   454

Treberfedd Farm
Dihewyd SA48 7NW
Tel: 01570 470672

Converted Barn: sleeps 9
Short breaks start from £89

Seasonal rare breed organic beef and lamb
from our farm

Soil Association

This award-winning barn conversion can sleep up to nine people. It provides the ideal country escape for families and groups. The accommodation was created from a traditional stone farm range. Many original features remain, with the beautifully crafted stone work of this Welsh building visible both inside and out. The main entrance to the house is through the archway which was originally made for the farm's horse-drawn cart. A large window in the kitchen / diner affords fantastic views of the valley and hills beyond. Our waymarked nature trail around the organic farm and woodland is great fun. Organic beef and lamb from the home farm is seasonally available to guests. Short breaks from just £89.

jack@treberfedd.co.uk www.treberfedd.co.uk/cart_house.php

LAMPETER *(S-C)*

THATCHED COTTAGE   455

Treberfedd Farm
Dihewyd SA48 7NW
Tel: 01570 470672

Cottage: sleeps 6
Short breaks start from £89

Seasonal rare breed organic beef and lamb
from our farm

Soil Association

The original thatched farmhouse at Treberfedd is surrounded by some of the finest scenery in Ceredigion. It sits in 67 acres of organic meadow and woodland that is yours to explore. The poet Dylan Thomas described this landscape as 'the most precious place in the world' – come and find out what makes it so special. Built in the late 1600s (and with original wall paintings to prove it), the house was modernised in 1802, and restored in 2002. It is furnished with beautiful Welsh country furniture. With its woodburning stove and underfloor heating, this Georgian farmhouse is the perfect place for a relaxing country break. Rare breed organic beef and lamb from our farm is seasonally available to guests.

jack@treberfedd.co.uk www.treberfedd.co.uk/thatched_cottage.php

LLANDYSUL *(B&B)*

BRONIWAN 456

Rhydlewis
Llandysul SA44 5PF
Tel: 01239 851261

Farmhouse Bed and Breakfast, £32 pppn
Evening Meal, £20 (by arrangement)

Our own Aberdeen Angus beef, eggs, soft
fruit, vegetables

Soil Association

A small farm (45 acres) with organic beef suckler cows in the far west of Wales. The grey stone house, with ancient ivy growing round the porch, was built in 1867. Its pine-panelled windows look towards the Preseli Hills. Delicious home-cooked meals with vegetarian options. We use our own organic produce, including eggs, beef, fruit and vegetables. Soups, cakes and marmalade are all homemade. Visitors may walk anywhere around the farm. There are sketch maps with rambles down to the stream or up to the high fields. Part of a Welsh conservation scheme, the front meadow is being devoted to new planting (crab apple, rowan, black thorn). The long, sandy Cardiganshire coast is ten minutes drive away.

broniwan@btinternet.com www.broniwan.com

LLANDYSUL *(B&B)*

NANTGWYNFAEN 457

Nantgwynfaen
Croeslan SA44 4SR
Tel: 01239 851914

B&B, ensuite from £60 pn (family 2+2 £85 pn)
Light Meal £7, Evening Meal £15

Meals include our own organic produce
(meat, vegetables, eggs, apple juice)

Soil Association

On our family farm we sell local organic food in our farm shop. We grow our own vegetables, and beef and sheep are reared on the farm. We have chickens (giving us fresh eggs), ponies, and pet lambs. Walk around the farm and see how organic animals are reared. Experience really great-tasting local organic food. We are passionate about food, and use all organic ingredients – flour, butter, eggs, cereal, juice, fruit and vegetables. Jam is homemade using our own organic fruit. We make most things here, but try to source local products (like honey and cheese), organic if possible as well. Children are welcome. This is a lovely area with walks from the farm, beaches, cliff top walks, and a good pub nearby too.

nantgwynfaen@hotmail.co.uk

LLANDYSUL *(S-C)*

THE LONGBARN 458

Penrhiw Farm
Capel Dewi SA44 4PG
Tel: 01559 363200

Bunkhouse: sleeps 34
Adult £8.50 pn (under 18 £6.50 pn)

Organic meat, local organic vegetables, dairy produce

Soil Association

Our traditional long stone barn provides comfortable bunkhouse accommodation in beautiful West Wales. The 18th-century fully converted barn is situated in the yard of a working organic farm involved in crop and livestock production. The yard is in a lovely position, with a spectacular view across the Teifi Valley. Our own organic meat is available to buy – pork, beef, lamb, poultry, sausages, burgers and bacon. Organic vegetable boxes can be ordered (by prior arrangement) and we can have organic milk, cheese, butter and yogurt delivered from Calon Wen. There is walking locally on footpaths, or our own farm trail. Both the stunning Ceredigion coast and the wild Cambrian Mountains are within easy reach.

cowcher@thelongbarn.co.uk   www.thelongbarn.co.uk

LLANDYSUL *(S-C)*

THE OLD COWSHED 459

Penbeili Mawr Farm
Coed Y Bryn SA44 5NA
Tel: 01239 851059

Cottage: sleeps 2
£260-£560 pw

Organic food is available locally

Soil Association

Penbeili Mawr is a small 87-acre organic sheep and beef farm nestling in the tranquil countryside of Ceredigion. We also have our own small apiary, and honey is available to visitors. Within the farm is a 25-acre wood, affording interesting walks and a wide variety of wildlife and flora, especially in the spring. The farm is well away from busy roads and towns and yet within easy reach are stunning coves and beaches, including the National Trust beach at Penbryn. The Old Cowshed was initially converted in 2001 and has been refurbished in 2007 by the new owners. It is a detached one bedroom cottage on ground level with full central heating. It has a private patio within a walled courtyard. Private parking.

penbeilicottages@hotmail.co.uk   www.penbeilicottages.co.uk

NEWPORT *(B&B)*

AWEN VEGETARIAN B&B 460

1 Penrhiwgwair Cottage
Twyn Road NP11 5AS
Tel: 01495 244615

Bed and Breakfast, £30-£40 pppn
Packed Lunch / Evening Meal (on request)

All food is locally sourced and organic wherever possible

A peaceful and cosy retreat from the modern world. Awen Vegetarian B&B, a converted 16th-century Welsh longhouse, nestles high on a mountainside in the heart of the Welsh valleys. Accommodation for up to six people consists of one bedroom with a double four-poster bed and a single bed, and a second bedroom with a double bed and a single bed. Packed lunches and evening meals are available on request. Delicious organic veggie breakfasts – vegetarian sausages, eggs, beans, tomatoes, mushrooms, toast, marmalade, jams, cereals, fresh fruit salad, yogurt and freshly baked bread. Organic soaps, shampoos and cleaning products are used in the house. Healing available on a donations basis.

info@awenbandb.com www.awenbandb.com

BALA *(B&B)*

CYSGODY GARN 461

Frongoch
Bala LL23 7NT
Tel: 01678 521457

Farmhouse Bed and Breakfast, £26-£34 pppn
Evening Meal (by arrangement)

Organic and local produce

Soil Association

Our small country farmhouse bed and breakfast stands in its own grounds, surrounded by beautiful organic farmland and spectacular rural Welsh views. Our family have been farming this land for two generations, and we are currently rearing sheep and the famous Welsh Black cattle. We are very proud of our farmhouse cuisine, and we are members of Blas ar Gymru (A Taste of Wales). Organic produce is used where possible for your tasty breakfast and evening meals. The three course evening meal (by prior arrangement) is from a set menu, cooked in the traditional way using fresh local produce. Our guests are most welcome to visit the farm during their stay, and farm tours are available on request.

carys@snowdoniafrongoch.co.uk www.snowdoniafrongoch.co.uk

CONWY *(S-C)*

BRYN DOWSI 462

Gyffin
Conwy LL32 8YF
Tel: 01492 592182

Cottages: sleep 2-6
Short Breaks (1 Oct-23 Mar)

Organic Welsh lamb and beef available direct from us

Organic Farmers & Growers

Bryn Dowsi is a 200-acre organic beef and sheep farm a mile from Conwy in North Wales. There are four hundred Welsh mountain sheep and twenty beef cattle on the farm, where for the last ten years conservation has been a high priority. Organic Welsh Black and Charolais cross beef and Welsh Mountain lamb raised on our farm are available direct from us (please contact us for more information on our meat). Traditional farm buildings have been converted into quality self-catering cottage accommodation. The cottages are ideally placed for exploring the whole of North Wales, including the lakes and mountains of Snowdonia, historic castles and gardens, and beaches from Llandudno to Anglesey and beyond.

berylanddafydd@bryndowsicottages.co.uk www.bryndowsicottages.co.uk

CONWY *(S-C)*

CONWY VALLEY BARN 463

Pyllau Gloewen Farm
Tal-y-Bont LL32 8YX
Tel: 01492 660504

Bunk Barn, £12.50 pppn (£200 pn sole use)
Breakfast £3.50, Packed Lunch £5

Home produced organic lamb and potatoes available to buy

Soil Association

Conwy Valley Barn is on a working farm called Pyllau Gloewen. Sturdy Welsh mountain sheep and Welsh black cattle are bred here, along with world renowned sheepdogs. Long meadows and marshlands stretch down towards the River Conwy, home to curlews, skylarks and herons. Our bunk barn has three dorms (sleep 4, 6, 10), a fully equipped kitchen and a spacious comfortable lounge area with traditional log fire. Breakfast can be ordered. Large barbecue area. We can prepare your food so when you get back you simply cook it on the ready-lit barbecue (£10 pp, min 15 pers). Buffet supper £10 pp. We sell our organic vegetables, Saltmarsh lamb and beef. Scones and Bara Brith can be ordered during your stay.

info@conwyvalleybarn.com www.conwyvalleybarn.com

DOLGELLAU *(S-C)*

PENTRE BACH 464

Llwyngwril
Dolgellau LL37 2JU
Tel: 01341 250294

Cottages: sleep 2, 4-6 and 7
£265-£830 pw

Organic fruit and vegetables, free-range eggs, organic bread, cakes, freezer meals, etc

Relax. Enjoy magnificent sunsets over Cardigan Bay and marvel at the stars in the night sky. There are mountains and sea on the doorstep, in Southern Snowdonia. Walk or cycle from the door of your holiday cottage up into the hills or nine hundred yards down to the quiet beach. Visit the Centre for Alternative Technology. Green practices include local buying, low energy use, minimum waste and recycling – all helping to provide a beautiful, caring and relaxing environment. Stroll around our organic no-dig walled kitchen garden. Taste our vegetables, fruit and free-range eggs. Remember to order some fresh homemade organic bread to be delivered to your door. Forget the 21st century for a while.

cottages@pentrebach.com www.pentrebach.com

DYFFRYN ARDUDWY *(S-C)*

YSTUMGWERN HALL 465

Ystumgwern Hall Farm, Ystumgwern
Dyffryn Ardudwy LL44 2DD
Tel: 01341 247249

Self-Catering: sleep 1-8
£220-£960 pw

Information given about where to buy organic food locally

Quality Welsh Food Certification Ltd

Luxury self-catering on a 16th-century traditional Welsh farm set between sea and mountains on the west coast of the Snowdonia National Park. The guest accommodation is in traditional stone farm buildings and farmhouses about a mile's walk from sandy beaches or rambling mountains. The properties have been awarded the highest grade of 5 stars by the Wales Tourist Board. We are a 1,000-acre working organic beef and sheep farm. There are numerous footpaths and ample opportunities to explore the open countryside with its breathtaking views. Snowdonia is a contrast of rugged mountains and wooded valleys, rushing streams and peaceful lakes, glorious beaches and boat dotted harbours.

ynys@ystumgwern.co.uk www.ystumgwern.co.uk

PENMACHNO (S-C)

TY NEWYDD UCHAF 466

Ty Newydd Uchaf
Penmachno LL24 0AJ
Tel: 01690 760350

Farmhouse: sleeps 4-5 people
£500-£850 pw

Organic eggs always available, meat and
poultry in season

Soil Association

Off-road traditional farmhouse, dating from the early 18th century, with stunning views of the Snowdonia mountains. It is situated in a peaceful rural location one mile from the village of Penmachno (near Betws-y-Coed). Recently restored using lime, it has an Aga cooker, underfloor heating, a working Victorian kitchen range and a woodburning stove. All rooms enjoy lovely views of the surrounding countryside. Ty Newydd is a 21-acre organic smallholding, specialising in organic egg and lamb production. Badger Face Welsh Mountain sheep, llamas and geese graze in the fields adjacent to the farmhouse. Organic eggs are always available, meat and poultry in season. Dogs and ponies are welcome.

clairebarnardburrows@yahoo.co.uk www.tnorganics.co.uk

PWLLHELI (S-C)

GWYNDY 467

Mur Crusto
Llangybi LL53 6LX
Tel: 01766 819109

Cottage: sleeps 4+cot
£185-£540 pw

Organic fruit and vegetables available
according to season

Soil Association

Small organic farm set between the lovely scenery and unspoilt beaches of the Lleyn Peninsula and Snowdonia National Park. We have lovingly converted our milking parlour into a beautifully furnished eco-cottage (Gwyndy) with underfloor heating and insulation, making it cosy and warm even in winter. Enjoy magnificent sea and mountain views from the conservatory. Stroll round our 13 acres of land, with ducks, sheep, and cows in summer, lake and nature reserve. We mainly grow vegetables and are Rick Stein Food Heroes. Organic vegetables are available to buy all year, organic fruit according to season. There are wonderful walks locally and a cycle route passes the end of our drive.

info@llangybi-organics.co.uk www.llangybi-organics.co.uk

PWLLHELI *(S-C)*

GWYNFRYN HOLIDAYS 468

Llannor
Pwllheli LL53 5UF
Tel: 01758 612536

Cottages: sleep 2-8
£210-£950 pw

Freshly cooked meals, made with local produce

Soil Association

Winner of Wales Tourist Board Self-Catering Award 2005. This 100-acre working organic dairy farm is a peaceful haven for nature lovers. Derelict farm buildings have been sympathetically transformed into quality houses in this idyllic rural setting. Indoor swimming pool, gym, tennis court, sauna and jacuzzi, and soft play area in the games room. Taste our creamy green top milk, straight from the cow. Homemade takeaway meals are available, made with local produce. Guests are welcome to help feed the animals, help bring in the cows for milking, or study the varied vegetation in the colourful meadows. The old market town of Pwllheli, the gateway to the beautiful Lleyn Peninsula, is a mile away.

sharon@gwynfryn.freeserve.co.uk www.gwynfrynfarm.co.uk

PWLLHELI *(S-C)*

ORGANIG PARC 469

Carnguwch
Llithfaen LL53 6NH
Tel: 01758 750000

Luxury Cottages: sleep 4-7
£335-£997 pw

Complimentary organic produce on arrival

Soil Association

Organig Parc offers a unique blend of eco-friendly design and 5-star luxury on a 300-acre working organic farm in the heart of the Llyn Peninsula. The five self-catering cottages have been designed and constructed using eco-friendly techniques, yet are fully equipped with modern conveniences. Situated in an Area of Outstanding Natural Beauty with some of the finest views in Cymru / Wales, Organig Parc is a short journey away from award-winning beaches and the mountains of Eryri / Snowdonia. Organig Parc has its own organic trout fishing lake. Running water is supplied by our own spring. We also supply organic linen and organic cleaning products. Complimentary organic produce on arrival.

info@organigparc.com www.organigparc.com

PWLLHELI *(Camping)*

RHOSFAWR PARK 470

Rhosfawr
Y Ffor LL53 6YA
Tel: 01766 810545

Touring Caravan and Camping Park
From £10 per day

Organic vegetables available in season

Soil Association

Rhosfawr Park is an award-winning, secluded, family-run site situated in the heart of the Llyn Peninsula. It offers a peaceful environment, panoramic views and space to enjoy. This quiet, sheltered, level site makes an ideal base either for exploring or simply taking it easy. Abersoch, Nefyn, Pwllheli, Criccieth, Porthmadog, Caernarfon and the Snowdonia National Park are all within easy access. You're never far from unspoilt beaches, fantastic scenery, magnificent mountains, historic castles. Also available to let are two holiday cottages sleeping 5 and 8 (£350-£750 per week), and a static caravan sleeping 6 (£200-£350 per week). A small selection of organic vegetables is grown in season.

Info@northwalesholidayhomes.co.uk www.northwalesholidayhomes.co.uk

PWLLHELI *(S-C)*

TREDDAFYDD CARAVAN 471

Llithfaen
Pwllheli LL53 6NL
Tel: 01758 750418

Caravan: sleeps 4-6, £195-£295 pw

Welcome grocery pack (on request)

Eggs, fresh vegetables and soft fruit available when in season

In Conversion

The caravan has stunning views across fields to the sea. Outside there's a private patio with seating and a barbecue. Our 7.5-acre organic smallholding is in a beautiful rural setting on the Lleyn Peninsula on the edge of Snowdonia. We have a flock of free-range hens, and produce soft fruit and vegetables. Farm gate sales of surplus seasonal fruit and vegetables (blueberries, strawberries, red / blackcurrants, potatoes, carrots, parsnips, swedes, sprouts, turnips, peas, runner beans, courgettes, cabbage, purple sprouting broccoli, beetroot, spinach, artichokes, etc). Children can help feed the hens and collect an egg each for breakfast. The Lleyn Coastal Path runs along the rear of the property. Short breaks £40 per night.

sharmear@aol.com www.treddafyddfarmholidays.co.uk

TALSARNAU *(Hotel)*

TREMEIFION HOTEL 472

Soar Road
Talsarnau LL47 6UH
Tel: 01766 770491

Vegetarian Country Hotel
Dinner Bed and Breakfast, £61-£72 pppn

Much of the produce is from our own organic garden

Situated deep within the Snowdonia National Park, with beautiful, unspoilt scenery all around. Excellent walks, historic interest, miles of safe sandy beaches, all on the doorstep. Exclusively vegetarian / vegan, we take pride in serving home cooked, high quality food which is both healthy and imaginative. We use organic ingredients whenever possible, including produce from our own organic fruit, vegetable and herb gardens. We offer a full cooked, American, or continental breakfast, and a 3 course evening meal. Wide range of organic wines and juices available. Wander in our 3 acres of garden. Enjoy superb views over the estuary to Portmeirion. Relax with a drink in the garden room and watch the sunset.

enquire@vegetarian-hotel.com   www.vegetarian-hotel.com

TYWYN *(S-C)*

GLAN MORFA BACH 473

Llanegryn
Tywyn LL36 9SN
Tel: 01654 710541

Cottage: sleeps 5
£250-£450 pw

Enjoy freshly picked produce from our smallholding

In Conversion

Glan Morfa Bach is an organic smallholding in Llanegryn in the beautiful Dysynni Valley. We are in organic conversion with Quality Welsh Food Certification Ltd, and can supply you with organic meat, vegetables and delicious homemade meals. You can relax in our peaceful gardens with spectacular views of the mountains, watching buzzards, red kites and badgers. Alternatively you can visit sandy beaches, go mountain biking, travel on the Tal-y-llyn steam railway, climb Cadair Idris, and visit the Centre for Alternative Technology. Then you can rest and refresh yourself at one of the cafés or delicatessens in the area and sample the local and organic produce, or simply relax in front of our log burning stove.

katiephilholidays@yahoo.co.uk   www.glanmorfa-cottages.co.uk

TYWYN *(S-C)*

THE PAD

Llanegryn
Tywyn LL36 9SN
Tel: 01654 710541

Cottage: sleeps 2
£180-£300 pw

Enjoy freshly picked produce from our smallholding

In Conversion

The Pad is a brilliant place for two on our organic smallholding in Llanegryn in the beautiful Dysynni Valley. We are in organic conversion with Quality Welsh Food Certification Ltd, and can supply you with organic meat, vegetables and delicious homemade meals. You can relax in our peaceful gardens with spectacular views of the mountains, watching buzzards, red kites and badgers. Alternatively you can visit sandy beaches, go mountain biking, travel on the Tal-y-llyn steam railway, climb Cadair Idris, and visit the Centre for Alternative Technology. Then you can rest and refresh yourself at one of the cafés or delicatessens in the area and sample some of the local and organic produce.

katiephilholidays@yahoo.co.uk   www.glanmorfa-cottages.co.uk

PENTRAETH *(B&B)*

BRONWEN COTTAGE

Bronwen
Rhoscefnhir LL75 8YS
Tel: 01248 450533

Guest House, £33 per person pn
Evening Meal, 2 course £15

We use organic / biodynamic fruit, vegetables and herbs all year round

Family-run peaceful guest house nestled in a cute hamlet near Red Wharf Bay. Food served at Bronwen Cottage is of a high quality and mainly organic. We prefer to use locally grown food, including our own organic / biodynamic produce all year round. We also utilise wild-crafted foods, superfoods and cold pressed oils, and cater for allergies and intolerances. Emma is a certified Plant Based Living Foods Practitioner, Ulrika a Yoga Teacher with the British Wheel of Yoga, Paddy an Environmental Biofuels Engineer (training in this area available). We are partially powered by solar, run our van on recycled vegetable oil, and plan to have a fresh water purification system in one of the kitchen areas.

bronwen_livingfoods@yahoo.co.uk   www.myspace.com/bronwen_livingfoods

YNYS MON *(S-C)*

SEAVIEW COTTAGE 476

Plas Llanfair
Tyn-y-Gongl LL74 8NU
Tel: 01248 852316

Cottage: sleeps 4-5, £225-£675 per week
Meal for your arrival on request

Seasonal organic fresh fruit, vegetables, jams, chutneys

Soil Association

An upstairs sitting room with a simple truss timbered roof and log burning stove takes advantage of extensive sea, countryside and mountain views. Ledged oak doors, Welsh green oak staircase, slate tiled finish to the ground floor, solid oak flooring upstairs. Half a mile from the coastal path, the village and the beach. Guests will be provided with a complimentary seasonal basket of our own organic produce on arrival. We are a three-hectare organic producer of a range of fruit and vegetables, specialising in soft fruits. We process the finest quality organic jams, preserves and chutneys from our own produce. Organic home-grown produce available for you to buy. On request, visitors may order a meal for their arrival.

plasllanfaircottages@fsmail.net www.plasllanfaircottages.co.uk

YNYS MON *(S-C)*

SWALLOW COTTAGE 477

Plas Llanfair
Tyn-y-Gongl LL74 8NU
Tel: 01248 852316

Cottage: sleeps 4, £200-£600 per week
Meal for your arrival on request

Seasonal organic fresh fruit, vegetables, jams, chutneys

Soil Association

Swallow Cottage is in a private and secluded setting with beautiful countryside and sea views from the patios and garden. The sitting room, with open king post and truss timbered roof, features a log burning stove. The land has a diverse range of species and habitats. Half a mile from the coastal path, the village and the beach. Guests will be provided with a complimentary seasonal basket of our own organic produce on arrival. We are a three-hectare organic producer of a range of fruit and vegetables, specialising in soft fruits. We process the finest quality organic jams, preserves and chutneys from our own produce. Organic home-grown produce is available to buy. On request, visitors may order a meal for their arrival.

mikeparker@fsmail.net www.plasllanfaircottages.co.uk

ABERGAVENNY *(B&B)*

PART-Y-SEAL 478

Grosmont
Abergavenny NP7 8LE
Tel: 01981 240814

Country House B&B, double £70 pn. Tea Room (morning coffee, lunch, afternoon tea)

Breakfasts use organic home-grown and homemade produce whenever possible

Part-Y-Seal is a peaceful and relaxing haven set in the beautiful Monnow Valley. Our rooms are ensuite with a choice of king-size, four-poster or twin beds, and all have magnificent views. Within our 4 acres of mature gardens is a large organic kitchen garden and greenhouses, where we try to produce crops for eating all year round. Our free-range chickens give us delicious eggs and our latest addition, bees, have provided us with organic honey. All food is homemade from breads to preserves. Guests are welcome to take their breakfast outside in summer, where you'll see the vast amount of birds and wildlife around, or by log fires in winter. A truly relaxing break which starts with complimentary cream teas on arrival.

fred@ong55.freeserve.co.uk   www.orientalsplendour.net/Part-Y-Seal.htm

TINTERN *(S-C)*

CRAIGO BARN 479

Craigo Farm
Botany Bay NP16 6SN
Tel: 01291 689757

Converted Barn: sleeps 5
£225-£385 pw

We can pre-arrange seasonal organic vegetable boxes if required

Renovated historic stone barn on our 9-acre smallholding (run on organic lines) with horses, sheep, chickens, a large pond and plenty of ducks. We'll be happy to source local organic produce (meat, vegetables, herbs, local wine) or recommend local growers. We have a Green Dragon certificate for our commitment to environmental management. Craigo Barn is in a delightful, quiet, rural area in the hills just above Tintern Abbey, midway between Chepstow and Monmouth. Set in thousands of acres of forestry woodlands in the heart of one of Europe's prime Areas of Outstanding National Beauty, the barn provides an excellent base for those interested in outdoor pursuits. Many scenic walks from the farm gate.

holidays@craigohouse.co.uk

TINTERN *(B&B)*

THE NURTONS 480

Tintern
Chepstow NP16 7NX
Tel: 01291 689253

Bed and Breakfast, from £30 pppn
Evening Platter (by arrangement)

We've been growing fruit and vegetables
organically here for more than 40 years

Soil Association

The Nurtons is situated on an historical site in an AONB. We have two suites, one twin with a double sofa bed, and one double. Both have their own private bathroom, sitting room and patio. A double ensuite room is also available in the house. Delicious organic breakfasts. Home produce and home baking. Organic evening platter (£30 for 2 persons) served at 7pm. The food is organically produced, as much homemade and home-grown as possible. We offer a selection of organic wines and beers. Our own spring water is available for drinking. The two suites open on to the garden and offer quiet seclusion. The 2.5-acre garden, organic for over forty years, is open under the National Gardens Scheme twice a year.

info@thenurtons.co.uk www.thenurtons.co.uk

CLYNDERWEN *(S-C)*

FFYNNON SAMSON 481

Llangolman
Clynderwen SA66 7QL
Tel: 01437 532542

Farmhouse: sleeps 4-5, £240-£530 per week
Home cooked organic meals (Fri, Sat, Sun)

Complimentary organic box of food,
vegetables and eggs

Soil Association

A working organic farm nestled beneath the enchanting Preseli hills. Located on the crest of a hill, the farm affords breathtaking views. On the border of the National Park, we link to a large network of footpaths and bridleways and the Bluestone cycle trails. You are welcome to roam on the farm which comprises of pastureland, mixed woodland, and a marshland hosting rare butterflies and orchids near the river border. An area is given over to an organic market garden, and seasonally produced vegetables, fruit and eggs are available for guests to order. Home cooked organic three course meals are on offer on Friday, Saturday and Sunday evenings. We do our utmost to use locally produced ingredients.

info@enjoypreseli.co.uk www.enjoypreseli.co.uk

CRYMYCH (S-C)

TAN Y BRYN 482

Brynberian
Crymych SA41 3TN
Tel: 01239 891294

Cottage: sleeps 8+
£375-£875 pw

Organic produce available locally

A traditional stone cottage with an interconnecting converted barn and conservatory. It is situated on a smallholding which is run on organic principles, in a tranquil valley in the Pembrokeshire Coast National Park. Furnished in a simple country style, the cottage has exposed beams, solid wood surfaces, quarry tiled floor and french doors to a stone-flagged grassy area outside. Tan y Bryn adjoins the beautiful and unspoilt countryside of the Preseli Hills, which is rich in birds and other wildlife. There are ancient oak woodlands and many prehistoric sites nearby. We are just four and a half miles from the breathtaking Pembrokeshire coastline, with its beautiful beaches and 180 miles of coastal footpath.

mansel@tanybryn.com   www.tanybryn.com

FISHGUARD (S-C)

HAYLOFT AND BARN 483

Ffynnonston
Dwrbach SA65 9QT
Tel: 01348 873004

Hayloft: sleeps 2, £225-£455 pw
Barn: sleeps 6, £250-£580 pw

Fresh organic produce available in season

Soil Association

This stone-built 18th-century hayloft is to be found down a little lane, set within an organic smallholding about a mile from Fishguard. The character of the building has been retained through stone walls, pine cladding and antique quarry tiles. Windows are small with glimpses of garden, lane and distant hills. One door opens onto a secluded garden, the other onto the old farmyard. There is also a stone barn, which sleeps six. A variety of fresh organic produce is available in season. The area is quiet and peaceful and there are many good walks. The Pembrokeshire Coast National Park, Gwaun Valley, Preseli Hills, beautiful secluded beaches are all within easy reach. We welcome dogs.

annhicks@waitrose.com

HAVERFORDWEST *(B&B)*   CUFFERN MANOR   484

Roch
Haverfordwest SA62 6HB
Tel: 01437 710071

Country House B&B, £30-£35 pppn
Vegetarian Evening Meal (by arrangement)

Meals are at least 90% organic (we aim for 100% organic)

Georgian manor house and a walled kitchen garden in three acres of woods. We can take groups of up to twenty. Ideal for family occasions or courses and conferences. Three double ensuites, two twin, two singles (each with wash hand basin) and three standard double rooms. A substantial packed lunch can be provided. Vegetarian / vegan evening meals available when required. All our own soft fruit and vegetables, from our one acre walled garden, are organic. We aim for 100% organic but sometimes buy fairtrade fruit, which may not be organic. Pembrokeshire Produce Award 2006 for 'best use of local food'. Cuffern Manor is three miles from the coastal path and the two mile long sandy beach at Newgale.

enquiries@cuffernmanor.co.uk   www.cuffernmanor.co.uk

HAVERFORDWEST *(B&B)*   LOWER DRUIDSTON B&B   485

Druidston
Haverfordwest SA62 3NE
Tel: 01437 781318

Farmhouse Bed and Breakfast
£26-£30 pppn

Home produce, local produce, organic produce

Lower Druidston Farm (WTB 4-stars) is situated at the end of a no-through road, 600 yards from the coastal path. On our 5-acre smallholding we grow a wide range of naturally produced vegetables and, in particular, soft fruit. Our own produce is served, in season, as part of your breakfast or packed lunch. Homemade preserves are a feature of both breakfasts and the welcoming afternoon teas. Other local produce, such as free-range eggs and organic meat, are obtained from farms within a mile of Lower Druidston. Druidston beach, a beautiful natural sandy beach with high cliffs, caves and rock pools, is twenty minutes walk away. Two other natural sandy beaches are within three miles, both ideal for families.

druidston@madasafish.com

HAVERFORDWEST *(S-C)*

LOWER DRUIDSTON   486

Druidston
Haverfordwest SA62 3NE
Tel: 01437 781318

Caravan: sleeps 4
£175-£295 pw

Chemical-free fruit and vegetables grown on the farm available to buy

Lower Druidston Farm is a five-acre smallholding, growing chemical-free fruit and vegetables. It is situated at the end of a no-through road, 600 yards from the 180 mile coastal path. Magnificent views of St Brides Bay can be enjoyed from the adjacent fields. The 28 foot caravan is situated in its own secluded area with private access. There is only one caravan on the farm and guests have access to two nearby fields. Chemical-free fruit and vegetables grown on the farm are available to buy. Druidston beach, a beautiful natural sandy beach with high cliffs, caves and rock pools, is just a twenty minute walk away. There are also two other natural sandy beaches within three miles of the caravan, both ideal for families.

druidston@madasafish.com

HAVERFORDWEST *(Camping)*

SHORTLANDS FARM   487

Druidston
Haverfordwest SA62 3NE
Tel: 01437 781234

Caravan: sleeps 4, £175-£270 per week
Camping, £3.50 pppn

Organic produce (lamb, beef and black puddings, fruit, vegetables) in season

Soil Association

Shortlands Farm, overlooking St Brides Bay within the Pembrokeshire Coast National Park, is home to a variety of traditional and rare breed cattle and sheep. We sell our organic beef, lamb and award-winning black puddings at local farmers' markets, and are recommended by Rick Stein as one of his 'local food heroes'. The caravan is just a short walk from a secluded sandy beach. It sleeps up to four adults in two bedrooms, and is available to rent from March to the end of October. The large sitting room, with dining area, has a gas fire, colour TV with video and DVD player. The well equipped kitchen has a full size gas cooker, fridge, microwave. The Pembrokeshire Coast Path runs through the farm.

info@bumpylane.co.uk   www.bumpylane.co.uk

HAVERFORDWEST *(S-C)*

THE OLD GRANARY   488

Shortlands Farm
Druidston SA62 3NE
Tel: 01437 781234

Converted Barn: sleeps 2-4
£285-£460 pw

Organic produce (lamb, beef and black puddings, fruit, vegetables) in season

Soil Association

A sympathetically restored stone and slate farm building available as a low-allergen holiday let. The lime mortar walls and timber have eco-friendly finishes, and the wood / slate floors, bedding, furniture and furnishings have been chosen to minimise problems for those with chemical sensitivities. Ideal for two people, with a double bed in the sleeping loft (accessed via a ladder), but could sleep four by using the bed settee. Our own organic rare breed lamb and beef, and home-grown organic fruit and vegetables, are available in season for guests to buy. There is a garden, with wooden furniture, for the exclusive use of visitors. The Old Granary has wonderful sea views, with a sandy beach ten minutes walk away.

info@bumpylane.co.uk   www.bumpylane.co.uk

HAVERFORDWEST *(Camping)*

TRELLYN CAMPING   489

Abercastle
Haverfordwest SA62 5HJ
Tel: 01348 837762

Yurts, Tipi, Camping
£140-£625 pw

On site home-grown vegetables, fresh local landed fish, lobster, crab, mackerel

A very small campsite with two yurts, two tipis and five pitches, set in 16 acres of a conservation project just yards from the sea in the Pembrokeshire National Park. We take a maximum of 40 guests or so on our holding. We provide wood and adjustable barbecue / grills, and encourage visitors to cook as much as possible on the open fire. Chill out around your very own campfire – this is what we are all about. Look up at the stars and watch the bats come out to play. The yurts and tipis provide a luxury camping experience that won't be spoilt by the weather. An organic ethos smallholding with meadows, ponds and woods to explore, aimed primarily at those looking for a low-impact family holiday.

camping@trellyn.co.uk   www.trellyn.co.uk

KILGETTY *(B&B)*

KNOWLES FARM 490

Lawrenny
Kilgetty SA68 0PX
Tel: 01834 891221

Farmhouse Bed and Breakfast, £30-£35 pppn
Evening Meal £12, 4 course organic £22

80% organic breakfast, organic meals on request

Soil Association

A lovely farmhouse amidst an organic arable and dairy farm, with a romantic estuary snaking its way around the boundary. The natural beauty of the farm, with its ancient hanging woods, teeming bird and wild animal life, makes for a holiday in itself. There are walks through the woods and along the shore, boating on the river, picnics on the front lawn – and then there's the coast. Only nine miles away you will find beaches, cliffs and coves. Castles, gardens, galleries, theme parks, fishing and riding – all these are only minutes away. Come and share our special corner of Pembrokeshire. See the stars and enjoy the peace. Bring your own wine and you can dine here on delicious organic meals in the evenings.

ginilp@lawrenny.org.uk   www.lawrenny.org.uk

LLANDISSILIO *(S-C)*

DOVE COTTAGE 491

Dyffryn Isaf
Llandissilio SA66 7QD
Tel: 01437 563657

Cottage: sleeps 4, £160-£340 pw
Short Breaks (October-April)

Honey, eggs, some home produced vegetables

Soil Association

Come and enjoy a relaxing holiday on our small organic farm. The holiday cottage has two bedrooms. We are located in a quiet valley, central for the beautiful Pembrokeshire coast and the Preseli Hills. You can also spend your time walking over our fields meeting our sheep, goats and chickens, learn about organic farming, or you can relax in the small private garden behind the cottage. Take a seat next to our pond and observe the wildlife, or enjoy a local walk through the quiet rural landscape around us. We also use and sell the wool from our Shetland sheep, so be inspired for your next craft project. Fresh farm produce for sale – normally we have home produced vegetables, eggs and honey available.

bettinab@dsl.pipex.com   www.pembrokeshire-organic-holidays.co.uk

NARBERTH *(S-C / Camping)*

ROSE PARK FARM 492

Llanteg
Narberth SA67 8QJ
Tel: 01834 831111

Cottage: sleeps 4, £470 pw
Camping, Caravan £10-£12 pn

Our own organic lamb sold at the farm shop in season

Soil Association

Rose Park is a 50-acre organic farm set in the heart of the beautiful Pembrokeshire countryside. Wake up to breathtaking views of Caldey Island and the beautiful Colby Lodge estate on our recently landscaped three and a half acre touring caravan and camping site. We have 28 hard standing pitches for tourers / motor homes, and a separate area for 20 tents. The newly built cottage has a patio with a picnic table. We have a newly restored bridleway and footpath running through the farm that leads on to the coastal path. Staying at Rose Park Organic Farm is an ideal retreat from the hustle and bustle of the towns, but within easy reach of Amroth, Saundersfoot, Pendine Sands and Tenby.

darranandwendy.james@virgin.net

NARBERTH *(S-C)*

BLACKMOOR FARM 493

Ludchurch
Narberth SA67 8JH
Tel: 01834 831242

Cottages: sleep 2-6, £280-£520 pw
Caravans: sleep 2-6, £180-£448 pw

Organic and local produce at Wisebuys Farm Shop (3 miles)

Soil Association

Blackmoor Farm, surrounded by our own 36 acres of pastureland, offers a relaxed holiday atmosphere where children can play in safety. The three cottages are set in an attractive sunny courtyard, architect-designed and purpose-built with country-style furniture and equipment. The caravans are set in a lawned area with a concrete path to each one and excellent parking facilities. The site is pleasantly sheltered by mature trees and there is every opportunity for a relaxed holiday away from the bustle of everyday life. The farm is within two miles of Amroth on the coast, with its large sandy beach backed by cliffs. The National Park footpath starts here, stretching for 168 miles around the Pembrokeshire coast.

ltecornth@aol.com   www.blackmoorfarm.co.uk

NEWPORT *(Camping)*

TYCANOL FARM 494

Newport
SA42 0ST
Tel: 01239 820264

Camping Barn: sleeps 4, £12 pppn
Caravan: sleeps 4 £25 p2pn, Camping £7 pppn

Organic food available locally

Soil Association

Tycanol is an organic farm close to the beautiful Pembrokeshire coast. The farm offers simple old-fashioned accommodation for four in a small camping barn with a fantastic view. There are no meals provided on this 2-star site but the camping barn has self-catering facilities. Organic produce can be bought from the wholefood shop in Newport, which is fifteen minutes walk away, and from Fishguard Farmers' Market (held fortnightly). For larger groups there is a camp site for tents and caravans which overlooks the whole of Newport Bay. There is a nature trail on the farm which contains badger setts. The camp site is situated on the coastal path, and we are just two minutes from our own beach.

www.caravancampingsites.co.uk/pembrokeshire/tycanolfarm.htm

ST DAVIDS *(S-C)*

CAERFAI BAY COTTAGES 495

Caerfai Organic Farm
St Davids SA62 6QT
Tel: 01437 720548

Cottages: sleep 1-6
£230-£870 pw

Organic farm shop (open May-August)

Soil Association

Caerfai Organic Farm, a 140-acre coastal farm, is just half a mile from St Davids. The farm's organic enterprises include milk ('green top' licensed), cheeses, potatoes, beef and cereals. We use our own organic unpasteurised milk to produce three types of cheese on the farm – Cheddar, Caerfilly, Caerfilly with leek and garlic. In high season (May-August) we operate a small organic shop. Set within the Pembrokeshire Coast National Park, the cottages once formed part of the old farmstead at Caerfai Farm. Each of the four cottages has its own grounds, away from the present farm buildings. It's only a 350 yard walk to beautiful Caerfai Bay, a sandy bathing cove with many colourful and fascinating rock pools.

chrismevans69@hotmail.com   www.caerfai.co.uk

ST DAVIDS *(B&B)*

CAERHYS FARM 496

Berea
St Davids SA62 6DX
Tel: 01348 831244

Farmhouse Bed and Breakfast
£30-£35 pppn

All produce is sourced organic and locally when possible

Soil Association

Enjoy an organic farm holiday at Caerhys Farm, on the picturesque coastline of north Pembrokeshire. Built in 1864, the farmhouse was extended and modernised in 1982. It includes a large sitting / breakfast room with lovely beamed ceilings and a beautiful stone fireplace. The two main windows in the room have fantastic sea views of Abereiddy. All produce for breakfast is sourced organic and local where possible. You are welcome to see the crops and animals on this unique organic coastal farm. See the rare breed 'Oxford Sandy and Black' pigs and Welsh Black suckler herd. We're half a mile from Abereiddy beach, home to the fantastic Blue Lagoon, and five miles from the white sands near St Davids.

caerhysbandb@hotmail.com   www.organic-holidays.co.uk

ST DAVIDS *(S-C)*

DAN Y GRAIG 497

Caerhys Farm
Berea SA62 6DX
Tel: 01348 831244

Cottage: sleeps 6
£250-£550 pw

Organic produce direct from the farmer

Soil Association

Enjoy an organic farm holiday at Caerhys Farm. A warm welcome awaits you at this appealing character cottage, set on a family-run organic farm in the beautiful countryside of the Pembrokeshire National Park. You are welcome to learn about organic farming, see the rare breed 'Oxford Sandy and Black' organic pigs and our Welsh Black suckler herd, or simply relax in the secluded garden. The coastal path, especially beautiful in May and June with all the flowers at their best, is less than ten minutes away. Wonderful views of Abereiddi and the coast from the farmyard. Pembrokeshire is well known for its beautiful coastline and unspoilt scenery, with a vast choice of activities waiting for you to explore.

ann@organic-holidays.co.uk   www.organic-holidays.co.uk/cottage.htm

ST DAVIDS *(Camping)*

TREGINNIS UCHAF 498

Treginnis Uchaf
St Davids SA62 6RS
Tel: 01437 720234

CL Caravan Site, from £6 pn
Open all year (phone to check availability)

Organic produce in St Davids (one and a half miles)

Soil Association

Spectacular views of the countryside can be seen from your caravan on the spacious level ground grass site. Sheep graze in the nearby fields, in March / April with their newborn lambs. Ducks, cormorants, and the occasional heron visit the man-made pond across the fields. Foxes and badgers can also be seen in the valley from the caravan site. The most spectacular sunsets can be enjoyed. Walking access to the Pembrokeshire Coastal Path is within five minutes to Porthllisky Bay with its fascinating rock pools and clear waters for bathing. Cold water drinking tap. Chemical disposal point with cold water tap. Batteries can be charged. Treginnis Uchaf is only one and a half miles from St Davids.

davies@treginnis.co.uk www.treginnis.co.uk/caravan/index.html

ST DAVIDS *(S-C)*

TY MORTIMER 499

Treginnis Uchaf
St Davids SA62 6RS
Tel: 01437 720234

Cottage: sleeps 5, £300-£660 per week
Short Breaks, from £160

Organic produce in St Davids (one and a half miles)

Soil Association

With outstanding views, Treginnis is situated in one of the most picturesque peninsula areas of the Pembrokeshire National Park. Ty Mortimer is set in a farmyard complex of traditional stone buildings. The quiet beach of Porthllisky, with its beautiful rock pools, is five hundred yards away. Easy accessibility to explore the magnificent coastal path. Many varied walks nearby – some coastal and spectacular, particularly with the sunsets – others more serene and gentle, capturing the essence of wild flowers and bird-watching. Porpoises and seals are a delight to see. Treginnis is a National Trust working organic farm with a breeding flock of 800 ewes. During spring and early summer lambs gambol in the fields.

davies@treginnis.co.uk www.treginnis.co.uk

ST DAVID'S *(Hotel)*

TYF ECO HOTEL 500

Caerfai Road
St David's SA62 6QS
Tel: 01437 721678

B&B £30-£40, HB £45-£55, FB £50-£60 pppn
Organic Restaurant

Almost all the food and drink we serve in
the restaurant is organic

Quality Welsh Food Certification Ltd

TYF Eco Hotel is an 18th-century converted windmill with green credentials. The hotel recently became the first organic certified hotel in Wales, through the Welsh Organic Scheme. The kitchen works with the rhythms of the seasons, and the core of our organic restaurant's repertoire is focused on high quality Welsh produce that's bursting with flavour. An excellent range of organic wine, beer and cider is available to complement your meal. The hotel is only a few minutes walk away from the beach, the Pembrokeshire Coast Path, and the centre of the historic city of St David's. This small city, surrounded by awe-inspiring landscapes and seascapes, is aiming to become Britain's first carbon neutral city.

stay@tyf.com www.tyf.com/?c=acc-felin

WHITLAND *(S-C)*

GWARMACWYDD FARM 501

Gwarmacwydd Farm
Llanfallteg SA34 0XH
Tel: 01437 563260

Cottages: sleep 2-6
£240-£570 pw

Local organic produce can be ordered

Organic Farmers & Growers

A country estate of over 450 acres set in the Vale of the River Taf. Our working organic farm uses a sustainable system of farming which respects the welfare needs of the land, environment, animals and people. Wildlife abounds. Enjoy the beauty of the south-west Wales countryside. Amble for one and a half miles along the river banks, or pause to fish for salmon or trout. Walk the old Whitland to Cardigan railway, a fantastic nature trail. Picnic amidst wooded glades. Explore the many paths that lead among grassy meadows. Walk through 50 acres of ancient oak and ash woodlands. Sandy beaches with rock pools and old county towns only 20 minutes drive. Book online via our website.

www.gwarmacwydd.co.uk

ABERCRAF *(B&B)*

THE PHOENIX RETREAT 502

School Road
Abercraf SA9 1XD
Tel: 01639 730218

Retreats, Courses, Therapies
See website for more information

Organic vegetarian and vegan food, at least
80% organic

A warm welcome to the Swansea valley, gateway to the south Brecon Beacons. All rooms are standard double, twin, or deluxe ensuite with naturally varnished wood floors, decorated with organic paints. It is an eco-friendly, chemical-free, mobile-free, EMF sanitised environment with vegan organic liquid soap in the bathrooms. Courses include meditation, vegetarian / vegan, self-empowerment, self-esteem, de-tox, healing, relax and rejuvenate. Bespoke courses can be created just for you, couples, groups or corporations. A great variety of therapies offered individually or to combine. Children and youths welcomed with parents / teachers. Special rates for groups of more than four and youth organisations

happiness@thephoenixretreat.co.uk www.thephoenixretreat.co.uk

BRECON *(S-C)*

BRYNIAU PELL 503

Aberhyddnant Organic Farm
Crai LD3 8YS
Tel: 01874 636797

Cottage: sleeps 4+2 cots, from £288 pw
Short Breaks, from £72 pn

A wide selection of organic produce is
available to order in advance

Quality Welsh Food Certification Ltd

Tranquil organic hill farm nestling in the breathtaking scenery of the Brecon Beacons National Park. The cottage has been converted to a high standard from an existing farm building providing comfortable accommodation with a cottage feel. Our 220-acre farm produces organic beef, pork and lamb, which you can buy along with our organic eggs and vegetables, whilst caring for the environment and abundant wildlife. The fields, sheltered by hedgerows and woodland, are managed under a whole farm environmental scheme. Farm stock includes cattle, sheep, pigs and chickens. Fresh spring water flows from the taps and there are thousands of acres of hillside adjoining the farm waiting to be explored.

info@abercottages.com www.abercottages.com

BRECON *(B&B)*

CASTLE ST. RESTAURANT   504

20 Castle Street
Brecon LD3 9BU
Tel: 01874 624392

Bed and Breakfast, £30-£60 room pn
Restaurant

Around 75% organic produce used in the
restaurant and breakfast

Good food and accommodation in the heart of the Brecon Beacons National Park. Our B&B and restaurant are in a Grade II listed townhouse less than five minutes walk from the centre of Brecon. We support local and small producers and aim to be organic and seasonal. All our dishes in the restaurant are freshly prepared and cooked to order. We use organic fruit and vegetables from Beacons Veggie Boxes, organic cheese from Caws Cenarth, organic wine from Vinceremos, as much other organic produce (flour, sugar, etc) as possible, and local caught fish. Salads are made using fresh local, mostly organic ingredients. We recycle our waste and aim to use environmental and recycled products.

carolynsharples@yahoo.co.uk www.castlestreetrestaurant.co.uk

BRECON *(S-C)*

NYTH Y WENNOL   505

Aberhyddnant Organic Farm
Crai LD3 8YS
Tel: 01874 636797

Cottage: sleeps 6+2 cots from £288 pw
Short Breaks, from £72 pn

Organic food and produce available to
visitors

Quality Welsh Food Certification Ltd

Tranquil organic hill farm nestling in the breathtaking scenery of the Brecon Beacons National Park. The cottage has been converted to a high standard from an existing farm building providing comfortable accommodation with a cottage feel. Our 220-acre farm produces organic beef, pork and lamb, which you can buy along with our organic eggs and vegetables, whilst caring for the environment and abundant wildlife. The fields, sheltered by hedgerows and woodland, are managed under a whole farm environmental scheme. Farm stock includes cattle, sheep, pigs and chickens. Fresh spring water flows from the taps. There are thousands of acres of hillside adjoining the farm waiting to be explored.

info@abercottages.com www.abercottages.com

BRECON *(S-C)*

PENPONT   506

Penpont
Brecon LD3 8EU
Tel: 01874 636202

Courtyard Wing: sleeps 13-17, from £1,350 pw
£800 2 night w/end, £900 3 night w/end

Our organic vegetables are available for guests to buy

Soil Association

Penpont is one of the finest houses situated within the heart of the Brecon Beacons National Park. This privately owned Grade I listed house has been home to the same family since it was first built in about 1666. It lies in the middle of a 2,000-acre working rural estate. Guest accommodation is in the courtyard wing. Around the house lie extensive grounds, sweeping lawns, the old Victorian rose and walled gardens, riverside and woodland walks, all weather tennis court. We are currently an organic demonstration unit, so host a number of conferences per year in conjunction with The Organic Centre Wales. Our organic vegetables are available for guests to buy (we suggest you pre-order before you arrive).

penpont@btconnect.com www.penpont.com

BRECON *(Hotel)*

PETERSTONE COURT   507

Llanhamlach
Brecon LD3 7YB
Tel: 01874 665387

Bed and Breakfast, double £90-£170 pn
Dinner B&B, double £150-£230 pn

Food from our family farm, all locally sourced and organic where possible

Peterstone Court country hotel and spa is situated in the heart of the Brecon Beacons National Park. The hotel is avant-garde and distinctive in its style, and the bedrooms are all large, light spaces. Food is of huge importance to us – most of the meat and poultry on our menu is reared on our family farm (Glaisfer Uchaf) just down the road, so we know exactly what our animals have been fed throughout their life. We hope this will help lessen our carbon impact on the environment. Our food is always seasonal, sustainable and simple, using fresh, organic where possible, home-reared ingredients. Our spa also uses only natural, organic products, a philosophy which has filtered down from the main house.

info@peterstone-court.com www.peterstone-court.com

BRECON *(B&B)*

PRIMROSE CENTRE B&B   508

Felindre
Hay-on-Wye LD3 0ST
Tel: 01497 847636

Bed and Breakfast
£22 pppn

Mainly organic and sourced locally where possible

Soil Association

Our B&B (one double, one twin, one single, two bathrooms) is traditional and simple but comfortable. We have a well established organic fruit and vegetable smallholding at the foot of the Black Mountains near Hay-on-Wye. Managed using organic and sustainable permaculture principles, it's a wonderful example of productivity in harmony with nature. The productive area includes half an acre of forest garden with a hundred varieties of fruit and nut trees. The holding is a Soil Association demonstration farm. We focus on creating healthy and wholesome food, using organic where possible, some straight from our abundant garden. Awarded Level 2 of the Green Dragon environmental standard.

jan.benham@ukonline.co.uk www.organic-sacred-earth.co.uk

BRECON *(B&B)*

PRIMROSE RETREATS   509

Felindre
Hay-on-Wye LD3 0ST
Tel: 01497 847636

Retreats and Residential Courses
£30 pppn (inc all meals), £200 pppw

Mainly organic food from the farm or sourced locally where possible

Soil Association

Variety of holistic courses encouraging respect for the earth. Courses on sound healing and sustainable living. Encouraging a connection with nature and the earth for grounding. Understanding of growing healthy food in harmony with the environment and creatively turning into nutritious and flavoursome meals. Quiet retreats for de-stressing from busy lives. Situated at the foot of the Black Mountains. A peaceful setting amidst beautiful gardens on a well established organic fruit and vegetable smallholding using permaculture principles. Simple but lovely retreat space in the peace garden. Alternatively one double, one twin, one single room available. Traditional but comfortable. Sorry no dogs, no TV.

jan.benham@ukonline.co.uk www.organic-sacred-earth.co.uk

BRECON *(Camping)*

SMALL FARMS CAMPSITE 510

Lower Porthamel
Talgarth LD3 0DL
Tel: 01874 712125

Camping, Adult £6, Child £2.50

Small children free of charge

Farm shop and café on site

Organic Farmers & Growers

Camp in the orchard at Lower Porthamel organic farm in the beautiful Wye Valley. Facilities include a loo block with hot showers, and a wash room. We have a small children's play area. Walk our Nature Trail through fields, down the old railway line and along the River Llynfi. The shop sells our own beef, lamb, pork, poultry. Fresh seasonal vegetables are available straight from the farm, and we have chosen the very best organic Welsh cheeses. Enjoy organic fairtrade coffee and tea, lemonade, and homemade cakes and tarts at our café. We can make up a delicious plate for you from our deli range, with garden salad leaves and healthy locally baked breads. Dogs very welcome with well trained owners.

joeldurrell@yahoo.com www.smallfarms.co.uk

BRECON *(B&B)*

UPPER MIDDLE ROAD FARM 511

Boughrood
Brecon LD3 0BX
Tel: 01874 754407

Farm Bed and Breakfast, £25 pppn
Evening Meal, £12-£15 (by arrangement)

Produce is from our own farm and garden or locally sourced

Set at 550 feet above the Wye Valley, our 5-acre working smallholding is run along organic lines. The house, once a wheelwright's cottage, is over 150 years old. We keep a small flock of sheep, which provide meat for the house and fleece to spin and dye. Two goats provide milk, which is regularly made into cheese. Free-range hens provide the eggs. Breakfast includes freshly home-baked bread using Doves Farm organic flour, homemade yogurt, jams and marmalade. Fruit from the garden available in season. All meals are freshly cooked with a Welsh flavour, using mainly produce from our own farm and garden, or locally sourced. We have achieved level two of the Green Dragon environmental award.

info@uppermiddleroad.co.uk www.uppermiddleroad.co.uk

BUILTH WELLS *(B&B)*

TRERICKET MILL 512

Erwood
Builth Wells LD2 3TQ
Tel: 01982 560312

Vegetarian Guest House, B&B £28-£32 pppn
Supper £7.50, Evening Meal from £13.50

Wholesome meals using organic and local
produce where possible

Grade II listed water corn mill overlooking the River Wye offering a range of informal accommodation. B&B in the guest house, a cosy traditional bunkhouse, and a campsite set in the old cider orchard. Trericket Mill has a unique historic atmosphere, complete with original milling machinery, log fires, books, games, a riverside garden within a designated SSSI. All the catering is vegetarian, from breakfast (£7) to simple suppers (£7.50) or evening meals (two course £13.50, three course £17.50), using wholefoods, organic, free-range and fairtrade produce wherever possible. Eggs are from our free-range ducks and hens during the laying season. Natural chemical-free water is provided by our private source.

mail@trericket.co.uk www.trericket.co.uk

CAERSWS *(S-C)*

THE HIDEAWAY 513

Gorfanc
Carno SY17 5JP
Tel: 01686 420423

Barn Loft: sleeps 2+2
£222-£251 pw, £87-£95 2 nights

Organically grown home produce in season

From the balcony entrance to The Hideaway you'll see only hills and woods. This fold in the hills of Trannon Moor is on the edge of the Cambrian Mountains. Surrounded by meadows, hedgerows and wild open upland you can walk for miles with only sheep paths to follow or potter along the tree-lined stream valley. Gorfanc is a traditional stone upland dwelling set in a peaceful and wild, but productive, garden. Organically grown produce from our garden may be available to buy, along with honey from our bees, homemade organic wholemeal bread, jams and pickles. Eggs come from Muriel's free-range hens at the bottom of the hill. Tents are also welcome (£4 pppn), in secluded locations with lovely views.

wildwood@deeppool.fsnet.co.uk

CRICKHOWELL *(S-C)*

OAKVIEW 514

Graig Barn Farm
Llangenny Lane NP8 1HB
Tel: 01873 810275

Apartments: sleep 2-6, £350-£500 pw
Short Breaks, £70-£100 pn (min 2 nights)

Can be ordered from Graig Farm Organics
on-line shop

Quality Welsh Food Certification Ltd

Superbly located barn conversion to two self-contained 4-star apartments with magnificent views over the Usk Valley. The top floor apartment caters for six, the ground floor accommodates four (both can be let as one unit for a maximum of ten). Significant reductions made for just two people staying. Drying room to facilitate walkers and cyclists. Outside there's a summerhouse with a barbecue area. To the rear of the property is a 10-acre bluebell wood. Graig Barn, our small family-run organic farm, is situated in the Brecon Beacons National Park. It's in a peaceful location on the slopes of the Black Mountains, near the quaint little town of Crickhowell. Our latest venture is an organic apple juice business.

johng.morris@virgin.net www.oakview-cottages.co.uk

LLANDRINDOD WELLS *(B&B)*

CWMLLECHWEDD FAWR 515

Llanbister
Llandrindod Wells LD1 6UH
Tel: 01597 840267

Farmhouse Bed and Breakfast, £30-£35 pppn
Evening Meal, £18

Around 75% organic

Soil Association

Cwmllechwedd Fawr is a 108-acre organic hill farm in the former county of Radnorshire, now part of Powys. The house is set back from the road and overlooks a broad shallow valley. Breakfast is served in the large farmhouse kitchen. After a day's excursion supper is served in the elegant dining room, with its stone floor and large woodburning stove. Where possible and according to the season, you will be served our own organically grown vegetables, salads, fruit and home produced meat. Explore the Welsh Borderlands (the Welsh Marches) – rich in history, or the wild Cambrian Mountains. The countryside is unspoilt, and is a haven for walkers, bird-watchers and those who enjoy a semi-wild landscape.

postmaster@cwmllechwedd.u-net.com www.cwmllechwedd.u-net.com

LLANDRINDOD WELLS (B&B)   PENLANOLE   516

Llanwrthwl
Llandrindod Wells LDI 6NN
Tel: 01597 810266

Bed and Breakfast
£25 pppn

Organic breakfast with bacon, sausages and eggs sourced from our own farm

Organic Farmers & Growers

Penlanole nestles in the breathtaking Wye Valley land. Our 40-acre organic farm is home to cows, sheep, and saddleback pigs ranging over ancient woodland, orchards and peat bog through to a kitchen garden, duck pond and hay meadow. Choose from a double room with an ensuite bathroom, or two double rooms with use of a shared bathroom, all with fabulous views of the surrounding countryside. Attic bedrooms are also available for children, or adults, who fancy something more adventurous. An organic breakfast, with bacon, sausages and eggs sourced from our own farm, can be served in the bright elegance of the dining room or in the warm informality of the family kitchen.

info@penlanole-organics.co.uk www.penlanole-organics.co.uk

LLANDRINDOD WELLS (Camping)   PENLANOLE   517

Llanwrthwl
Llandrindod Wells LDI 6NN
Tel: 01597 810266

Stable: sleeps 4, £50 pn
Camping

Buy fresh organic produce from the farm

Organic Farmers & Growers

A family of four or a group of friends can take over the converted stable block, which has a youth hostel-style shared sleeping platform, loo and basin, and basic cooking facilities. For the more outdoorsy types, camping pitches are available in the apple orchard and well-drained field close to the main house. In October / November the annual apple harvesting and pressing party yields delicious fresh organic apple juice, which we sell as a speciality. We welcome and encourage volunteers of all ages to join in with farm tasks and seasonal activities such as haymaking, lambing and apple pressing. Exhausted farm hands can then collapse under the stunning star-spangled Penlanole night sky.

info@penlanole-organics.co.uk www.penlanole-organics.co.uk

LLANWRTYD WELLS *(Hotel)* LASSWADE HOTEL 518

Station Road
Llanwrtyd Wells LD5 4RW
Tel: 01591 610515

Small Hotel, B&B from £37.50 pppn
Restaurant (3 course dinner £28)

Choose from a selection of fresh, local,
mostly organic food

Comfortable period country house hotel offering friendly hospitality, magnificent views and high quality food and drink in the heart of Wales, between the Cambrian Mountains and the Brecon Beacons. All our produce is sourced fresh, local and mostly organic, with a daily changing menu. We use single estate tea, coffee and fairtrade products. We have an AA Rosette for our restaurant. Good Food Guide listed 2004-2008. We were the first eco-friendly and organic hotel and restaurant in Wales. Other accolades include the Green Dragon Environmental Award and Considerate Hoteliers Award. We are the pioneers of food transportation by railway. A discount is available for those travelling here by train.

info@lasswadehotel.co.uk www.lasswadehotel.co.uk

MACHYNLLETH *(Camping)* ECO RETREATS 519

Dyfi Valley
SY20 8PG
Tel: 01654 781375

Furnished Tipis and Yurts
From £295 per tipi for 2 nights

Organic and fairtrade basic provisions
provided

Organic Farmers & Growers

Romantic and secluded tipi and yurt retreats on an organic Welsh hill farm far from anywhere, deep in the Dyfi Forest. Our tipis are beautifully and simply furnished with woodburning stoves, cushions and luxurious fabrics. Each tipi is set in its own space on our breathtaking site, so you can just enjoy being together. We pride ourselves on our ethical stance and take the time to source good quality certified organic fare, from tea and coffee to wine, from the sheepskins to the shampoo. We're in the process of replacing all our sheets and towels with organic fairtrade unbleached cotton. We include a holistic therapy and twilight meditation session, as well as tickets for the Centre for Alternative Technology.

chananb@ecoretreats.co.uk www.ecoretreats.co.uk

MACHYNLLETH *(S-C)*

GLANLLYNMAWR 520

Nant-y-Nodyn
Dinas Mawddwy SY20 9AG
Tel: 01650 531330

Farmhouse: sleeps 6
£240-£560 pw

Organic and local produce at the Quarry
Shop and Café in Machynlleth

Soil Association

This 17th-century farmhouse nestles in the valley above the River Dovey. The interior of the house retains its traditional character with a wealth of original beams and is tastefully furnished. Mawddwy is an unspoilt, quiet valley in the superb scenery of the southern Snowdonia National Park. Nant-y-Nodyn's four self-catering cottages, a quarter of a mile apart, are situated in this valley about two miles from the wool village of Dinas Mawddwy and near the highest pass in Wales, which leads to Lake Vyrnwy and Bala Lake. The cottages are part of a sheep and beef organic farm, which has been positively managed with conservation in mind, and guests are welcome to explore and enjoy the wildlife.

elwyn@nantynodyn.fsnet.co.uk www.nantynodyn.co.uk

MACHYNLLETH *(B&B)*

GWALIA FARM B&B 521

Cemmaes
Machynlleth SY20 9PZ
Tel: 01650 511377

Vegetarian Bed and Breakfast, £25 pppn
Evening Meal (by arrangement)

Wholefood, homemade, organic meals

Gwalia Farm is a peaceful, traditional smallholding with goats, hens and sheep in the remote hills of Mid Wales. The large organic garden provides an abundance of vegetables and soft fruit for home cooked, wholefood vegetarian meals, together with our own milk, free-range eggs and homemade jams. A conservation area has a tranquil lake with native trees and amazing pond life, and here you will also find a diving board and canoes. There are beautiful views of the mountains at the southern edge of Snowdonia National Park. Enjoy a log fire, spring water, good walking, bird-watching, dragonflies, stargazing – and silence. The Centre for Alternative Technology is about seven miles from the farm.

www.gwaliafarm.co.uk

MACHYNLLETH (S-C)

HENDRERON COTTAGE 522

Penyglog
Aberhosan SY20 8SG
Tel: 01654 702033

Cottage: sleeps 6
£220-£500 pw

Local organic food is readily available in
Machynlleth (4 miles)

In Conversion

The tastefully renovated 18th-century miner's cottage is part of an organic beef and sheep farm with glorious views of the surrounding unspoilt Mid-Wales countryside. Renovated to a high standard, it has three bedrooms sleeping six people with all linen provided. The kitchen / diner is all electric, and there is a large family lounge with the original beams, inglenook and original bread oven retained. Outside is an enclosed garden with a barbecue and garden furniture. Visitors are more than welcome to take walks on the farm to see the abundant wildlife and wide variety birds, especially the red kite. Local organic food is readily available in the small country market town of Machynlleth (4 miles).

d.b.evans@btinternet.com

MACHYNLLETH (S-C)

LLANERCH   523

Nant-y-Nodyn
Dinas Mawddwy SY20 9AG
Tel: 01650 531330

Farmhouse: sleeps 6
£240-£560 pw

Organic and local produce at the Quarry
Shop and Café in Machynlleth

Soil Association

This 16th-century Grade II listed farmhouse is surrounded by lovely, peaceful mountain scenery near the River Dovey. Beautifully restored with original oak beams and an inglenook fireplace. Mawddwy is an unspoilt, quiet valley in the superb scenery of the southern Snowdonia National Park. Nant-y-Nodyn's four self-catering cottages, a quarter of a mile apart, are situated in this valley about two miles from the wool village of Dinas Mawddwy and near the highest pass in Wales, which leads to Lake Vyrnwy and Bala Lake. The cottages are part of a sheep and beef organic farm, which has been positively managed with conservation in mind, and guests are welcome to explore and enjoy the wildlife.

elwyn@nantynodyn.fsnet.co.uk www.nantynodyn.co.uk

MACHYNLLETH *(S-C)*

TY'N Y FFORDD   524

Nant-y-Nodyn
Dinas Mawddwy SY20 9AG
Tel: 01650 531330

Cottage: sleeps 6
£360-£740 pw

Organic and local produce at the Quarry
Shop and Café in Machynlleth

Soil Association

This is an enchanting Grade II listed beamed whitewashed cottage. The accommodation is on the ground floor. French doors open onto a patio from where you can enjoy glorious views. Mawddwy is an unspoilt, quiet valley in the superb scenery of the southern Snowdonia National Park. Nant-y-Nodyn's four self-catering cottages, a quarter of a mile apart, are situated in this valley about two miles from the wool village of Dinas Mawddwy and near the highest pass in Wales, which leads to Lake Vyrnwy and Bala Lake. The cottages are part of a sheep and beef organic farm, which has been positively managed with conservation in mind, and guests are welcome to explore and enjoy the wildlife.

elwyn@nantynodyn.fsnet.co.uk   www.nantynodyn.co.uk

MACHYNLLETH *(S-C)*

YR EFAIL   525

Nant-y-Nodyn
Dinas Mawddwy SY20 9AG
Tel: 01650 531330

Cottage: sleeps 2
£320-£453 pw

Organic and local produce at the Quarry
Shop and Café in Machynlleth

Soil Association

This is a beautifully renovated stone smithy, refurbished to a luxuriously high standard. All the accommodation is on the ground floor. Enclosed garden with barbecue and garden furniture. Mawddwy is an unspoilt, quiet valley in the superb scenery of the southern Snowdonia National Park. Nant-y-Nodyn's four self-catering cottages, a quarter of a mile apart, are situated in this valley about two miles from the wool village of Dinas Mawddwy and near the highest pass in Wales, which leads to Lake Vyrnwy and Bala Lake. The cottages are part of a sheep and beef organic farm, which has been positively managed with conservation in mind, and guests are welcome to explore and enjoy the wildlife.

elwyn@nantynodyn.fsnet.co.uk   www.nantynodyn.co.uk

MONTGOMERY *(Camping)*

BACHELDRE CAMPSITE 526

Churchstoke
Montgomery SY15 6TE
Tel: 01588 620489

Caravan and Campsite
£10 per pitch (based on 1-2 people)

Small shop selling basic provisions and stoneground flour from the mill

Soil Association

Caravan and campsite set in the grounds of a traditional working watermill. Graded WTB 4 stars, the small site (2 acres) is secluded and tranquil, providing a high degree of privacy and security. Surrounded by streams, mature trees and farmland, and situated next to our mill there are 25 mainly level and grassy pitches, most with electric hook-ups. With modern clean shower and toilet facilities, we offer a quality location for you to enjoy your holiday. At Bacheldre Watermill we are artisan millers of exceptional flours, our grain is organically grown and we always purchase the highest quality grain available. The Soil Association certifies our entire production process from start to finish ensuring high quality.

info@bacheldremill.co.uk www.bacheldremill.co.uk/holidaycampsite.htm

MONTGOMERY *(S-C)*

BACHELDRE WATERMILL 527

Churchstoke
Montgomery SY15 6TE
Tel: 01588 620489

Apartments: sleep 2-4, £195-£275 per week
Short Breaks, from £40-£60 pn

Shop sells a range of organic stoneground flours

Soil Association

Holiday accommodation in the grounds of a unique 18th-century working watermill in the Welsh Marches. Millers of stoneground strong organic and traditional flours, Bacheldre Watermill have been consistent award winners in the Organic Food Awards. There are four self-contained apartments in the peaceful and relaxed atmosphere of a traditional old brick barn conversion (formerly an 18th-century grain store) adjacent to the watermill itself. There's a large shared lawn area, overlooking the millpond, with a barbecue area and picnic tables with stunning views to the Kerry Ridgeway. Excellent local walking with Offa's Dyke (half a mile), Kerry Ridgeway, Long Mynd and the Stiperstones are all close by.

info@bacheldremill.co.uk www.bacheldremill.co.uk/holidaymain.htm

RHAYADER *(S-C)*

THE CLYN   528

Elan Valley
Rhayader LD6 5HP
Tel: 01597 810120

Cottage: sleeps 7, £247-£623 per week
Granary: sleeps 4, £242-£403 pw

Seasonal home produce (organically grown vegetables, soft fruit, meat, honey, eggs)

The cottages are on a remote smallholding, which has organically reared sheep, poultry, bees, and sometimes pigs, as well as extensive vegetable, fruit and flower gardens. The focus is on 'green living', with electricity from renewable sources (wind and water turbines) and solar water-heating panels. A range of home produce is available in season. Pure spring water on tap. The Clyn is in a superb setting, high on the edge of open moorland, and ideally situated for walking, mountain biking, fishing, bird-watching. National Trust / Elan Valley Trust moorland, RSPB reserves and the Elan Valley reservoirs are literally on the doorstep. Children, and dogs on leads welcome. Short breaks are available.

theclyn@tiscali.co.uk www.clyncottages.co.uk

SHREWSBURY *(B&B)*

LANE FARM   529

Criggion
Shrewsbury SY5 9BG
Tel: 01743 884288

Farmhouse Bed and Breakfast
£23-£25 pppn

Full Welsh breakfast using local produce

Organic Farmers & Growers

A warm welcome awaits you at our traditional family-run working organic farm, set beneath the Breidden Hills in the picturesque Severn Valley. At Lane Farm a large farmhouse breakfast is assured, using local produce and when possible our own eggs. Relax and enjoy the house farm and gardens. You are welcome to walk around our tranquil 400 acres, but remember this is a working farm with moving machinery and animals and children must always be supervised. Private free fishing is available on the River Severn (please bring your own rods). For those feeling energetic, a walk to the top of the Breiddens to Rodney's Pillar will afford spectacular views of the Severn Valley on a clear day.

lane.farm@ukgateway.net www.lanefarmbedandbreakfast.co.uk

GOWER *(S-C)*

HARDINGSDOWN 530

Lower Hardingsdown Farm
Llangennith SA3 1HT
Tel: 01792 386222

Bunkhouse: sleeps 14, £15 pppn shared
£180 pn sole occupancy

Organic fruit and vegetables can be
delivered

Soil Association

Hardingsdown Bunkhouse at Lower Hardingsdown Farm is a renovated stone barn situated on an organic working farm on the Gower Peninsula. The bunkhouse provides comfortable self-catering accommodation for families or groups, sleeping up to fourteen people. Fully equipped kitchen, three shower / toilet rooms, living room with comfy sofas, chairs and two single sofa beds, four bedrooms. Fully centrally heated throughout with underfloor heating downstairs. Patio area and lawned garden. Separate drying room and lock up for storage. Ample parking. Shops and pubs nearby. Access to all that the Gower Peninsula has to offer within easy reach. Level 2 Green Dragon Environmental Award Scheme achieved.

bunkhousegower@tiscali.co.uk www.bunkhousegower.co.uk

ACCOMMODATION INDEX

FEEDBACK FORM

We would welcome your feedback on the contents or organisation of this second edition of **Organic Places to Stay**. If you have any comments, or would like to suggest places for inclusion in the next edition, please email them to us at sales@greenbooks.co.uk, or write them below and post this form to Green Books, Foxhole, Dartington, Totnes, Devon TQ9 6EB.

....

....

....

....

....

....

....

....

....

....

....

Your name and address, or email (for our identification purposes only – these details will not be disclosed to any other party):

....

....

....

....

....

❏ Please tick here if you would like to receive information about future editions of **Organic Places to Stay** or related books that we publish.

Thank you for your help.